About Aspen Publishers

Aspen Publishers, headquartered in New York City, is a leading information provider for attorneys, business professionals, and law students. Written by preeminent authorities, our products consist of analytical and practical information covering both U.S. and international topics. We publish in the full range of formats, including updated manuals, books, periodicals, CDs, and online products.

Our proprietary content is complemented by 2,500 legal databases, containing over 11 million documents, available through our Loislaw division. Aspen Publishers also offers a wide range of topical legal and business databases linked to Loislaw's primary material. Our mission is to provide accurate, timely, and authoritative content in easily accessible formats, supported by unmatched customer care.

To order any Aspen Publishers title, go to *http://lawschool.aspenpublishers.com* or call 1-800-638-8437.

For more information on Loislaw products, go to *www.loislaw.com* or call 1-800-364-2512.

For Customer Care issues, e-mail *CustomerCare@aspenpublishers.com*; call 1-800-234-1660; or fax 1-800-901-9075.

Aspen Publishers
a Wolters Kluwer business

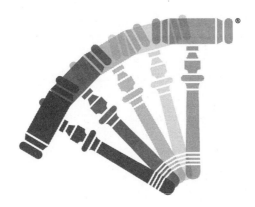

Casenote™ Legal Briefs

CRIMINAL PROCEDURE

Keyed to Courses Using

**Kamisar, LaFave, Israel, and King's
Modern Criminal Procedure**

Eleventh Edition

ΛSPEN

PUBLISHERS

111 Eighth Avenue, New York, NY 10011
http://lawschool.aspenpublishers.com

This publication is designed to provide accurate and authoritative information in regard to the subject matter covered. It is sold with the understanding that the publisher is not engaged in rendering legal, accounting, or other professional services. If legal advice or other expert assistance is required, the services of a competent professional person should be sought.

> — From a *Declaration of Principles* adopted jointly by a Committee of the American Bar Association and a Committee of Publishers and Associates

© 2006 Aspen Publishers, Inc.
a Wolters Kluwer business
http://lawschool.aspenpublishers.com

Aspen Publishers
Permissions Dept.
111 Eighth Avenue, 7th Floor
New York, NY 10011-5201

Printed in the United States of America.

ISBN 0-7355-5954-6

1 2 3 4 5 6 7 8 9 0

Format for the Casenote Legal Brief

Nature of Case: This section identifies the form of action (e.g., breach of contract, negligence, battery), the type of proceeding (e.g., demurrer, appeal from trial court's jury instructions) or the relief sought (e.g., damages, injunction, criminal sanctions).

Fact Summary: This is included to refresh your memory and can be used as a quick reminder of the facts.

Rule of Law: Summarizes the general principle of law that the case illustrates. It may be used for instant recall of the court's holding and for classroom discussion or home review.

Facts: This section contains all relevant facts of the case, including the contentions of the parties and the lower court holdings. It is written in a logical order to give the student a clear understanding of the case. The plaintiff and defendant are identified by their proper names throughout and are always labeled with a (P) or (D).

Palsgraf v. Long Island R.R. Co.
Injured bystander (P) v. Railroad company (D)

N.Y. Ct. App., 248 N.Y. 339, 162 N.E. 99 (1928).

NATURE OF CASE: Appeal from judgment affirming verdict for plaintiff seeking damages for personal injury.

FACT SUMMARY: Helen Palsgraf (P) was injured on R.R.'s (D) train platform when R.R.'s (D) guard helped a passenger aboard a moving train, causing his package to fall on the tracks. The package contained fireworks which exploded, creating a shock that tipped a scale onto Palsgraf (P).

🏛 **RULE OF LAW**
The risk reasonably to be perceived defines the duty to be obeyed.

FACTS: Helen Palsgraf (P) purchased a ticket to Rockaway Beach from R.R. (D) and was waiting on the train platform. As she waited, two men ran to catch a train that was pulling out from the platform. The first man jumped aboard, but the second man, who appeared as if he might fall, was helped aboard by the guard on the train who had kept the door open so they could jump aboard. A guard on the platform also helped by pushing him onto the train. The man was carrying a package wrapped in newspaper. In the process, the man dropped his package, which fell on the tracks. The package contained fireworks and exploded. The shock of the explosion was apparently of great enough strength to tip over some scales at the other end of the platform, which fell on Palsgraf (P) and injured her. A jury awarded her damages, and R.R. (D) appealed.

ISSUE: Does the risk reasonably to be perceived define the duty to be obeyed?

HOLDING AND DECISION: (Cardozo, C.J.) Yes. The risk reasonably to be perceived defines the duty to be obeyed. If there is no foreseeable hazard to the injured party as the result of a seemingly innocent act, the act does not become a tort because it happened to be a wrong as to another. If the wrong was not willful, the plaintiff must show that the act as to her had such great and apparent possibilities of danger as to entitle her to protection. Negligence in the abstract is not enough upon which to base liability. Negligence is a relative concept, evolving out of the common law doctrine of trespass on the case. To establish liability, the defendant must owe a legal duty of reasonable care to the injured party. A cause of action in tort will lie where harm,

though unintended, could have been averted or avoided by observance of such a duty. The scope of the duty is limited by the range of danger that a reasonable person could foresee. In this case, there was nothing to suggest from the appearance of the parcel or otherwise that the parcel contained fireworks. The guard could not reasonably have had any warning of a threat to Palsgraf (P), and R.R. (D) therefore cannot be held liable. Judgment is reversed in favor of R.R. (D).

DISSENT: (Andrews, J.) The concept that there is no negligence unless R.R. (D) owes a legal duty to take care as to Palsgraf (P) herself is too narrow. Everyone owes to the world at large the duty of refraining from those acts that may unreasonably threaten the safety of others. If the guard's action was negligent as to those nearby, it was also negligent as to those outside what might be termed the "danger zone." For Palsgraf (P) to recover, R.R.'s (D) negligence must have been the proximate cause of her injury, a question of fact for the jury.

▶ **ANALYSIS**
The majority defined the limit of the defendant's liability in terms of the danger that a reasonable person in defendant's situation would have perceived. The dissent argued that the limitation should not be placed on liability, but rather on damages. Judge Andrews suggested that only injuries that would not have happened but for R.R.'s (D) negligence should be compensable. Both the majority and dissent recognized the policy-driven need to limit liability for negligent acts, seeking, in the words of Judge Andrews, to define a framework "that will be practical and in keeping with the general understanding of mankind." The Restatement (Second) of Torts has accepted Judge Cardozo's view.

▬▬

Quicknotes
FORESEEABILITY A reasonable expectation that change is the probable result of certain acts or omissions.

NEGLIGENCE Conduct falling below the standard of care that a reasonable person would demonstrate under similar conditions.

PROXIMATE CAUSE The natural sequence of events without which an injury would not have been sustained.

▬▬

Party ID: Quick identification of the relationship between the parties.

Concurrence/Dissent: All concurrences and dissents are briefed whenever they are included by the casebook editor.

Analysis: This last paragraph gives you a broad understanding of where the case "fits in" with other cases in the section of the book and with the entire course. It is a hornbook-style discussion indicating whether the case is a majority or minority opinion and comparing the principal case with other cases in the casebook. It may also provide analysis from restatements, uniform codes, and law review articles. The analysis will prove to be invaluable to classroom discussion.

Issue: The issue is a concise question that brings out the essence of the opinion as it relates to the section of the casebook in which the case appears. Both substantive and procedural issues are included if relevant to the decision.

Holding and Decision: This section offers a clear and in-depth discussion of the rule of the case and the court's rationale. It is written in easy-to-understand language and answers the issues(s) presented by applying the law to the facts of the case. When relevant, it includes a thorough discussion of the exceptions to the case as listed by the court, any major cites to the other cases on point, and the names of the judges who wrote the decisions.

Quicknotes: Conveniently defines legal terms found in the case and summarizes the nature of any statutes, codes, or rules referred to in the text.

Aspen Publishers is proud to offer *Casenote Legal Briefs*—continuing thirty years of publishing America's best-selling legal briefs.

Casenote Legal Briefs are designed to help you save time when briefing assigned cases. Organized under convenient headings, they show you how to abstract the basic facts and holdings from the text of the actual opinions handed down by the courts. Used as part of a rigorous study regime, they can help you spend more time analyzing and critiquing points of law than on copying out bits and pieces of judicial opinions into your notebook or outline.

Casenote Legal Briefs should never be used as a substitute for assigned casebook readings. They work best when read as a follow-up to reviewing the underlying opinions themselves. Students who try to avoid reading and digesting the judicial opinions in their casebooks or on-line sources will end up shortchanging themselves in the long run. The ability to absorb, critique, and restate the dynamic and complex elements of case law decisions is crucial to your success in law school and beyond. It cannot be developed vicariously.

Casenote Legal Briefs represent but one of the many offerings in Aspen's Study Aid Timeline, which includes:

- Casenote *Legal Briefs*
- Emanuel *Law Outlines*
- *Examples & Explanations* Series
- *Introduction to Law* Series
- Emanuel *Law in a Flash* Flashcards
- Emanuel *CrunchTime* Series

Each of these series is designed to provide you with easy-to-understand explanations of complex points of law. Each volume offers guidance on the principles of legal analysis and, consulted regularly, will hone your ability to spot relevant issues. We have titles that will help you prepare for class, prepare for your exams, and enhance your general comprehension of the law along the way.

To find out more about Aspen Study Aid publications, visit us on-line at *www.aspenpublishers.com* or e-mail us at *legaledu@aspenpubl.com*. We'll be happy to assist you.

Free access to Briefs on-line!

Download the cases you want in your notes or outlines using the full cut-and-paste feature accompanying our on-line briefs. Please fill out this form for full access to this useful feature. No photocopies of this form will be accepted.

Name	Phone
	( )

Address	Apt. No.

City	State	ZIP Code

Law School	Year (check one)
	☐ 1st ☐ 2nd ☐ 3rd

Cut out the UPC found on the lower left-hand corner of the back cover of this book. Staple the UPC inside this box. Only the original UPC from the book cover will be accepted. No photocopies or store stickers are allowed.

Attach UPC inside this box.

E-mail (Print LEGIBLY or you may not get access!)

Title of this book (course subject)

Used with which casebook (provide author's name)

Mail the completed form to:

Aspen Publishers, Inc.
Legal Education Division
Casenote On-line Access
675 Massachusetts Ave., 11th floor
Cambridge, MA 02139

I understand that on-line access is granted solely to the purchaser of this book for the academic year in which it was purchased. Any other usage is not authorized and will result in immediate termination of access. Sharing of codes is strictly prohibited.

Signature _____

Upon receipt of this completed form, you will be e-mailed codes so that you may access the Briefs for this Casenote Legal Brief. On-line Briefs may not be available for all titles. For a full list of available titles, please check *http://lawschool.aspenpublishers.com.*

A. Decide on a Format and Stick to It

Structure is essential to a good brief. It enables you to arrange systematically the related parts that are scattered throughout most cases, thus making manageable and understandable what might otherwise seem to be an endless and unfathomable sea of information. There are, of course, an unlimited number of formats that can be utilized. However, it is best to find one that suits your needs and stick to it. Consistency breeds both efficiency and the security that when called upon you will know where to look in your brief for the information you are asked to give.

Any format, as long as it presents the essential elements of a case in an organized fashion, can be used. Experience, however, has led *Casenotes* to develop and utilize the following format because of its logical flow and universal applicability.

NATURE OF CASE: This is a brief statement of the legal character and procedural status of the case (e.g., "Appeal of a burglary conviction").

There are many different alternatives open to a litigant dissatisfied with a court ruling. The key to determining which one has been used is to discover *who is asking this court for what.*

This first entry in the brief should be kept *as short as possible.* Use the court's terminology if you understand it. But since jurisdictions vary as to the titles of pleadings, the best entry is the one that addresses who wants what in this proceeding, not the one that sounds most like the court's language.

RULE OF LAW: A statement of the general principle of law that the case illustrates (e.g., "An acceptance that varies any term of the offer is considered a rejection and counter-offer").

Determining the rule of law of a case is a procedure similar to determining the issue of the case. Avoid being fooled by red herrings; there may be a few rules of law mentioned in the case excerpt, but usually only one is *the* rule with which the casebook editor is concerned. The techniques used to locate the issue, described below, may also be utilized to find the rule of law. Generally, your best guide is simply the chapter heading. It is a clue to the point the casebook editor seeks to make and should be kept in mind when reading every case in the respective section.

FACTS: A synopsis of only the essential facts of the case, i.e., those bearing upon or leading up to the issue.

The facts entry should be a short statement of the events and transactions that led one party to initiate legal proceedings against another in the first place. While some cases conveniently state the salient facts at the beginning of the decision, in other instances they will have to be culled from hiding places throughout the text, even from concurring and dissenting opinions. Some of the "facts" will often be in dispute and should be so noted. Conflicting evidence may be briefly pointed up. "Hard" facts must be included. Both must be *relevant* in order to be listed in the facts entry. It is impossible to tell what is relevant until the entire case is read, as the ultimate determination of the rights and liabilities of the parties may turn on something buried deep in the opinion.

Generally, the facts entry should not be longer than three to five *short* sentences.

It is often helpful to identify the role played by a party in a given context. For example, in a construction contract case the identification of a party as the "contractor" or "builder" alleviates the need to tell that that party was the one who was supposed to have built the house.

It is always helpful, and a good general practice, to identify the "plaintiff" and the "defendant." This may seem elementary and uncomplicated, but, especially in view of the creative editing practiced by some casebook editors, it is sometimes a difficult or even impossible task. Bear in mind that the *party presently* seeking something from this court may not be the plaintiff, and that sometimes only the cross-claim of a defendant is treated in the excerpt. Confusing or misaligning the parties can ruin your analysis and understanding of the case.

ISSUE: A statement of the general legal question answered by or illustrated in the case. For clarity, the issue is best put in the form of a question capable of a "yes" or "no" answer. In reality, the issue is simply the Rule of Law put in the form of a question (e.g., "May an offer be accepted by performance?").

The major problem presented in discerning what is *the* issue in the case is that an opinion usually purports to raise and answer several questions. However, except for rare cases, only one such question is really the issue in the case. Collateral issues not necessary to the resolution of the matter in controversy are handled by the court by language known as *"obiter dictum"* or merely *"dictum."* While dicta may be included later in the brief, they have no place under the issue heading.

To find the issue, ask *who wants what* and then go on to ask *why did that party succeed or fail in getting it.* Once this is determined, the "why" should be turned into a question.

The complexity of the issues in the cases will vary, but in all cases a single-sentence question should sum up the issue.

In a few cases, there will be two, or even more rarely, three issues of equal importance to the resolution of the case. Each should be expressed in a single-sentence question.

Since many issues are resolved by a court in coming to a final disposition of a case, the casebook editor will reproduce the portion of the opinion containing the issue or issues most relevant to the area of law under scrutiny. A noted law professor gave this advice: "Close the book; look at the title on the cover." Chances are, if it is Property, you need not concern yourself with whether, for example, the federal government's treatment of the plaintiff's land really raises a federal question sufficient to support jurisdiction on this ground in federal court.

The same rule applies to chapter headings designating sub-areas within the subjects. They tip you off as to what the text is designed to teach. The cases are arranged in a casebook to show a progression or development of the law, so that the preceding cases may also help.

It is also most important to remember to *read the notes and questions* at the end of a case to determine what the editors wanted you to have gleaned from it.

HOLDING AND DECISION: This section should succinctly explain the rationale of the court in arriving at its decision. In capsulizing the "reasoning" of the court, it should always include an application of the general rule or rules of law to the specific facts of the case. Hidden justifications come to light in this entry; the reasons for the state of the law, the public policies, the biases and prejudices, those considerations that influence the justices' thinking and, ultimately, the outcome of the case. At the end, there should be a short indication of the disposition or procedural resolution of the case (e.g., "Decision of the trial court for Mr. Smith (P) reversed").

The foregoing format is designed to help you "digest" the reams of case material with which you will be faced in your law school career. Once mastered by practice, it will place at your fingertips the information the authors of your casebooks have sought to impart to you in case-by-case illustration and analysis.

B. Be as Economical as Possible in Briefing Cases

Once armed with a format that encourages succinctness, it is as important to be economical with regard to the time spent on the actual reading of the case as it is to be economical in the writing of the brief itself. This does not mean "skimming" a case. Rather, it means reading the case with an "eye" trained to recognize into which "section" of your brief a particular passage or line fits and having a system for quickly and precisely marking the case so that the passages fitting any one particular part of the brief can be easily identified and brought together in a concise and accurate manner when the brief is actually written.

It is of no use to simply repeat everything in the opinion of the court; record only enough information to trigger your recollection of what the court said. Nevertheless, an accurate statement of the "law of the case," i.e., the legal principle applied to the facts, is absolutely essential to class preparation and to learning the law under the case method.

To that end, it is important to develop a "shorthand" that you can use to make margin notations. These notations will tell you at a glance in which section of the brief you will be placing that particular passage or portion of the opinion.

Some students prefer to underline all the salient portions of the opinion (with a pencil or colored underliner marker), making marginal notations as they go along. Others prefer the color-coded method of underlining, utilizing different colors of markers to underline the salient portions of the case, each separate color being used to represent a different section of the brief. For example, blue underlining could be used for passages relating to the rule of law, yellow for those relating to the issue, and green for those relating to the holding and decision, etc. While it has its advocates, the color-coded method can be confusing and time-consuming (all that time spent on changing colored markers). Furthermore, it can interfere with the continuity and concentration many students deem essential to the reading of a case for maximum comprehension. In the end, however, it is a matter of personal preference and style. Just remember, whatever method you use, underlining must be used sparingly or its value is lost.

If you take the marginal notation route, an efficient and easy method is to go along underlining the key portions of the case and placing in the margin alongside them the following "markers" to indicate where a particular passage or line "belongs" in the brief you will write:

N   (NATURE OF CASE)
RL   (RULE OF LAW)
I   (ISSUE)
HL   (HOLDING AND DECISION, relates to the RULE OF LAW behind the decision)
HR   (HOLDING AND DECISION, gives the RATIONALE or reasoning behind the decision)
HA   (HOLDING AND DECISION, APPLIES the general principle(s) of law to the facts of the case to arrive at the decision)

Remember that a particular passage may well contain information necessary to more than one part of your brief, in which case you simply note that in the margin. If you are using the color-coded underlining method instead of margin notation, simply make asterisks or checks in the margin next to the passage in question in the colors that indicate the additional sections of the brief where it might be utilized.

The economy of utilizing "shorthand" in marking cases for briefing can be maintained in the actual brief writing process itself by utilizing "law student shorthand" within the brief. There are many commonly used words and phrases for which abbreviations can be substituted in your briefs (and in your class notes also). You can develop abbreviations that are personal to you and which will save you a lot of time. A reference list of briefing abbreviations can be found on page xii of this book.

C. Use Both the Briefing Process and the Brief as a Learning Tool

Now that you have a format and the tools for briefing cases efficiently, the most important thing is to make the time spent in briefing profitable to you and to make the most advantageous use of the briefs you create. Of course, the briefs are invaluable for classroom reference when you are called upon to explain or analyze a particular case. However, they are also useful in reviewing for exams. A quick glance at the fact summary should bring the case to mind, and a rereading of the rule of law should enable you to go over the underlying legal concept in your mind, how it was applied in that particular case, and how it might apply in other factual settings.

As to the value to be derived from engaging in the briefing process itself, there is an immediate benefit that arises from being forced to sift through the essential facts and reasoning from the court's opinion and to succinctly express them in your own words in your brief. The process ensures that you understand the case and the point that it illustrates, and that means you will be ready to absorb further analysis and information brought forth in class. It also ensures you will have something to say when called upon in class. The briefing process helps develop a mental agility for getting to the *gist* of a case and for identifying, expounding on, and applying the legal concepts and issues found there. The briefing process is the mental process on which you must rely in taking law school examinations; it is also the mental process upon which a lawyer relies in serving his clients and in making his living.

Abbreviations for Briefs

acceptance	acp	offer	O
affirmed	aff	offeree	OE
answer	ans	offeror	OR
assumption of risk	a/r	ordinance	ord
attorney	atty	pain and suffering	p/s
beyond a reasonable doubt	b/r/d	parol evidence	p/e
bona fide purchaser	BFP	plaintiff	P
breach of contract	br/k	prima facie	p/f
cause of action	c/a	probable cause	p/c
common law	c/l	proximate cause	px/c
Constitution	Con	real property	r/p
constitutional	con	reasonable doubt	r/d
contract	K	reasonable man	r/m
contributory negligence	c/n	rebuttable presumption	rb/p
cross	x	remanded	rem
cross-complaint	x/c	res ipsa loquitur	RIL
cross-examination	x/ex	respondeat superior	r/s
cruel and unusual punishment	c/u/p	Restatement	RS
defendant	D	reversed	rev
dismissed	dis	Rule Against Perpetuities	RAP
double jeopardy	d/j	search and seizure	s/s
due process	d/p	search warrant	s/w
equal protection	e/p	self-defense	s/d
equity	eq	specific performance	s/p
evidence	ev	statute of limitations	S/L
exclude	exc	statute of frauds	S/F
exclusionary rule	exc/r	statute	S
felony	f/n	summary judgment	s/j
freedom of speech	f/s	tenancy in common	t/c
good faith	g/f	tenancy at will	t/w
habeas corpus	h/c	tenant	t
hearsay	hr	third party	TP
husband	H	third party beneficiary	TPB
in loco parentis	ILP	transferred intent	TI
injunction	inj	unconscionable	uncon
inter vivos	I/v	unconstitutional	unconst
joint tenancy	j/t	undue influence	u/e
judgment	judgt	Uniform Commercial Code	UCC
jurisdiction	jur	unilateral	uni
last clear chance	LCC	vendee	VE
long-arm statute	LAS	vendor	VR
majority view	maj	versus	v
meeting of minds	MOM	void for vagueness	VFV
minority view	min	weight of the evidence	w/e
Miranda warnings	Mir/w	weight of authority	w/a
Miranda rule	Mir/r	wife	W
negligence	neg	with	w/
notice	ntc	within	w/i
nuisance	nus	without prejudice	w/o/p
obligation	ob	without	w/o
obscene	obs	wrongful death	wr/d

Table of Cases

The Right to Counsel; Equality and the Adversary System

Quick Reference Rules of Law

Betts v. Brady

Farmhand (D) v. Court (P)

316 U.S. 455 (1942).

NATURE OF CASE: Criminal prosecution for robbery.

FACT SUMMARY: Betts (D) was indicted for robbery and his request to have counsel appointed for his trial was denied under a local law which allowed appointed counsel only for rape and murder cases.

🏛 RULE OF LAW

The right to counsel is not fully applicable to the states because the Sixth Amendment's guarantee of counsel is not completely incorporated by the Fourteenth Amendment, but the failure to appoint counsel is a violation of due process, if, under the circumstances of the case, it results in a conviction that is lacking in fundamental fairness.

FACTS: Betts (D), an indigent, was indicted for robbery. He was an unemployed farmhand of ordinary intelligence but uneducated. He requested to have counsel appointed for him because he was too poor to afford an attorney, but his request was denied under a local rule which allowed the appointment of counsel only in rape and murder cases. Betts's (D) defense to the charge was the presentation of an alibi, so the only issue involved in the trial was the veracity of the prosecution and defense witnesses. Betts (D) elected to have a trial without a jury and didn't take the stand in his own defense; the trial resulted in a conviction and an 8-year sentence.

ISSUE: Is the State's failure to appoint counsel for an indigent defendant a violation of the Fourteenth Amendment guarantee of due process?

HOLDING AND DECISION: (Roberts, J.) No. The Fourteenth Amendment's guarantee of due process does not require the appointment of counsel for indigent defendants in all criminal cases. Under the Sixth Amendment, which applies only to federal courts, appointment of counsel is required for all criminal cases if the defendant is unable to afford counsel and he does not intentionally and competently waive his right to counsel. But the Fourteenth Amendment does not incorporate all aspects of the Sixth Amendment, so the federal rule of appointment of counsel for all criminal cases is not applicable to the states. The Sixth Amendment is not fully incorporated because the appointment of counsel is not a fundamental right essential to preserve the fairness of all trials. This proposition is shown by the fact that in most states the appointment of counsel is not considered required for all cases but is essen-

tially a question of legislative policy. However, in most states the court does have the power to appoint counsel where it is necessary in the interest of fairness. Affirmed.

DISSENT: (Black, J.) First, the Fourteenth Amendment makes the Sixth Amendment guarantee of counsel fully applicable to the states, but this view is not accepted by the majority. Nonetheless, even if the majority's view of incomplete incorporation is adopted, the nature of the offense and the circumstances of the trial show that the denial of counsel was a violation of due process.

▶ ANALYSIS

This case is important only for historical reasons because its holding that the Sixth Amendment is not fully applicable to the States through the Fourteenth Amendment was reversed in the following case of *Gideon v. Wainwright*, 72 U.S. 335 (1963). But the rule had vitality until 1963. Under the Betts rule, the court was willing to find special circumstances which made the denial of appointed counsel violation of due process.

Quicknotes

PROCEDURAL DUE PROCESS The constitutional mandate that if the state or federal government acts so as to deny a citizen of a life, liberty or property interest the individual is first entitled to notice and the right to be heard.

RIGHT TO COUNSEL Right conferred by the Sixth Amendment that the accused shall be provided effective legal assistance in a criminal proceeding.

Gideon v. Wainwright

Non-capital felon (D) v. Court (P)

372 U.S. 335 (1963).

NATURE OF CASE: Appeal of denial of petition for habeas corpus relief.

FACT SUMMARY: Gideon (D) appealed his criminal conviction for a noncapital felony on the grounds that the trial court's refusal to appoint counsel for him was unconstitutional.

🏛 RULE OF LAW
The right to counsel is one of those rights that is "fundamental and essential to a fair trial" and is thus made obligatory upon the states by the Fourteenth Amendment.

FACTS: Gideon (D) was convicted of a noncapital felony after the Florida trial court refused to appoint counsel for him because the law allowed such appointment only in capital cases. His petition for habeas corpus relief was denied, but the U.S. Supreme Court granted certiorari to consider his contention that the denial of appointed counsel had been unconstitutional.

ISSUE: Is the right to counsel a fundamental right that is made obligatory upon the states by the Fourteenth Amendment?

HOLDING AND DECISION: (Black, J.) Yes. A provision of the Bill of Rights which is "fundamental and essential to a fair trial" is made obligatory upon the states by the Fourteenth Amendment. *Betts v. Brady*, 316 U.S. 455 (1942), was correct in so assuming. However, the *Betts* Court was wrong in concluding that the Sixth Amendment's guarantee of counsel is not one of those fundamental rights. It is. In deciding it was not, the *Betts* Court made an abrupt break with its own well considered precedents. Today, this Court returns to these old precedents by recognizing that the right to counsel of one charged with a crime is deemed fundamental and essential to a fair trial in our country. Reversed.

CONCURRENCE: (Clark, J.) The Constitution makes no distinction between capital and noncapital cases. It requires due process for a deprivation of "liberty" just as for a deprivation of "life."

CONCURRENCE: (Harlan, J.) While *Betts* should be overruled, to say that it represented "an abrupt break with well-considered precedents" is wrong. *Betts* recognized that special circumstances similar to those which made denial of counsel unconstitutional in capital cases could exist in non-capital cases, but it required they be shown in order to establish a denial of due process. The special circumstances rule has been abandoned in capital cases and it is time that it now be abandoned in noncapital cases which carry the possibility of a substantial prison sentence.

▶ ANALYSIS

The flip side of the right to have counsel is the right not to have counsel, i.e., self-representation. The ABA has taken the position that the right to counsel is so fundamental that except in the simplest trials the court should appoint "standby counsel" when a defendant chooses to represent himself. Most courts that have addressed the issue have decided that a defendant need not specifically be informed of his right to represent himself.

■■■

Quicknotes

PROCEDURAL DUE PROCESS The constitutional mandate that if the state or federal government acts so as to deny a citizen of a life, liberty or property interest the individual is first entitled to notice and the right to be heard.

RIGHT TO COUNSEL Right conferred by the Sixth Amendment that the accused shall be provided effective legal assistance in a criminal proceeding.

■■■

Douglas v. California

Indigent appellant (D) v. State (P)

372 U.S. 353 (1963).

NATURE OF CASE: Appeal from criminal conviction.

FACT SUMMARY: After his conviction, Douglas (D) was denied appointed counsel for assistance in pursuing his right of first appeal. The denial came after the appellate court had reviewed the transcript of his trial and, pursuant to state law, had determined that counsel would not be of help to the defendant.

RULE OF LAW

An indigent is entitled to appointed counsel to prepare an appellate brief where the appeal pursued is granted as a matter of right to all defendants.

FACTS: Douglas (D) was convicted in a state proceeding and was sentenced. He served notice that he wished to appeal his conviction and that he was in need of appointed counsel due to indigency. The first appeal after a trial conviction is granted as a matter of right in California (P). However, Douglas (D) was denied the appointment of counsel to prosecute the appeal. The denial came after the appellate court had reviewed the transcript and determined that appointed counsel would not be of help to either Douglas or the court. The decision was in line with a state rule providing for this procedure.

ISSUE: Is an indigent entitled to appointed counsel to assist in preparation of an appeal from a state criminal conviction where the appeal is granted to all defendants as a manner of right?

HOLDING AND DECISION: (Douglas, J.) Yes. In spite of California's (P) otherwise forward-looking favorable treatment of indigents, the problem presented by this case is the same as that presented by *Griffin v. Illinois*, 351 U.S. 12 (1956), i.e., discrimination against the indigent. By the system employed, only a defendant affluent enough to retain counsel will obtain a full judicial review of his conviction. The indigent is entitled to no more than a review of the bare transcript by the appellate court. Not all appealable issues will appear on the face of a transcript. While the Fourteenth Amendment does not demand absolute equality, due process cannot be denied by "invidious discrimination." While the rich man can employ counsel to focus on appealable issues and to raise hidden objections to the conduct of the trial, the indigent is denied this same right. Our decision is not directed toward discretionary appeals, but toward appeals granted as a matter of right to all defendants. In such an instance, the indigent is entitled to appointed counsel.

DISSENT: (Harlan, J.) The majority appears to rely on both the Equal Protection Clause and the Due Process Clause of the Fourteenth Amendment. I do not think the former is applicable or the letter violated in this case. The Equal Protection Clause prohibits discrimination between rich and poor "as such." The California (P) procedure affords everyone the right to appeal and to transcript of the trial. The difference comes in determining whether appointed counsel is necessary. California (P) has determined appointed counsel is not necessary in nonmeritorious cases. To compel counsel in all cases is to say that the State is obligated to provide absolute equality of all services which is both an impossibility and not mandated by the Equal Protection Clause. In *Griffin v. Illinois*, this Court, while finding that a transcript must be furnished to the indigent appellant, also said that the State could find other means of affording adequate and effective appellate review to indigent defendants. This is what California (P) has done and yet the majority strikes down the procedure California (P) has apparently gone beyond what this Court has recently required for indigents in federal courts, yet it has been found insufficient. A state can legitimately advance its own economic interests in the face of needless expense. That is what California (P) has done. The indigent is not denied appellate review or counsel in a meritorious case, but the State need not fund frivolous appeals.

ANALYSIS

Some commentators have viewed the Douglas decision as a precursor to a requirement for appointed counsel whenever retained counsel is permitted. In fact, some lower courts (not a majority) have held that the difference between appeals of right and discretionary appeals is not a barrier to the right to appointive counsel. However, the weight of the commentaries appears to favor viewing the *Douglas–Griffin* decisions as interposing the right to counsel only where the lack of such counsel, in relation to retained counsel cases, works an inequality so significant as to amount to fundamental unfairness. On that basis, the right to counsel on a discretionary appeal is not found since such appeals rarely delve into new ground not covered in the first appeal and involve broad policy decisions fully developed in the first appeal.

Continued on next page.

Quicknotes

EQUAL PROTECTION A constitutional guarantee that no person shall be denied the same protection of the laws enjoyed by other persons in life circumstances.

INVIDIOUS DISCRIMINATION Unequal treatment of a class of persons that with particularly malicious or hostile.

PROCEDURAL DUE PROCESS The constitutional mandate that if the state or federal government acts so as to deny a citizen of a life, liberty or property interest the individual is first entitled to notice and the right to be heard.

■▬■

Ross v. Moffitt

Forgery convict (D) v. Court (P)

417 U.S. 600 (1974).

NATURE OF CASE: Appeal from a conviction for forgery.

FACT SUMMARY: Ross (D) contended that he was entitled to appointed counsel to represent him in a petition for discretionary review by the Supreme Court.

RULE OF LAW
There is no constitutional right to appointed counsel for discretionary appellate proceedings.

FACTS: Ross (D) was convicted of forgery in a North Carolina state court. He was represented at trial and in his appeal of right to the intermediate appellate court by a public defender. He was denied such representation in his discretionary appeal to the state supreme court. The United States Supreme Court granted review.

ISSUE: Is there a constitutional right to appointed counsel for discretionary appellate proceedings?

HOLDING AND DECISION: (Rehnquist, J.) No. There is no constitutional right to appointed counsel for discretionary appellate proceedings. At the trial stage, the state's responsibility is to ensure the defendant's rights are protected. The state has channeled resources toward convicting a defendant, thus in an adversarial arena it is only just that counsel be appointed. However, on appeal, the defendant initiates the process in order to overturn a lower court. The defendant is thus not in need of protection from state action. He is the aggressor. No constitutional right exists in this circumstance. Reversed.

DISSENT: (Douglas, J.) The indigent defendant, whose liberty is at stake, is at a great disadvantage on appeal whether such is of right or discretionary. He is entitled to appointed counsel.

ANALYSIS

This case rejects the equal protection argument that wealthy defendants have a better chance in discretionary appeal than indigent defendants. Wealth is not a suspect classification and thus indigence does not necessarily entitle the defendant to increased access to appellate review.

Quicknotes

EQUAL PROTECTION A constitutional guarantee that no person shall be denied the same protection of the laws enjoyed by other persons in life circumstances.

SUSPECT CLASSIFICATION A class of persons that have historically been subject to discriminatory treatment; statutes drawing a distinction between persons based on a suspect classification, i.e. race, nationality or alienage, are subject to a strict scrutiny standard of review.

Gagnon v. Scarpelli

Convict on probation (D) v. Court (P)

411 U.S. 778 (1973).

NATURE OF CASE: Appeal from denial of writ of habeas corpus.

FACT SUMMARY: Scarpelli (D) had his probation revoked and the suspended sentence imposed without either a hearing on the matter or with the assistance of counsel.

RULE OF LAW

A probationer or parolee does not have an absolute due process right to the assistance of counsel at a hearing to revoke probation or parole; such right exists only as determined on a case-by-case basis.

FACTS: Scarpelli (D) pled guilty to a charge of armed robbery. He was given a suspended sentence of fifteen years and placed on probation for seven years. Scarpelli (D) was apprehended one month later during an attempted burglary. After having been advised of his constitutional rights, Scarpelli (D) admitted to the police that he had unlawfully broken into the house. Scarpelli (D) now asserts that the statement was made under duress and is false. His probation from the earlier conviction was revoked on the grounds that Scarpelli (D) had been involved in a burglary and that he had associated with a known criminal in the perpetration of the burglary. At no time was Scarpelli (D) afforded a hearing on the new charges and the probation revocation. Scarpelli's (D) suspended sentence was imposed.

ISSUE: Does a probationer or a parolee have an absolute due process right to the assistance of counsel at all probation and parole revocation hearings?

HOLDING AND DECISION: (Powell, J.) No. While a probationer or a parolee does have a due process right to a preliminary and final revocation hearing, there is no absolute due process right to the assistance of counsel at these hearings. Whether due process requires the State to appoint a counsel for indigents at a parole or probation revocation hearing must be determined on a case-by-case basis. Considerable discretion must be allowed the revocation agency. The indigent must be informed of his right to request counsel. Presumptively, counsel should be afforded if the indigent claims he did not commit the alleged violation, or if he argues mitigating reasons that would be difficult for him to develop. The revocation agency, in passing on a request, should consider the indigent's ability to speak for himself and, in denying a request, should state its reasons for the record. Whether, under this test, counsel is afforded or not to an indigent, there still exists a due process right to a preliminary and a final revocation hearing. *Morrissey v. Brewer*, 408 U.S. 471 (1972), which prescribed the due process right to a hearing for parole revocation, is held to be applicable to probation revocation. Scarpelli (D) was neither afforded a hearing nor was he afforded assistance of counsel. Because of the denial of a hearing, the case must be remanded. In light of Scarpelli's (D) subsequent denial of the voluntariness and truth of his admission to the police, his denial of counsel should be reexamined in the light of this opinion, although ordinarily an admission such as that made by Scarpelli (D) is exactly the type of situation in which counsel is not necessary to protect the defendant's due process rights.

ANALYSIS

This case continues the trend evidenced in *Mempa v. Rhay*, 389 U.S. 128 (1967), of the Court's continuing inquiry into the correctional stage of criminal proceedings. In *Morrissey v. Brewer*, 408 U.S. 471 (1972), the Court laid down fairly specific rules concerning procedural due process, both at the time that a parolee is arrested and at parole revocation hearings. The Court held that even though these procedures were not strictly part of a criminal prosecution, they did constitute a deprivation of liberty and thus procedural due process required a hearing before parole or probation could be revoked. This case extends the rule in Morrissey to include probation revocation hearings. However, the Court resisted extending the right to counsel in these hearings. The case-by-case approach is an attempt by the Court to avoid laying down an absolute rule requiring the presence of counsel. Thus, parole and probation revocation hearings are not a critical stage in the criminal prosecution, though they do amount to a deprivation of liberty. The Court is limiting its inquiry into the correctional stage to the requirement of an established hearing procedure and the requirement of counsel only where it is absolutely necessary to insure a fair and adequate hearing. The right to counsel in this stage of the criminal process becomes a function of a fair hearing, and is not an absolute requirement on its own merits.

Continued on next page.

Quicknotes

CRITICAL STAGE OF PROCEEDINGS That stage in criminal proceedings, when an accused's right to counsel arises, at which some action may be taken that will prejudice later proceedings.

PROCEDURAL DUE PROCESS The constitutional mandate that if the state or federal government acts so as to deny a citizen of a life, liberty or property interest the individual is first entitled to notice and the right to be heard.

■▬■

The Role of Counsel

Quick Reference Rules of Law

Faretta v. California

Grand theft defendant (D) v. State (P)

422 U.S. 806 (1975).

NATURE OF CASE: Appeal from conviction for grand theft.

FACT SUMMARY: Faretta (D) was convicted following a trial court's refusal to allow him to represent himself.

> ## 🏛 RULE OF LAW
> A criminal defendant has a Sixth Amendment right to conduct a pro se defense.

FACTS: Faretta (D) was charged with grand theft. Before trial, he indicated that he wished to conduct his own defense. Faretta (D) was a high school graduate and had once before represented himself. The trial court compelled him to allow an attorney to represent him, and he was convicted. Faretta's (D) appeals were rejected in the state courts. Faretta (D) appealed to the Supreme Court.

ISSUE: Does a criminal defendant have a Sixth Amendment right to conduct a pro se defense?

HOLDING AND DECISION: (Stewart, J.) Yes. A criminal defendant has a Sixth Amendment right to conduct a pro se defense. The protections afforded a defendant in the Sixth Amendment are personal to him. The right to counsel is just that—a right. Rights may be waived. To thrust counsel upon an unwilling defendant would violate the language of the Amendment. As long as waiver of counsel is intelligently made, the state cannot force one upon a defendant. Reversed.

DISSENT: (Burger, C.J.) The Sixth Amendment guarantees a defendant a full defense, and allowing a defendant to waive the right to counsel violates this spirit.

DISSENT: (Blackmun, J.) The overriding interest in any criminal prosecution is that justice be done. Without counsel, justice often will not be done to a defendant.

▌ANALYSIS

The rule here was later lessened somewhat. In *McKaskle v. Wiggins*, 465 U.S. 168 (1984), the Court held that a court could force a defendant to have counsel in a consultant role while conducting his defense. Obviously, where consultation ends and outright representation starts is not a question easily answered.

***

Quicknotes

GRAND THEFT The illegal taking of another's property with the intent to deprive the owner thereof, the value of which is greater than the statutory amount.

PRO SE DEFENSE Representing oneself at trial rather than retaining a lawyer.

***

Iowa v. Tovar

State (P) v. Drunk driver (D)

541 U.S. 77 (2004).

NATURE OF CASE: Appeal from conviction on a guilty plea to charge of driving under the influence of alcohol.

FACT SUMMARY: The Iowa Supreme Court reversed Tovar's (D) guilty plea and conviction for failure of a proper Sixth Amendment waiver of right to counsel on the grounds that the trial judge, at time of sentencing, failed specifically (1) to advise Tovar (D) that waiving counsel entails the risk that a viable defense will be overlooked; and (2) to admonish Tovar (D) that by waiving counsel he would lose the opportunity to obtain an independent opinion on the wisdom of pleading guilty.

🏛 RULE OF LAW
The Sixth Amendment right to counsel is satisfied by informing the accused of the nature of charges, right to be counseled, and range of allowable punishments.

FACTS: Tovar (D), a college student, after being arrested for driving under the influence of alcohol, was brought before a district court judge for his first appearance where he was advised of the charges against him and of his right to court-appointed counsel, which he expressly waived. At the arraignment, he also waived his right to counsel, and after again being informed of his right to jury trial and right to counsel, he waived both and pleaded guilty. Finally, at sentencing, he was again advised of the sentence range and of his right to counsel to assist at sentencing, which he expressly waived. The Iowa Supreme Court reversed the conviction, holding that the Sixth Amendment mandates that before accepting a guilty plea and waiver of counsel, a court must specifically (1) advise the defendant that waiving counsel entails the risk that a viable defense will be overlooked; and (2) admonish the defendant that by waiving counsel he will lose the opportunity to obtain an independent opinion on the wisdom of pleading guilty. Ultimately, Iowa (P) appealed this holding.

ISSUE: Is the Sixth Amendment right to counsel satisfied by informing the accused of the nature of charges, right to be counseled, and range of allowable punishments?

HOLDING AND DECISION: (Ginsburg, J.) Yes. The Sixth Amendment right to counsel is satisfied by informing the accused of the nature of charges, right to be counseled, and range of allowable punishments. While the Constitution does not force a lawyer upon a defendant, it does require that any waiver of the right to counsel be knowing, voluntary, and intelligent. This occurs when the defendant knows what he is doing and his choice is made "with eyes open." However, this Court has not prescribed any formula or script to be read to a defendant who states he elects to proceed without counsel. The information he must possess to make an intelligent election will depend on a range of case-specific factors, including the defendant's education or sophistication, the complex or easily grasped nature of the charge, and the stage of the proceeding. Here, Tovar (D) waived counsel at his initial appearance, affirming this at the plea hearing, and again declined counsel at time of sentencing. The Sixth Amendment does not require a court to give a rigid and detailed admonishment to a pro se defendant pleading guilty of the usefulness of an attorney, that an attorney may provide an independent opinion whether it is wise to plead guilty, and that without an attorney the defendant risks overlooking a defense. Tovar (D) never claimed that he did not fully understand the charge or the range of punishment for the crime prior to pleading guilty. Reversed.

▶ ANALYSIS

In its *Tovar* decision, the U.S. Supreme Court went on to say that the states are free to adopt by statute, rule, or decision any guides to the acceptance of an uncontested plea they deem useful and held only that the two admonitions the Iowa Supreme Court ordered were not required by the federal Constitution.

■=■

Quicknotes

PRO SE An individual appearing on his own behalf.

RIGHT TO COUNSEL Right conferred by the Sixth Amendment that the accused shall be provided effective legal assistance in a criminal proceeding.

WAIVER The intentional or voluntary forfeiture of a recognized right.

■=■

Caplin & Drysdale, Chartered v. United States

Law firm (P) v. Federal government (D)

491 U.S. 617 (1989).

NATURE OF CASE: Review of adjudication of third-party interest in seized proceeds.

FACT SUMMARY: Caplin & Drysdale (P), a law firm, contended that funds earmarked for a criminal defendant's counsel could not be seized.

RULE OF LAW
Funds earmarked for a criminal defendant's counsel may be seized.

FACTS: Reckmeyer was indicted for violations of various drug laws. Pursuant to 21 U.S.C. § 848, a large portion of his assets were seized by federal authorities. Included in the seized assets was $25,000 Reckmeyer had earmarked to pay for his defense costs. As part of a plea bargain, Reckmeyer agreed to forfeit almost all of his assets, which left him unable to pay his attorneys' fees. Caplin & Drysdale (P), his attorneys, petitioned for release of the $25,000 contending that forfeiture thereof was contrary to the Sixth Amendment. The district court granted the petition, but the Fourth Circuit reversed. The Supreme Court accepted review.

ISSUE: May funds earmarked for a criminal defendant's counsel be seized?

HOLDING AND DECISION: (White, J.) Yes. Funds earmarked for a criminal defendant's counsel may be seized. The Sixth Amendment gives a defendant the right to select an attorney to represent him. It does not guarantee him the funds to pay for such counsel. The law permitting seizure does not prevent the defendant from using nonseizable assets or utilizing pro bono counsel. Thus, the burden placed on the defendant is a limited one. The Sixth Amendment does not give a defendant the right to use ill-gotten gains in his defense, and the law in question does no more than prevent that. Therefore, the law is not in conflict with the Sixth Amendment. Affirmed.

DISSENT: (Blackmun, J.) Our system of criminal justice is built upon a truly equal presentation of the case, and the trust necessary for such equality can only exist when a defendant chooses his counsel. The seizure law unfairly gives the government the power to, as a practical matter, deprive a class of defendants from choosing their own counsel.

▶ ANALYSIS

Per a part of 21 U.S.C. § 853, title to the proceeds of illegal drug enterprises vests in the United States at the time of the act giving rise to forfeiture. This "relation back" provision is what gives the government its right to seize. In effect, the fund never belonged to the violator, much as a bank robber never obtains true title to stolen funds.

■=■

Strickland v. Washington

Confessing convict (D) v. State (P)

466 U.S. 668 (1984).

NATURE OF CASE: Appeal from denial of writ of habeas corpus.

FACT SUMMARY: Strickland (D) contended he was denied effective assistance of counsel when his attorney failed to present character evidence which might have reduced his sentence.

> **RULE OF LAW**
> A defendant must, in order to show he was denied the effective assistance of counsel, establish that: (1) counsel's performance was deficient; and (2) the deficient performance prejudiced the defense.

FACTS: Strickland (P) confessed to several crimes including murder, torture, and kidnapping. After he was convicted, he stated at the sentencing hearing that he was sorry for and regretted his crimes. His appointed counsel chose not to introduce any character evidence and to allow the court to pass sentence based solely on Strickland's (D) statements. The attorney knew the judge favored such repentance and that introducing character evidence would subject Strickland (D) to cross-examination. Strickland (D) was sentenced to death. He petitioned the district court for a writ of habeas corpus, contending he was denied effective assistance of counsel. The district court found that any errors made by counsel were not prejudicial and denied the writ. The court of appeals reversed, and the Supreme Court granted certiorari.

ISSUE: Must a defendant show that his defense was prejudiced by his counsel's deficient performance in order to sustain a claim he was denied effective assistance of counsel?

HOLDING AND DECISION: (O'Connor, J.) Yes. In order to establish that he was denied effective assistance of counsel, a defendant must show: (1) counsel's performance was deficient; and (2) the deficient performance prejudiced his defense. This requires that the defendant show that counsel's errors were so serious as to deprive him of a fair trial. In this case, Strickland's (D) counsel gave him reasonably effective assistance by pursuing a reasonable defense strategy. Further, any further character evidence submitted at the hearing would have been cumulative and ineffective. Therefore, any errors committed were not prejudicial. As a result, Strickland (D) failed to establish he was denied effective counsel. Reversed.

CONCURRENCE AND DISSENT: (Brennan, J.) The death penalty is cruel and unusual punishment and cannot be constitutionally imposed. However, the principles concerning the effective assistance of counsel were properly applied by the Court.

DISSENT: (Marshall, J.) The prejudice standard here established by the majority is so malleable that, in practice, it will either have no grip at all or will yield excessive variation in the manner in which the Sixth Amendment is interpreted and applied by different courts. To tell lawyers and lower courts that counsel for a criminal defendant must behave "reasonably" and must act like "a reasonably competent attorney" is to tell them almost nothing.

▶ ANALYSIS

In this case, the Court stated that the "benchmark for judging any claim of ineffectiveness must be whether counsel's conduct so undermined the proper functioning of the adversarial process that the trial cannot be relied on as having produced a just result." From this point of departure, it broke the test down to two parts: performance and prejudice.

Quicknotes

CHARACTER EVIDENCE Evidence of someone's moral standing in a community based on reputation.

Mickens v. Taylor

Convicted murderer (P) v. State (D)

535 U.S. 162 (2002).

NATURE OF CASE: Appeal from a murder conviction.

FACT SUMMARY: When Mickens (P) discovered that his court-appointed defense counsel for his capital murder trial, had also represented the victim, Mickens (P) argued for automatic reversal of his conviction on the grounds of attorney conflict of interest.

RULE OF LAW
To establish his counsel's conflict of interest, a defendant must show both an actual conflict of interest and an adverse effect even if the trial court fails to inquire into a potential conflict about which it reasonably should have known.

FACTS: A Virginia jury in 1993 convicted Mickens (P) of murder. In 1998 he filed a habeas petition based on ineffective assistance when he discovered that his court-appointed attorney (Bryan Saunders) had a conflict of interest at trial in that Saunders had also represented Hall (Mickens's (P) victim) on assault and concealed weapons charges. Saunders had never disclosed to the court, to his co-counsel, or to Mickens (P) that he had previously represented Hall. The federal district court denied Mickens's (P) petition for relief, and the federal circuit court affirmed. Mickens (P) appealed.

ISSUE: To establish his counsel's conflict of interest, must a defendant show both an actual conflict of interest and an adverse effect even if the trial court fails to inquire into a potential conflict about which it reasonably should have known?

HOLDING AND DECISION: (Scalia, J.) Yes. To establish his counsel's conflict of interest, a defendant must show both an actual conflict of interest and an adverse effect even if the trial court fails to inquire into a potential conflict about which it reasonably should have known. Mickens's (P) proposed rule of automatic reversal when there existed a conflict that did not affect counsel's performance, but the trial judge failed to make its mandated inquiry, makes little policy sense. Prejudice is to be presumed only if the conflict has substantially affected counsel's performance—thereby rendering the verdict unreliable. The trial court's awareness of a potential conflict neither renders it more likely that counsel's performance was significantly affected nor in any other way renders the verdict unreliable. Nor does the trial judge's dereliction in making the mandated conflict-inquiry cause it to be harder for reviewing courts to determine conflict and effect, particularly since those

courts may rely on evidence and testimony whose importance only becomes established at the trial. Nor, finally, is automatic reversal simply an appropriate means of enforcing this Court's mandate of inquiry. This Court does not presume that judges are as careless or as partial as those police officers who need the incentive of the exclusionary rule. Affirmed.

CONCURRENCE: (Kennedy, J.) Here, the district court properly found that Saunders did not believe he had any obligation to his former client (Hall) that would interfere with the litigation. Although Saunders probably did learn some matters that were confidential, nothing the attorney learned was relevant to the subsequent murder case.

DISSENT: (Stevens, J.) The lawyer who represented Mickens (P) had a duty to disclose his prior representation of the victim to Mickens (P) and to the trial judge; that duty was here violated. Setting aside Mickens's (P) conviction is the only remedy that can maintain public confidence in the fairness of the procedures employed in capital cases.

DISSENT: (Souter, J.) Since here the state judge was on notice of a prospective potential conflict, this case calls for application of the rule that the remedy for the judge's dereliction of duty should be an order vacating the conviction and affording a new trial.

DISSENT: (Breyer, J.) The facts of this case categorically warrant and require an automatic reversal. To carry out a death sentence when the defendant's appointed attorney, as here, had previously represented the victim, would invariably diminish faith in the fairness and integrity of our criminal justice system.

▶ ANALYSIS

As the Supreme Court notes in its Mickens decision, the existing rule, which requires proof of effect upon representation but (once such effect is shown) presumes prejudice, already creates an "incentive" for a court to inquire into a potential conflict. In those cases where the potential conflict is in fact an actual one, only inquiry will enable the judge to avoid all possibility of reversal by either seeking waiver or replacing a conflicted attorney.

Continued on next page.

Quicknotes

CONFLICT OF INTEREST Refers to ethical problems that rise, or may be anticipated to arise, between an attorney and his client if the interests of the attorney, another client or a third party conflict with those of the present client.

PREJUDICE A preference of the court toward one party prior to litigation.

■═■

Wheat v. United States

Drug conspirator (D) v. Federal government (P)

486 U.S. 153 (1988).

NATURE OF CASE: Appeal from conviction for conspiracy.

FACT SUMMARY: Wheat (D) contended he was deprived of his right to counsel when the district court disqualified his attorney of choice for conflict of interest.

RULE OF LAW

A criminal defendant is not entitled to have counsel of his choice where his representation would create an inherent conflict of interest.

FACTS: Wheat (D) was arrested along with Gomez-Barajas and Bravo on drug conspiracy charges. Iredale, an attorney, represented Gomez-Barajas and Bravo. Bravo pled guilty, and Gomez-Barajas was acquitted. He was scheduled to be tried separately on the other charge; however, he offered to plead guilty pursuant to a plea bargain. After this agreement was made, but before it was accepted by the court, Wheat (D) sought to have Iredale represent him. The Government (P) moved to disqualify Iredale on the basis that such representation would require the cross-examination of Gomez-Barajas and Bravo and thus presented a conflict of interest. The court denied the request for Iredale to represent Wheat (D), rejecting Wheat's (D) contention that the denial violated his constitutional right to counsel. Wheat (D) was convicted and appealed. The court of appeals affirmed and the Supreme Court granted a hearing.

ISSUE: Is a criminal defendant entitled to have counsel of his own choice where his representation would create an inherent conflict of interest?

HOLDING AND DECISION: (Rehnquist, C.J.) No. A criminal defendant is not entitled to have counsel of his choice where his representation creates an inherent conflict of interest. The right to counsel does not always include the right to counsel of choice. In this case, representation of all three co-conspirators would incurably compromise counsel's ability to represent all his clients. As a result, the representation was properly denied. Affirmed.

DISSENT: (Marshall, J.) A constitutional right to counsel of choice exists and is fully applicable in this case. The right to control the defense rests solely with the defendant. Thus, such right overcomes any potential conflict of interest.

DISSENT: (Stevens, J.) The majority here gives inadequate weight to the informed and voluntary character of the clients' waiver of their right to conflict-free representation. Specifically, the majority virtually ignores the fact that the additional counsel representing petitioner had provided him with sound advice concerning the wisdom of a waiver and would have remained available during the trial to assist in the defense.

ANALYSIS

In general, counsel may represent conflicting interests after full disclosure and a written waiver. Some cases, such as this one, present such a pronounced conflict that such cannot be waived. It is felt that while the right to counsel of choice is upheld, the right to effective counsel is sacrificed.

■=■

Quicknotes

CONFLICT OF INTEREST Refers to ethical problems that arise, or may be anticipated to arise, between an attorney and his client if the interests of the attorney, another client or a third party conflict with those of the present client.

CROSS EXAMINATION The interrogation of a witness by an adverse party either to further inquire as to the subject matter of the direct examination or to call into question the witness's credibility.

■=■

Arrest, Search, and Seizure

Quick Reference Rules of Law

Wolf v. Colorado

Abortion physician (D) v. State (P)

338 U.S. 25 (1949).

NATURE OF CASE: Appeal from conviction of conspiracy to commit abortion.

FACT SUMMARY: Dr. Wolf (D) was convicted of conspiracy to commit abortion, such conviction resting in part upon evidence seized from his office.

🏛 RULE OF LAW
In a prosecution in a state court for a state crime, the Fourteenth Amendment does not forbid the admission of evidence obtained by an unreasonable search and seizure.

FACTS: Appointment books were seized from Dr. Wolf's (D) office. Partly on the basis of this evidence, Dr. Wolf (D) was convicted in a state court of conspiracy to commit abortion. Under Colorado law, evidence seized in an unreasonable search and seizure is admissible against the accused. Had the case been brought in federal court, the evidence would have been inadmissible under the exclusionary rule as being in violation of Dr. Wolf's (D) Fourth Amendment rights.

ISSUE: Does a conviction by a state court for a state offense deny a defendant his due process rights under the Fourteenth Amendment solely because evidence was obtained by a search and seizure which was illegal under the Fourth Amendment, and thus would have been excluded if the case had been brought in a federal court?

HOLDING AND DECISION: (Frankfurter, J.) No. While the Fourth Amendment's prohibition against unreasonable searches and seizures is incorporated under the due process clause of the Fourteenth Amendment and thus is binding upon the states, the federal exclusionary rule is not binding on the states. The exclusion of illegally obtained evidence is not fundamental to the concept of ordered liberty. It is merely one means of securing compliance with the Fourth Amendment and thus deterring unreasonable searches and seizures. The states are free to fashion other remedies to deter violations of defendants' due process rights, as long as they do indeed provide some means of redress. It is not a departure from the basic standards of individual rights to remand such individuals to the remedies of private action and to such protection as the internal discipline of the police. While it is true that exclusion of such evidence is an effective means of deterring unreasonable searches, the Supreme Court will not condemn a state's reliance upon methods which, if consistently enforced, would be equally effective. The public opinion within the state can be more effectively exerted against the local police than can local opinion be exerted against federal officers.

CONCURRENCE: (Black, J.) The exclusionary rule is not a command of the Fourth Amendment, but is merely a judicially created rule of evidence and thus should not be incorporated within the Fourteenth Amendment.

DISSENT: (Murphy, J.) There are no real alternative remedies to the exclusionary rule, and thus the exclusionary rule must be binding on the states. District attorneys would not prosecute themselves or those working for them for illegally obtaining evidence. An action for trespass is subject to far too many defenses, and also provides little inducement in the way of damages to discourage illegal searches and seizures.

DISSENT: (Douglas, J.) Without the exclusionary rule, the Fourth Amendment loses its meaning and validity.

▶ ANALYSIS

In *Weeks v. U.S.*, 232 U.S. 383 (1914), the Supreme Court first held that, under the Fourth Amendment, evidence obtained by federal officials by means of an unreasonable search and seizure is inadmissible as evidence in a federal court. Evidence procured by state officials in violation of the Fourth Amendment is also inadmissible in federal court (*Elkins v. U.S.*, 364 U.S. 206 (1960)). In *Wolf*, the Court established two basic propositions: first, the Fourth Amendment's prohibition against unreasonable search and seizure is binding on the states through the Due Process Clause of the Fourteenth Amendment; and second, the rule of Weeks, excluding all evidence seized in an unreasonable search, is not commanded by the Fourth Amendment but is a judicially created rule of evidence for federal courts and is, therefore, not binding on the states. Under *Wolf*, then, although unreasonable search and seizure by state officials is unconstitutional, it is permissible for the state courts to use such illegally obtained evidence in state trials, if the state has some procedure other than the exclusionary rule to discourage unreasonable searches. Although this case held that the exclusionary rule is not implicit in the Fourteenth Amendment's concept of ordered liberty and fundamental justice, the following case of *Mapp v. Ohio*, 67 U.S. 643 (1961), using the same standard, overturned Wolf and found that the exclusionary rule was a part of the Fourteenth Amendment, binding on the states.

Mapp v. Ohio

Homeowner (D) v. State (P)

367 U.S. 643 (1961).

NATURE OF CASE: Certiorari from conviction of possession of lewd and lascivious materials.

FACT SUMMARY: Evidence obtained when officers broke into and conducted an unlawful search of Miss Mapp's (D) home, was used for her conviction (by an Ohio State Court) of possession of lewd and lascivious materials.

🏛 RULE OF LAW
The Fourth Amendment is incorporated in the Fourteenth Amendment Due Process Clause, and requires that the state courts exclude evidence obtained by unlawful searches and seizures.

FACTS: On May 23, 1957, three Cleveland police officers arrived at Miss Mapp's home (D) pursuant to information that a person wanted for questioning in connection with a bombing and a large amount of "policy paraphernalia" could be found there. When Miss Mapp (D) (after telephoning her attorney) refused to allow the officers in without a search warrant, they waited for more officers and then forcibly broke into the house. The officers then proceeded to conduct a warrantless search of Miss Mapp's (D) entire house. At her subsequent trial, evidence seized from this search was used to convict her of the possession of lewd and lascivious books, pictures, and photographs. The Supreme Court of Ohio found that her conviction was valid, even though it was based upon unlawfully seized evidence. Thereupon, Miss Mapp (D) was granted certiorari by this Court.

ISSUE: Can evidence obtained in an unlawful search and seizure be used as evidence in a state trial of the accused?

HOLDING AND DECISION: (Clark, J.) No. The Fourth Amendment is incorporated by the Fourteenth Amendment Due Process Clause, and requires that state courts exclude evidence obtained by unlawful searches and seizures. The Fourth Amendment right to be free from unreasonable searches and seizures was first extended to the states under the Fourteenth Amendment in *Wolf v. Colorado*, 338 U.S. 25 (1949). Although this Court refused in *Wolf* to apply the exclusionary rule to the states as essential to the protection of that right, it was well established even then (by this Court in *Weeks*, 232 U.S. 383 [1914]) that, in federal prosecutions, the Fourth Amendment bars the use of any evidence secured through any illegal search and seizure. Today, for compelling reasons, the same sanction of exclusion must be applied to the states.

First, as a minor consideration, it must be recognized that *Wolf* was based upon factual considerations no longer true today. At the time of *Wolf*, two-thirds of the states were opposed to the use of the exclusionary rule, but today more than half have wholly or partially adopted it. Second, and more importantly, the exclusionary rule is essential to the protection of the right to be free from unreasonable searches and seizures, and to the integrity of the judiciary. The purpose of the exclusionary rule is "to compel respect for the constitutional guaranty in the only effectively available way—by removing the incentive to disregard it." Without this rule, the Fourth and Fourteenth Amendments' protection against unreasonable searches and seizures would be a valueless "form of words." Furthermore, the "judicial integrity" of our system requires that government, for its own preservation, observe its own laws, especially the charter of its own existence." Miss Mapp's (D) conviction must be reversed. Reversed and remanded.

DISSENT: (Harlan, J.) There are several problems with the Court's decision today. First, the pivotal issue is not a reexamination of *Wolf*, but whether the "mere knowing possession of obscene materials" can be considered criminal, consistent with the rights of the free thought and expression. Second, even if the issue is the reexamination of *Wolf*, this Court's reasoning that the basic federal remedy for a violation of the Fourth Amendment rights must apply to the states is unjustifiable. *Wolf* did not hold that the Fourth Amendment, as such, is applicable to the states through the Fourteenth Amendment, but only that problem does not involve the substantive commands of the Fourth Amendment, but the flexible Due Process Clause of the Fourteenth Amendment. The Court should refrain from hindering the states in their own criminal law enforcement with the adamant exclusionary rule.

▶ ANALYSIS

This case illustrates the trend of the Court in incorporating the Bill of Rights into the Due Process Clause of the Fourteenth Amendment. However, the Court has not applied a "total incorporation theory" (as it did here) to all of those rights so far incorporated. For example, in the case of the right to a trial by jury, the federal requirement of a unanimous verdict of the twelve-man jury for conviction is not applicable to the states, although the right to a jury trial is, because such a requirement is not "essential" to the right.

Continued on next page.

Note, finally that the Fourth Amendment applies only to the government (state or federal), and as such the prosecution may use evidence obtained by private parties even if the methods such parties used were illegal.

■═■

Quicknotes

BILL OF RIGHTS   Refers to the first ten Amendments to the federal Constitution, setting forth individual rights and liberties.

EXCLUSIONARY RULE   A rule precluding the introduction at trial of evidence unlawfully obtained in violation of the federal constitutional safeguards against unreasonable searches and seizures.

PRIVILEGE AGAINST SELF-INCRIMINATION   A privilege guaranteed by the Fifth Amendment to the federal Constitution in a criminal proceeding for communications made by an accused and protecting an accused or witness from having to give testimony that may incriminate himself.

■═■

United States v. Leon

Federal government (P) v. Owner of illegally seized evidence (D)

468 U.S. 897 (1984).

NATURE OF CASE: Appeal from the suppression of evidence.

FACT SUMMARY: The court of appeals held that evidence seized pursuant to a facially valid warrant had to be suppressed due to a lack of probable cause to issue the warrant even though the police had acted in good faith.

🏛 RULE OF LAW
The Fourth Amendment does not require the exclusion of evidence seized pursuant to a facially valid warrant where the police have acted in good faith.

FACTS: The district court granted Leon's (D) motion to suppress evidence seized on good faith pursuant to a facially valid warrant issued by the neutral magistrate which was subsequently found to be based on an affidavit which did not sufficiently establish probable cause. The court of appeals affirmed, refusing to recognize a good faith exception to the exclusionary rule. The Supreme Court granted certiorari.

ISSUE: Does the Fourth Amendment require the exclusion of evidence seized pursuant to a facially valid warrant where the police have acted in good faith?

HOLDING AND DECISION: (White, J.) No. The Fourth Amendment does not require the exclusion of evidence seized pursuant to a facially valid warrant where the police have acted in good faith. The exclusionary rule is applied only in cases where it would be consistent with its rationale. The rule is imposed to deter police conduct which denies the defendant his constitutional rights. Where the police act in good faith, under the authorization of a neutral and detached magistrate, the deterrent purpose does not apply. As a result, the rule should not be applied in this case. Reversed.

CONCURRENCE: (Blackmun, J.) Because the Court correctly recognized that the exclusionary rule is not constitutionally mandated, it correctly limited its scope to cases where the deterrent purpose will be served.

DISSENT: (Brennan, J.) The exclusionary rule is indirectly compelled by the Fourth Amendment. Also, the good faith exception will simply allow police to infringe on constitutional rights by limiting the information included in affidavits supporting search warrants.

▶ ANALYSIS

The Court stated in this case that suppression remains a viable tool if the magistrate or judge, in issuing a warrant, was misled by information in an affidavit that the affiant knew was false. Suppression will also be allowed where the police could not have acted in good faith because the warrant was obviously invalid.

Quicknotes

EXCLUSIONARY RULE A rule precluding the introduction at trial of evidence unlawfully obtained in violation of the federal constitutional safeguards against unreasonable searches and seizures.

GOOD FAITH EXCEPTION TO WARRANT REQUIREMENT The exception to the rule that evidence obtained as the result of an unlawful search and seizure is nevertheless admissible at trial if the officers had a reasonable, good faith belief that they acted pursuant to legal authority.

PROBABLE CAUSE A reasonable basis for believing that a crime has been committed.

Katz v. United States

Telephone better (D) v. Federal government (P)

389 U.S. 347 (1967).

NATURE OF CASE: Appeal from criminal conviction for transmitting betting information over the phone.

FACT SUMMARY: Katz (D) was arrested for transmitting wagering information by telephone to another state; at his trial, the government introduced recordings of his conversation made by attaching a listening and recording device to the outside of a phone booth.

🏛 RULE OF LAW
The Fourth Amendment protects a person from search and seizure if, under the circumstances, he has a justifiable expectation of privacy, regardless of whether an actual physical trespass occurred.

FACTS: Katz (D) was arrested and convicted for transmitting betting information by telephone to another state in violation of a federal statute. At his trial, the prosecution introduced recordings of phone conversations Katz (D) had made. These recordings were made by attaching a recording and listening device to the outside of a phone booth that Katz (D) used to make his calls. There was no search warrant. The government used this device only after it had made an investigation which indicated that the phone booth was being used to transmit such information, and they only recorded conversation that Katz (D) personally had.

ISSUE: Is the attachment of a listening device to the outside of a public telephone booth a search and seizure within the meaning of the Fourth Amendment?

HOLDING AND DECISION: (Stewart, J.) Yes. The Fourth Amendment protects persons' justifiable expectations of privacy, and protects people and not places. Whatever a person knowingly exposes to the public, even in his own home, is therefore not protected by the Fourth Amendment, but what a person keeps private, even in a public place, may be protected. Earlier cases stated that a surveillance without a trespass or seizure of a material object is outside of the Fourth Amendment, and now these cases must be overturned. Even though the phone booth was a public place, and there was no physical trespass (the device was on the outside of the booth), there was a search because the government violated the privacy upon which Katz (D) justifiably relied. There also is a seizure even though no tangible property was taken because the recording of a statement overheard, even if there is no trespass, is a seizure. The remaining question, then, is whether the government complied with the constitutional standards of the Fourth Amendment. Although the government reasonably believed that the phone booth was being illegally used, and their search and seizure was carefully limited both in scope and duration, the action cannot be upheld because there was no search warrant issued. A search warrant is a safeguard in several ways: a neutral magistrate, on the basis of information presented to him, determines whether a warrant should issue; the search warrant carefully limits the scope of the search; and the government must report back on the evidence it finds. Without such safeguards, even if the search was in fact reasonable, it cannot be upheld. Reversed.

CONCURRENCE: (Harlan, J.) In order to be protected by the Fourth Amendment, a person must have an actual subjective expectation of privacy, and also, that expectation of privacy must be reasonable.

DISSENT: (Black, J.) When the Fourth Amendment was adopted, eavesdropping was a common practice, and if the framers of the Constitution wished to limit that procedure, they would have used appropriate language. This case, then, goes against the plain meaning of the Fourth Amendment which was solely aimed at limiting the practice of breaking into buildings and seizing tangible property. Therefore, wiretapping, which is a form of eavesdropping, is not subject to the Fourth Amendment.

▶ ANALYSIS

Katz rejects the old rule which held that there was no search unless there was a physical trespass and substitutes a new rule based on the defendant's expectation of privacy. One facet of this privacy concept is the place involved—for example, if, unlike Katz (D), the defendant was engaged in conversation in a public place that was audible to others, there would be no search within the meaning of the Fourth Amendment. Also, the privacy concept turns on the action of the defendant. If he had engaged in a loud conversation, even in his own home, which was audible to a person standing outside of his door, there would be no search since the conversation was exposed by the defendant to the public.

Quicknotes

EXPECTATION OF PRIVACY Requirement that in order to invoke the Fourth Amendment's protection against unreasonable searches and seizures, the individual must have a reasonable expectation of privacy in respect to the location searched or thing seized.

Kyllo v. United States

Resident (D) v. Federal government (P)

533 U.S. 27 (2001).

NATURE OF CASE: Appeal from indictment of manufacturing marijuana.

FACT SUMMARY: Federal agents suspected Kyllo (D) of growing marijuana in his residence and used a thermal scanner to prove he was doing so.

🏛 RULE OF LAW
Where the government uses a device that is not in general public use to explore details of the home that would previously have been unknowable without physical intrusion, the surveillance is a "search" and is presumptively unreasonable without a warrant.

FACTS: Federal agents suspected Kyllo (D) was growing marijuana in his home and used a thermal imager to scan the residence. The agents concluded that Kyllo (D) was using halide lights to grow marijuana in his house and a magistrate issued a search warrant on the basis of the thermal scan, tips from informants, and Kyllo's (D) heating bills. Kyllo (D) was indicted and unsuccessfully moved to suppress the evidence. The court of appeals remanded the case for an evidentiary hearing regarding the intrusiveness of the thermal imaging. The district court upheld the warrant and affirmed denial of the motion. The court of appeals affirmed.

ISSUE: Does the use of a thermal-imaging device aimed at a private home from the street to detect relative amounts of heat within the home constitute a "search" within the meaning of the Fourth Amendment?

HOLDING AND DECISION: (Scalia, J.) Yes. Where the government uses a device that is not in general public use to explore details of the home that would previously have been unknowable without physical intrusion, the surveillance is a "search" and is presumptively unreasonable without a warrant. Remanded to the district court to determine whether probable cause existed independent of the evidence from the thermal visioning. Reversed and remanded.

DISSENT: (Stevens, J.) There is a distinction between "through-the-wall surveillance" that gives the observer direct access to information in a private area and the thought processes used to draw inferences from information in the public domain. The Court has crafted a rule that purports to deal with direct observation of the inside of the home. This case, however, involves indirect deductions from observations of the exterior of the home.

▶ ANALYSIS

The Court upholds the test of "reasonableness" set forth in *Katz v. United States*, 389 U.S. 347 (1967), that whether the individual has an expectation of privacy depends on whether society is prepared to recognize such expectation as reasonable. The Court rejects the erosion of Fourth Amendment protection by technological advances, concluding that any such technological "intrusion into a constitutionally protected area" constitutes a search, especially if the product of the use of a device not available to the general public.

Quicknotes

FOURTH AMENDMENT Provides that persons be secure as to their person and private belongings against unreasonable searches and seizures.

PROBABLE CAUSE A reasonable basis for believing that a crime has been committed.

SEARCH An inspection conducted in order to obtain evidence to be utilized for the prosecution of a crime.

WARRANT An order issued by a court directing an officer to undertake a certain act (e.g., arrest or search).

Andresen v. Maryland

Law office owner (D) v. State (P)

427 U.S. 463 (1976).

NATURE OF CASE: Appeal from a criminal conviction on Fifth Amendment grounds.

FACT SUMMARY: State (P) authorities with search warrants found specified documents in Andresen's (D) law office pertaining to a fraudulent land sale, and those papers were admitted at trial against him.

🏛 RULE OF LAW
The seizure of a defendant's business records and their admission against him at trial do not violate the Fifth Amendment protection against self-incrimination.

FACTS: Andresen's (D) law office and corporate offices were searched by state (P) authorities with search warrants for specified documents pertaining to a fraudulent land sale. The papers were found and were admitted against Andresen (D) at his trial where he was convicted. Andresen (D) appealed, arguing that the seizure and admission of the records violated his Fifth Amendment privilege against self-incrimination.

ISSUE: Do the seizure of a defendant's business records and their admission against him at trial violate the Fifth Amendment protection against self-incrimination?

HOLDING AND DECISION: (Blackmun, J.) No. The seizure of a defendant's business records and their admission against him at trial do not violate the Fifth Amendment protection against self-incrimination. Andresen (D) was not compelled to say or do anything personally. The seized records contained statements that Andresen (D) voluntarily put on paper. Although the Fifth Amendment may protect an individual from complying with a subpoena for the production of his personal records in his possession because the very act of production may constitute a compulsory authentication of incriminating information, a seizure of the same materials by law enforcement officers differs in a crucial respect—the individual against whom the search is directed is not required to say or do anything under penalty of sanction.

DISSENT: (Brennan, J.) "The matter cannot be resolved on any simplistic notion of compulsion. Search and seizure is as rife with elements of compulsion as subpoena . . . and compulsion does not disappear merely because the individual is absent at the time of the search and seizure."

▶ ANALYSIS

The Court based its decision upon *Fisher v. United States*, 425 U.S. 391. In that case, it was held that an attorney's production, pursuant to lawful summons of his client's tax records in his hands, did not violate the Fifth Amendment privilege of the taxpayer "because enforcement against a taxpayer's lawyer would not 'compel' the taxpayer to do anything—and certainly would not compel him to be a 'witness' against himself." The Court also cited a principle stated by Justice Holmes, "A party is privileged from producing the evidence but not from its production." The gist of Justice Brennan's dissent was that the effect of the holding was to get around the prohibition against forcing a defendant to produce the papers himself.

Quicknotes

PRIVILEGE AGAINST SELF-INCRIMINATION A privilege guaranteed by the Fifth Amendment to the federal Constitution in a criminal proceeding for communications made by an accused and protecting an accused or witness from having to give testimony that may incriminate himself.

SUBPOENA A mandate issued by court to compel a witness to appear at trial.

Spinelli v. United States

Gambler (D) v. Federal government (P)

393 U.S. 410 (1969).

NATURE OF CASE: Appeal from conviction of violation of gambling statutes.

FACT SUMMARY: Spinelli (D) was convicted upon evidence seized with a search warrant, which was issued based upon an affidavit containing a statement from an anonymous informer and information from FBI agents.

🏛 RULE OF LAW

If an affidavit to obtain a search warrant is based upon an informer's tip (i.e., hearsay), then the affidavit must state why the informer is "reliable" and the "underlying circumstances" from which the informer drew his conclusions, so as to enable an independent magistrate to conclude that the informer's information provides probable cause for the search.

FACTS: Spinelli (D) was convicted of violation of gambling statutes based upon evidence seized by the FBI under a search warrant. The FBI obtained this warrant based upon an affidavit containing the following information: (1) the FBI had been informed by a reliable informer that Spinelli (D) was using two specific telephones to conduct gambling operations; (2) that Spinelli (D) had been seen entering the apartment in which these two telephones were located; and (3) that Spinelli (D) had a reputation as a gambler. Upon conviction, and affirmance of that conviction by the court of appeals, Spinelli (D) brought a petition of certiorari to this Court challenging the constitutionality of the issuance of the search warrant.

ISSUE: Is an affidavit based primarily upon an informer's tip, which does not state why the informer is reliable or the "underlying circumstances" as to how the informer obtained his information, sufficient to establish probable cause for the issuance of a search warrant?

HOLDING AND DECISION: (Harlan, J.) No. If an affidavit to obtain a search warrant is based upon an informer's tip (i.e., hearsay), then the affidavit must state why the informer is "reliable" and the "underlying circumstances" from which the informer drew his conclusions, so as to enable an independent magistrate to conclude that the informer's information provides probable cause for the search. Of course, in the absence of a statement detailing how the informer's tip was gathered, a search warrant may still issue if: (1) the tip describes the accused's criminal activity in such detail (Draper) that a magistrate may conclude that it was gained in a reliable manner, or (2) there is sufficient independent corroboration of criminal activity in the affidavit so that a magistrate may conclude that there is probable cause that a crime is being committed. Here, first, the tip is insufficient for the issuance of a warrant. The affidavit neither states why the informer was considered reliable nor how he obtained his information. Second, there is no sufficient corroboration of the tip. The fact that Spinelli (D) entered an apartment with two telephones contains no suggestion of criminal activity by itself, and the fact that Spinelli (D) is known as a gambler is only "suspicion" entitled to no weight. Judgment reversed.

CONCURRENCE: (White, J.) It is difficult to understand how the majority can claim to embrace *Draper*. The Court in *Draper* did not base its decision on the basis that a tip was sufficiently detailed, but rather on the basis that an informer must be considered reliable because of his past reliability. In *Draper*, several innocent collateral details given by an informer were corroborated by officers' personal observations of the suspect. Under such circumstances, the Court concluded that the officers had "reasonable grounds" to believe another of the informer's details (i.e., the critical detail that Draper was carrying narcotics). But past reliability has never been, and is not in *Spinelli*, considered sufficient for establishing current reliability.

▶ ANALYSIS

This case illustrates the two-pronged Aguilar test applicable to affidavits for search warrants based upon hearsay, and *Harris v. U.S.* (1971) further specified a situation in which a search warrant may be issued on the basis of hearsay. In *Harris*, a warrant was upheld based upon hearsay because the affidavit contained sufficient information to allow the magistrate to determine that there was probable cause for a search warrant. The affidavit contained: (1) the informer's "personal and recent observations" of the accused's criminal activity; (2) the informer's statement which was against his own penal interest; and (3) the fact that the officer himself had certain knowledge of the accused's background consistent with the illegal activity alleged. Note, finally that police do not have to reveal the identity of their informer on a hearing on the issue of probable cause, although they must do so when it is material at trial to establish guilt or innocence.

■=■

Quicknotes

HEARSAY An out-of-court statement made by a person other than the witness testifying at trial that is offered in order to prove the truth of the matter asserted.

■=■

Illinois v. Gates

State (P) v. Drug trafficker (D)

462 U.S. 213 (1983).

NATURE OF CASE: Appeal of an order to suppress evidence gained through an illegal search.

FACT SUMMARY: The Illinois Supreme Court suppressed evidence seized from Lance and Sue Gates (D) holding that the information in an anonymous letter failed to adequately show the reliability of the informant and his basis of knowledge and therefore showed insufficient probable cause to issue the search warrant.

🏛 RULE OF LAW

A magistrate must evaluate the totality of the circumstances presented to him, including, but not limited to, the reliability of an informant and the basis of his knowledge, in determining whether probable cause exists to issue a search warrant.

FACTS: An Illinois (P) magistrate issued a search warrant for the car and residence of Larry and Sue Gates (D) based on an affidavit prepared by Mader, a Bloomingdale police detective which stated he had initiated an investigation of the Gates (D) based on information received in an anonymous letter which alleged in some detail the Gateses' (D) drug trafficking activities between Florida and Illinois (P) and said that on a particular date, they would follow this procedure and pick up over $100,000 in drugs. The affidavit further stated that Mader's investigation had corroborated this information in that among other things, the Gates (D) had traveled to Florida on the day predicted, and had left the next morning travelling toward Chicago. Pursuant to the warrant, the Bloomingdale police searched the Gateses' (D) car and residence upon their return, and seized drugs, weapons, and other contraband. The trial court suppressed the evidence and the appellate court affirmed. The Illinois Supreme Court affirmed on the basis that probable cause could be found only if sufficient facts were presented to show both the relationship of the informant and the basis of his knowledge. It found the affidavit insufficient in this regard and held there was no probable cause to issue the warrant. Illinois (P) appealed.

ISSUE: May a magistrate evaluate the totality of the circumstances presented to him, including, but not limited to, the reliability of the informant and the basis of his knowledge, in determining whether probable cause exists to issue a search warrant?

HOLDING AND DECISION: (Rehnquist, J.) Yes. A magistrate must evaluate the totality of the circumstances presented to him, including, but not limited to, the reliability of an informant and his basis of knowledge, in determining whether probable cause exists to issue a search warrant. In determining probable cause, reliability and basis of knowledge are more useful as interacting issues, where a weak showing of one can be compensated for by a strong showing in the other, than as separate requirements. To require strict adherence to the two-pronged test would severely curtail the use of anonymous information essential to effective police investigations. In this case, the affidavit showing corroboration of the letter coupled with the specificity of detail contained in the letter, adequately show the reliability of the informant based on a totality of the circumstances, and, therefore, it was within the power of the issue magistrate to find that probable cause existed and to issue the warrant. Reversed.

CONCURRENCE: (White, J.) The warrant should be upheld, yet on the basis that it meets the two-pronged test of reliability and basis of knowledge and not on the more expansive totality of circumstances test. Instead of adopting an overly expansive test, the two-pronged test should be clarified to avoid undue rigidness.

DISSENT: (Brennan, J.) By rejecting the two-pronged test, the Court provides no standards to aid lay magistrates in making probable cause determinations. Further, the totality of circumstances test adopted by the Court opens the door to probable cause determinations made on less-than-reliable information from credible sources.

DISSENT: (Stevens, J.) The facts and circumstances in this case show nothing more than a corroboration of events which are just as easily explainable as innocent travel as they are of criminal activity. Because of the lack of sufficient specificity of detail in the letter, it cannot itself be said to show reliability, and therefore no probable cause existed to issue the warrant using either the two-pronged test or the totality of the circumstances test.

▶ ANALYSIS

This case shows the Court encouraging the issuance of search warrants by lowering the standards required to find probable cause. The two-pronged test derived from the cases of *Aguilar v. Texas*, 378 U.S. 108 (1964), and *Spinelli v. United States*, 393 U.S. 410 (1969), had evolved to the point

Continued on next page.

where the Court felt that effective police functions were being undercut by overly expansive interpretations of Fourth Amendment rights. It is argued that the adoption of the totality of the circumstances test is actually a retention of the two-pronged test with recognition of a good faith exception to the exclusionary rule.

■▬■

Quicknotes

AFFIDAVIT   A declaration of facts written and affirmed before a witness.

PROBABLE CAUSE   A reasonable basis for believing that a crime has been committed.

■▬■

Maryland v. Pringle

State (P) v. Convicted drug possessor (D)

540 U.S. 366 (2003).

NATURE OF CASE: Appeal by state from reversal of conviction for cocaine possession.

FACT SUMMARY: When Pringle (D) was arrested for cocaine possession when he was a front-seat passenger in a vehicle and the cocaine was found in the back seat, he argued that he did not have sufficient possession of the cocaine to show probable cause for his arrest, hence any confession resulting from such arrest would be invalid.

RULE OF LAW

The passenger of a vehicle, even if separated from the drugs, has sufficient constructive possession of drugs located in the vehicle to give rise to probable cause for the passenger's arrest.

FACTS: A police officer stopped an automobile for speeding. There were three occupants in the car. Pringle (D) was the front-seat passenger. When the driver opened the glove compartment to get the registration, the officer observed a large amount of rolled-up cash. The driver consented to a vehicle search, which yielded $763 from the glove-compartment and cocaine from behind the back-seat armrest. Pringle (D) and both other occupants were arrested. Pringle (D) waived his Miranda rights and confessed the cocaine belonged to him. The trial court denied Pringle's (D) motion to suppress the confession as fruit of an illegal arrest, holding the officer had probable cause for the arrest. Pringle (D) was convicted of cocaine possession, however the Court of Appeals of Maryland reversed, holding that the mere finding of cocaine in the back armrest when Pringle (D) was simply a passenger in the front seat, failed to establish probable cause to arrest Pringle (D) for possession. Maryland (P) appealed.

ISSUE: Does the passenger of a vehicle, even if separated from the drugs, have sufficient constructive possession of drugs located in the vehicle to give rise to probable cause for the passenger's arrest?

HOLDING AND DECISION: (Rehnquist, C.J.) Yes. The passenger of a vehicle, even if separated from the drugs, has sufficient constructive possession of drugs located in the vehicle to give rise to probable cause for the passenger's arrest. Maryland law authorizes police officers to execute warrantless arrests, inter alia, for felonies committed in an officer's presence or where the officer has probable cause to believe a felony has been, or is being, committed. Here, the officer, upon recovering the plastic bags of cocaine, had probable cause to believe a felony had been committed. As to whether there was probable cause to believe Pringle (D) had committed that crime, Maryland law defines "possession" as the exercise of actual or constructive dominion over a thing by one or more persons. The probable cause standard is incapable of precise definition or quantification into percentages because it deals with probabilities and depends on the totality of the circumstances. In the instant case, Pringle (D) was one of three men riding in the car in the early morning hours when a large amount of rolled up cash and five baggies of cocaine were found. The cocaine was "accessible" to all three of the occupants, including Pringle (D). It was an entirely reasonable inference from these facts that any or all three of the occupants had knowledge of, and exercised dominion and control over, the cocaine. Thus, a reasonable officer could conclude there was probable cause to believe Pringle (D) committed the crime of possession of cocaine, either solely or jointly. Reversed and remanded.

▶ ANALYSIS

As the U.S. Supreme Court makes clear in Pringle, the probable cause standard is a practical, nontechnical conception that deals with the factual and practical considerations of everyday life on which reasonable and prudent persons, "not legal technicians," act. Probable cause is a "fluid concept"—turning on the assessment of probabilities in particular factual contexts, not readily, or even usually, reduced to a neat set of legal rules.

Quicknotes

FELONY A criminal offense of greater seriousness than a misdemeanor; felonies are generally defined pursuant to statute as any crime that is punishable by death or by a term of imprisonment exceeding one year.

United States v. Watson

Federal government (P) v. Credit card thief (D)

423 U.S. 411 (1976).

NATURE OF CASE: Appeal from reversal of a conviction for theft of credit cards from the malls.

FACT SUMMARY: Watson (D) was arrested without a warrant by a government (P) postal inspector who, on the basis of information from a reliable informant, had time to obtain an arrest warrant for theft of credit cards from the malls.

🏛 RULE OF LAW
A law officer may arrest a suspect without a warrant for a felony committed in his presence as well as for a felony not committed in his presence if he has reasonable grounds for making the arrest.

FACTS: A reliable informant told a government (P) postal inspector that Watson (D) had supplied him with a stolen credit card and had agreed to furnish more cards later. Subsequently, the informant met with Watson (D) in a restaurant. When Watson (D) indicated that he had the cards, the informant signaled to the inspector, who arrested Watson (D) without a warrant. Watson's (D) conviction was reversed by the court of appeals on the ground that the inspector had time to obtain an arrest warrant but failed to do so. The government (P) appealed.

ISSUE: May a law officer arrest a suspect without a warrant for a felony committed in his presence as well as for a felony not committed in his presence if he has reasonable grounds for making the arrest?

HOLDING AND DECISION: (White, J.) Yes. Never has any case indicated that an arrest warrant is required under the Fourth Amendment to make an arrest for a felony. At common law, no such warrant was required, and in 1792, the Second Congress saw no inconsistency between the Fourth Amendment and giving federal marshals the same power as state officers to make warrantless arrests. Reversed.

CONCURRENCE: (Powell, J.) The holding creates an anomaly because great discretion is given in making warrantless arrests while rarely can a warrantless search be made even though it would appear that an arrest is a greater personal invasion. "But logic sometimes must defer to history and experience."

DISSENT: (Marshall, J.) The case should have simply been decided on the ground that the inspector had probable cause to believe that an offense was taking place in his presence (at the restaurant), and that the suspect was then in possession of the evidence. The Court need not have gone beyond that; having done so, it must be said that the common-law rule provides no support for the far-reaching modern rule fashioned here. And, as a matter of doctrine, the longstanding existence of a government practice does not immunize it from scrutiny under the Constitution.

▶ ANALYSIS

The ALI Model Code of Pre-Arraignment Procedure (1975) § 120.1 provides that a law officer, if he has reasonable cause, may make warrantless arrests for felonies and, under certain circumstances, for misdemeanors. The commentary to that section states: "This section does not require an officer to arrest under a warrant even if a reasonable opportunity to obtain a warrant exists. As to arrests on the street, such a requirement would be entirely novel."

Quicknotes

FELONY A criminal offense of greater seriousness than a misdemeanor; felonies are generally defined pursuant to statute as any crime that is punishable by death or by a term of imprisonment exceeding one year.

MISDEMEANOR Any offense that does not constitute a felony, which is generally less severe and for which a lesser punishment is imposed.

United States v. Robinson

Federal government (P) v. Heroin possessor (D)

414 U.S. 218 (1973).

NATURE OF CASE: Action against Robinson (D) for possession and facilitation of concealment of heroin.

FACT SUMMARY: A police officer arrested Robinson (D) for a traffic violation. It was conceded that he had probable cause for the arrest. During his search of Robinson (D), the officer found a cigarette package containing heroin.

> 🏛 **RULE OF LAW**
> A full search of a person incident to a lawful arrest is a reasonable search under the Fourth Amendment and need not be limited to a frisk for weapons in cases involving crimes, such as traffic violations, where there would be no further evidence of such crimes.

FACTS: As a result of a previous investigation of Robinson's (D) driver's permit, Officer Jenks decided that there was reason to believe that Robinson (D) was driving without a license. He signalled Robinson (D) to stop his car, and when he did, Jenks arrested him. It was conceded that Jenks had probable cause for the arrest. In accordance with police department procedures, Jenks searched Robinson (D). He felt an object in Robinson's (D) coat, but couldn't tell its size or what it was. He pulled it out and found a crumbled cigarette package. He opened it and found heroin capsules inside. The court of appeals held that since no further evidence could have been obtained from a search in this case, Jenks should have only conducted a search for weapons.

ISSUE: Are there circumstances in which a police officer may not conduct a full search of an arrestee's person following a lawful arrest?

HOLDING AND DECISION: (Rehnquist, J.) No. A search incident to a lawful arrest is a traditional exception to the warrant requirement of the Fourth Amendment. The validity of the search of the person of the arrestee is well established and is considered to be a reasonable search under the Fourth Amendment. The court of appeals felt that in a case involving a traffic violation, the principles of *Terry v. Ohio*, 392 U.S. 1 (1968), should be applied and only a search for weapons could be justified. *Terry v. Ohio* held that a frisk incident to an investigative stop based on less than probable cause must be limited to a search for weapons. That decision recognizes a sharp distinction between such frisks and searches incident to arrests for probable cause. That case affords no basis for extending the limitation placed on a stop-and-frisk search without probable cause to a probable cause arrest. The court of appeals, in effect, determined that the only reason supporting a full search incident to a lawful arrest was the possibility of discovering evidence. However, the reason for a full search rests equally on the need to disarm the arrestee. The danger to the officer is far greater in the case of the extended proximity which follows the custodial arrest of a suspect than in a stop-and-frisk encounter. Further, the danger to the officer flows from the arrest itself, rather than from the grounds for arrest. The search of Robinson's (D) person conducted by Jenks and the seizure of the heroin were permissible under the Fourth Amendment. Officer Jenks was not required to limit the search to a search for weapons. Reversed.

DISSENT: (Marshall, J.) The vast majority of the several state and federal courts which have considered this question have held that absent special circumstances, a police officer has no right to conduct a full search of the person incident to a lawful arrest for violation of a motor vehicle violation. Here, the majority attempts to avoid case-by-case adjudication of Fourth Amendment issues. However, "there is no formula for the determination of reasonable, each case is to be decided on its own facts and circumstances." Further, the powers granted to the police in this case are strong ones, subject to potential abuse. There is always the possibility that a police officer, lacking probable cause to obtain a search warrant, will use a traffic arrest as a pretext to conduct a search. In this case, Jenks's removal of the cigarette package, which he said he did not believe was a weapon, exceeded the limitation of the Terry frisk for weapons. May a police officer, when effecting an arrest of a traffic offender, make a fuller search of the person than Terry permits? To answer this question, the individual's interest in remaining free from unnecessarily intrusive invasions of privacy must be balanced with society's interest that police officers not take unnecessary risks in performing their duties. It is not necessary to solve this balancing question here, but empirical evidence does support the court of appeals' decision rather than the result reached by the majority. This evidence indicates that "virtually all of the killings of officers in the line of duty are caused by guns and weapons, the very type of weapons which will not go undetected in a properly conducted weapon search. In this case, however, Jenks's search extended beyond Robinson's (D) person to a separate search of effects found on his person.

Continued on next page.

Assuming, arguendo, that it was reasonable for Jenks to remove the cigarette package from Robinson's (D) person, there was no justification consistent with the Fourth Amendment for his looking inside the package. Once in Jenks's hands, even if the package did contain a weapon, it was out of Robinson's (D) reach. Opening the package, therefore, did not further the protective purpose of the search.

▶ ANALYSIS

Most courts have upheld inventory of the items found on the arrestee's person as a part of the booking process, on the ground that it is a reasonable means of safeguarding the accused's property while they are in jail, and ensuring that weapons and contraband are not introduced into the jail. Some courts have limited the inventory authority somewhat by ruling that evidence found in an inventory must be suppressed if the police conducted the inventory without a correct determination of whether the arrestee would, of necessity, be held in jail. As to an officer's power to seize items uncovered in a search incident to an arrest in *State v. Elkins*, 245 Or. 279 (1966), it was held that before an officer can seize implements of a crime other than that for which the arrest was made, he must have reasonable grounds to believe that the article is contraband.

■■■

Quicknotes

CONTRABAND Items that are illegal to have in one's possession or to trade or produce.

INVESTIGATORY STOP A brief, nonintrusive stop, requiring the police officer to have a reasonable suspicion that a crime has been committed based on specific and articulable facts.

PROBABLE CAUSE A reasonable basis for believing that a crime has been committed.

■■■

Chimel v. California

Burglary convict (D) v. State (P)

395 U.S. 752 (1969).

NATURE OF CASE: Appeal from burglary conviction.

FACT SUMMARY: Police officers, after lawfully arresting Chimel (D) in his house, conducted a search, over his objections, of his entire house, which produced evidence used to obtain his conviction on two charges of burglary.

RULE OF LAW

Under the Fourth and Fourteenth Amendments, a warrantless search conducted incident to a lawful arrest may only extend to a search of the arrestee's person and to the area "within his immediate control" (i.e., the area within which he might obtain a weapon or destructible evidence).

FACTS: Late one afternoon, police officers arrived at Chimel's (D) home with a warrant authorizing his arrest for the burglary of a coin shop. Chimel's (D) wife allowed the officers to enter the house and wait for Chimel (D) to return from work. When Chimel (D) entered his home, the officers arrested him and then conducted a search, over his objection, of his entire three-bedroom house, including the attic, the garage, and a small workshop. During this search, the officers seized a number of coins, several medal tokens, and other objects, used subsequently at Chimel's (D) trial to obtain his conviction on two charges of burglary. Upon affirmance of this conviction, Chimel (D) brought a petition for certiorari to this court.

ISSUE: When a suspect is lawfully arrested in one room of his house, can a search of his entire house be constitutionally justified as incident to that arrest?

HOLDING AND DECISION: (Stewart, J.) No. Under the Fourth and Fourteenth Amendments, a warrantless search conducted incident to a lawful arrest may only extend to a search of the arrestee's person and to the area "within his immediate control" (i.e., the area within which he might obtain a weapon for destructible evidence). The past decisions of this Court on such searches have been far from consistent, and this case marks the final determination of which one of two divergent lines of cases applies. On one hand, the *Harris*, 331 U.S. 145 (1947), and *Rabinowitz*, 339 U.S. 56 (1950), line of cases have given a broad scope to warrantless searches conducted incident to arrest. Under these cases, anything within the "possession" of the arrestee (as broadly defined to include

a search of the arrestee's entire apartment in Harris, and to include a search of the arrestee's one-room business office in Rabinowitz) may be searched at the time of his arrest, in order to seize any evidence connected with his suspected crime. On the other hand, the *Go-Bart*, 282 U.S. 344 (1931), *Lefkowitz*, 285 U.S. 452 (1932), and *Trupiano*, 334 U.S. 699 (1948), line of cases limits warrantless charges incident to arrest. In both *Go-Bart* and *Lefkowitz*, such searches were limited to evidence which was "visible and accessible and in the offender's immediate custody." In *Trupiano*, the Court stated that a search warrant is always required absent some showing of "necessity" and there must be something more of a necessity for a warrantless search than mere arrest. The decision of this Court today is an attempt to define, along the line of the *Trupiano* case, when such necessity exists. As this Court stated in *Trupiano*, the burden is upon those seeking an exemption from the warrant requirement to show that it is justified by necessity. Such justification in the case of warrantless searches incident to arrest may extend no further than the arrestee's person and the area within his immediate control. It is reasonable for an officer to search the arrestee's person for his own safety, since the arrestee may have concealed weapons, and it is reasonable to search the area within the arrestee's control to prevent him from reaching a weapon or destroying evidence. But, any extension beyond such an area would lead to the "evaporation" of the Fourth Amendment's right against unreasonable searches and seizures. Here, the search of Chimel's (D) house was far beyond that area considered reasonable. As such, the judgment is reversed.

CONCURRENCE: (Harlan, J.) Today's decision raised a problem of implementation, since the states have widely varying local law enforcement problems and it is not known to what extent they are prepared to administer the greatly expanded warrant system required by this decision. However, *Harris* and *Rabinowitz* are bad Fourth Amendment law, and cannot be upheld.

DISSENT: (White, J.) When there is probable cause to search and there are exigent circumstances making it "impracticable" to obtain a search warrant, a warrantless search is reasonable under the Fourth Amendment. Such an exigent circumstance is supplied by the fact of an arrest. Almost always, there is a strong possibility that if officers leave the scene of the arrest to obtain a warrant, confederates of the arrestee

Continued on next page.

will remove that evidence for which the officers had probable cause to search. It is, therefore, unreasonable, assuming that there is probable cause to search the premises where a person is lawfully arrested, to require the police to obtain a search warrant.

▶ *ANALYSIS*

This case illustrates the limited scope of a warrantless search conducted incident to a lawful arrest. Whenever police take an arrested person into custody, it is "reasonable" to make a "full search" of his person, regardless of the reason for his arrest. But this decision leaves open the question of whether a "full search," or only a limited search for weapons, may be conducted when the person is not taken into custody after his arrest. Note, however, that after a lawful arrest, when the suspect is taken into custody, a warrantless search of his clothing and the property in his immediate possession may be done "after he has been brought to the station house" and "after a substantial period of time during his incarceration"—at least when there is probable cause linking the clothes to his crime.

Quicknotes

EXIGENT CIRCUMSTANCES Circumstances requiring an extraordinary or immediate response; an exception to the prohibition on a warrantless arrest or search when police officers believe probable cause to exist and there is no time for obtaining a warrant.

SEARCH INCIDENT TO LAWFUL ARREST EXCEPTION PLAIN VIEW Exception to the requirement of a valid warrant for a search or seizure so long as the officer is lawfully in the location where the evidence is obtained and it is apparent that the thing seized is evidence.

Payton v. New York

Murder convict (D) v. State (P)

445 U.S. 573 (1980).

NATURE OF CASE: Appeal from convictions for murder.

FACT SUMMARY: Without a warrant, the police entered Payton's (D) apartment to arrest him for murder and, even though he was not there, seized a shell casing that was in plain sight and was later admitted into evidence at his trial.

> 🏛 **RULE OF LAW**
> Absent exigent circumstances, the police may not make a warrantless, nonconsensual entry into a private residence to make a routine felony arrest.

FACTS: Having probable cause to believe Payton (D) had murdered a gas station manager, the police entered his apartment to effect a routine felony arrest. Although he was not home, the police found a 30-caliber shell casing in plain sight in the apartment and seized it for ultimate use as evidence at his trial. Payton's (D) motions to suppress the evidence were denied and he was convicted of murder. On appeal, he argued that the statute authorizing warrantless entries to make routine felony arrests violated the Fourth Amendment. The court of appeals affirmed the conviction.

ISSUE: Under normal circumstances, is it constitutional for the police to make a warrantless, nonconsensual entry into a private residence to effect a routine felony arrest?

HOLDING AND DECISION: (Stevens, J.) No. The Fourth Amendment does not permit the police to make a warrantless and nonconsensual entry into a private residence to effect a routine felony arrest in the absence of exigent circumstances. The Fourth Amendment, made applicable to the states by the Fourteenth Amendment, draws a firm line at the entrance to the house. Absent exigent circumstances, that threshold may not reasonably be crossed without a warrant. Inasmuch as no warrant was obtained, the police acted impermissibly in entering Payton's (D) apartment, and the evidence found therein should not have been admitted into evidence at trial. Reversed.

DISSENT: (White, J.) Instead of adopting a rule which will severely hamper effective law enforcement, the Court should embrace a clear and simple rule comporting with the carefully crafted restrictions on the common-law power of arrest entry. That is, after knocking and announcing their presence, police may enter the home to make a daytime arrest without a warrant when there is a probable cause to believe that the person to be arrested committed a felony and is present in the house.

▶ ANALYSIS

At the time this case was decided, some states had already passed laws requiring a warrant as a precondition to a felony arrest in the home. The Court noted that no proof had been offered that such a requirement had caused law enforcement in those states to suffer.

Quicknotes

EXIGENT CIRCUMSTANCES Circumstances requiring an extraordinary or immediate response; an exception to the prohibition on a warrantless arrest or search when police officers believe probable cause to exist and there is no time for obtaining a warrant.

KNOCK AND ANNOUNCE Requirement that a police officer must first knock and announce his intention before he enters an individual's home in the execution of a valid warrant.

California v. Carney

State (P) v. Drug dealer (D)

471 U.S. 386 (1985).

NATURE OF CASE: Appeal from conviction for drug trafficking.

FACT SUMMARY: Carney (D) was accused of trading drugs for sexual favors.

🏛 RULE OF LAW
The "automobile exception" to the warrant requirement applies to motor homes.

FACTS: A Drug Enforcement Agency (DEA) agent placed the motor home of Carney (D) under surveillance. When a youth exited the motor home, he was stopped by Williams, a DEA agent. The youth told him that he had received marijuana in return for sexual favors. Williams and other agents searched the motor home and found marijuana and related paraphernalia. Carney (D) was charged with possession for sale. He moved to suppress the evidence as the agents did not have a search warrant. The trial court denied the motion, but the California Supreme Court reversed.

ISSUE: Does the "automobile exception" to the warrant requirement apply to motor homes?

HOLDING AND DECISION: (Burger, C.J.) Yes. The "automobile exception" to the warrant requirement applies to motor homes. The reason for the exception is twofold. Autos are inherently mobile and can be taken away before a warrant is issued. Also, autos, unlike homes, are subject to regulations that lower the owner's expectation of privacy. The motor home here, while having homelike qualities, is also inherently mobile and is subject to the same state licensing as a regular automobile. Therefore, the rationales for the auto exception apply to mobile homes. Reversed.

DISSENT: (Stevens, J.) Where, as here, agents have the element of surprise on their side, and the motor home is parked, the exigencies justifying the auto exception do not apply.

▶ ANALYSIS

While auto searches do not require warrants, probable cause is still necessary. For this reason, the scope of an auto search is limited. It may not be more intrusive than that necessary to obtain the required evidence.

Quicknotes

AUTOMOBILE EXCEPTION Exception to the requirement of a valid warrant if a police officer has probable cause to believe that a vehicle contains evidence of a crime or contraband; the officer may search the entire vehicle.

EXIGENT CIRCUMSTANCES Circumstances requiring an extraordinary or immediate response; an exception to the prohibition on a warrantless arrest or search when police officers believe probable cause to exist and there is no time for obtaining a warrant.

EXPECTATION OF PRIVACY Requirement that in order to invoke the Fourth Amendment's protection against unreasonable searches and seizures, the individual must have a reasonable expectation of privacy in respect to the location searched or thing seized.

PROBABLE CAUSE A reasonable basis for believing that a crime has been committed.

California v. Acevedo

State (P) v. Contraband possessor (D)

500 U.S. 565 (1991).

NATURE OF CASE: Appeal from acceptance of motion to suppress evidence.

FACT SUMMARY: In California's (P) criminal action against Acevedo (D) for possession of contraband, the appellate court, reversing the district court's ruling, accepted Acevedo's (D) motion to suppress evidence relating to his contraband possession.

RULE OF LAW
The warrantless search of an automobile or any closed containers within it is reasonable under the Fourth Amendment if there is probable cause for the search.

FACTS: Officers, who had probable cause to believe that contraband was in a residence which they had under surveillance, watched Acevedo (D) enter the address, stay for ten minutes, and reappear carrying a full, brown paper bag. Subsequently, Acevedo (D) placed this bag in the trunk of his car and started to drive away. However, the officers, fearing loss of evidence, stopped him, opened his trunk and the bag without a warrant, and found contraband. At the criminal proceedings brought against Acevedo (D) for possession of contraband, Acevedo (D) moved to suppress the contraband evidence, arguing that since the officers' probable cause was directed specifically at the bag and not at his car, common law dictated that the officers obtain a warrant prior to searching the bag's contents. Notwithstanding Acevedo's (D) argument, the district court denied his motion. On appeal, however, the California Court of Appeal reversed, and the Supreme Court affirmed. California (P) appealed.

ISSUE: Is the warrantless search of an automobile or any closed containers within it reasonable under the Fourth Amendment if there is probable cause for the search?

HOLDING AND DECISION: (Blackmun, J.) Yes. The warrantless search of an automobile or any closed containers within it is reasonable under the Fourth Amendment if there is probable cause for the search. This rule rectifies the two apparently dichotomous common law rules governing the warrantless search of an automobile and the warrantless search of a closed container within the automobile. The dichotomy dictates that if there is probable cause to search a car, then the entire car—including any closed container found therein—may be searched without a warrant, but if there is probable cause only as to a container in the car, the container may be held but not searched until a warrant is obtained. However, the line between probable cause to search a vehicle and probable cause to search a package in that vehicle is not always clear, and separate rules that govern the two objects to be searched may enable police to broaden their power to make warrantless searches to the detriment of privacy interests. Furthermore, the protection of privacy interests afforded by disallowing the warrantless search of closed container contained within an automobile is minimal since, in an overwhelming majority of cases, a warrant is routinely given after a closed container is seized. Finally, the discrepancy between the two rules has led to confusion for law enforcement officers. Hence, to avoid these anomalous results, necessity dictates that the common law rule requiring a warrant to search closed containers contained within an automobile be overruled. In the instant case, although the police merely had probable cause as to the contraband, their search of the paper bag was reasonable under the Fourth Amendment. Reversed and remanded.

CONCURRENCE: (Scalia, J.) Reversal was proper not because a closed container carried inside a car becomes subject to the "automobile" exception to the general warrant requirement but because the search of a closed container, outside a privately owned building, with probable cause to believe that the container contains contraband, is not one of those searches whose Fourth Amendment reasonableness depends upon a warrant.

DISSENT: (Stevens, J.) It is a cardinal principle that searches conducted outside the judicial process, without prior approval by judge or magistrate, are per se unreasonable under the Fourth Amendment—subject only to a few specifically established and well-delineated exceptions. Moreover, the circumstances in the present case are not so exceptional as to justify invasion of an individual's privacy interest outside the presence of a neutral magistrate.

▶ ANALYSIS

In considering the above rule, the next logical step for the court may be to permit warrantless searches of luggage or personal belongings being transported on foot as opposed to within a motor vehicle since there is a possibility that evidence can be lost, i.e., through the transporter taking flight or through the evidence being hidden, only to be retrieved later. Obviously, the possibility of these two things happening dictates whether such a rule would be adopted. Moreover, a significant increase in drug activity across the country may also make such a rule thinkable.

Thornton v. United States

Drug and firearms defendant (P) v. Federal government (D)

541 U.S. 615 (2004).

NATURE OF CASE: Appeal from denial of a motion to suppress evidence.

FACT SUMMARY: When a police officer, after lawfully arresting Marcus Thornton (D) who had just alighted from his vehicle, searched the interior of the vehicle and found incriminating evidence, Thornton (D) contended that, under *New York v. Belton*, it is only when an officer makes a lawful custodial arrest of an "occupant" of a vehicle that the Fourth Amendment allows a search of the vehicle's interior.

🏛 RULE OF LAW
So long as an arrestee is a recent occupant of a vehicle, officers may search that vehicle incident to the arrest.

FACTS: A suspicious police officer observed Marcus Thornton (D) drive his vehicle into a parking lot and exit the vehicle. The officer accosted Thornton (D) and informed him his license tags did not match the vehicle he was driving. Thornton (D) agreed to a pat down; the officer found drugs, placed Thornton (D) under arrest, and searched the interior of the vehicle where he found a handgun under the driver's seat. The district court denied Thornton's (D) motion to suppress evidence of the gun. Thornton (D) was convicted of drug and gun charges. The court of appeals affirmed, and Thornton (D) appealed.

ISSUE: So long as an arrestee is a recent occupant of a vehicle, may officers search that vehicle incident to the arrest?

HOLDING AND DECISION: (Rehnquist, C.J.) Yes. So long as an arrestee is a recent occupant of a vehicle, officers may search that vehicle incident to the arrest. In *New York v. Belton*, 453 U.S. 454 (1981), this Court held that when an officer makes a lawful custodial arrest of an occupant of an automobile, the Fourth Amendment allows a search of the passenger compartment. Today we hold that *Belton* governs even when an officer does not make the vehicle search until the person has left the vehicle. In all relevant aspects, the arrest of a suspect who is next to a vehicle presents identical concerns regarding officer safety and the destruction of evidence as the arrest of one who is inside the vehicle. An officer may search a suspect's vehicle under *Belton* only if the suspect is arrested. A custodial arrest is fluid and the danger to the police officer flows from the fact of the arrest, and its attendant proximity, stress, and uncertainty. The stress is no less merely because the arrestee exited his or her car before the officer initiated contact, nor is an arrestee less likely to attempt to lunge for a weapon or to destroy evidence if he or she is outside of, but still in control of, the vehicle. In either case, the officer faces a highly volatile situation. It would make little sense to apply two different rules to what is, at bottom, the same situation. Furthermore, in some circumstances it may be safer and more effective for officers to conceal their presence from a suspect until he or she has left the vehicle; certainly that is a judgment officers should be free to make without jeopardizing their ability to maintain their own safety or to prevent evidence destruction. Affirmed.

CONCURRENCE: (O'Connor, J.) Lower court decisions seem now to treat the ability to search a vehicle incident to the arrest of a recent occupant as a police entitlement rather than as an exception justified by the rationales of *Chimel v. California*, 395 U.S. 752 (1969).

CONCURRENCE: (Scalia, J.) If *Belton* searches are justifiable, it is not because the arrestee might grab a weapon or evidentiary item from the car, but simply because the car might contain evidence relevant to the crime for which he was arrested. Here, Thornton (D) was lawfully arrested for a drug offense, and it was reasonable for the officer to believe that further contraband might be found in the vehicle from which he had just alighted and which was still in the vicinity at the time of the arrest. I would affirm on that ground.

DISSENT: (Stevens, J.) The only genuine justification for extending *Belton* to cover search of a vehicle after the arrestee has exited, is the interest in uncovering potentially valuable evidence. Such a goal must give way to the citizen's constitutionally protected interest in privacy when there is already in place a well-defined rule limiting the permissible scope of a search of an arrested pedestrian.

▶ ANALYSIS

Not all contraband in the passenger compartment or other interior part of a vehicle is likely to be readily accessible to a recent occupant. However, in *Thornton*, the firearm and the passenger compartment in general were no more inaccessible than were the contraband and the passenger compartment in *Belton*. The need for a clear rule, readily understood by police officers and not depending on differing estimates of what items were or were not within reach of an arrestee at any particular moment, justifies the sort of generalization which *Belton* enunciated.

■=■

Colorado v. Bertine

State (P) v. DUI arrestee (D)

479 U.S. 367 (1987).

NATURE OF CASE: Appeal of order to suppress evidence.

FACT SUMMARY: A routine inventory of Bertine's (D) auto after Bertine's (D) driving under the influence (DUI) arrest produced closed containers which, when opened, revealed contraband.

RULE OF LAW
A police inventory inspection may involve the opening of closed containers.

FACTS: Bertine (D) was arrested for drunk driving. Following the arrest, Bertine's (D) auto was inventoried. Sealed containers were found which, when opened, revealed illegal drugs. Bertine (D) moved to suppress the contents of the containers. The trial court granted the motion on state constitutional grounds. The state supreme court upheld the suppression, but on federal constitutional grounds. The State (P) appealed.

ISSUE: May a police inventory inspection involve the opening of closed containers?

HOLDING AND DECISION: (Rehnquist, C.J.) Yes. A police inventory inspection may involve the opening of closed containers. Inventory searches are a well-defined exception to the Fourth Amendment's warrant requirement, and probable cause does not figure into the analysis, provided that the inspection was in fact routine and not a subterfuge for a criminal investigation. The state has a legitimate interest in ensuring against theft and fraudulent claims of property loss, and, therefore, an inventory is proper. It is not possible to know the contents of a closed container without opening it, so the opening of a closed container during inventory is proper. Reversed.

CONCURRENCE: (Blackmun, J.) The opening of a closed container is permissible only if done as part of routine procedures mandating such opening every time.

DISSENT: (Marshall, J.) The procedure here afforded the police officer excessive discretion.

▶ ANALYSIS

The police department in this instance had at least two options, one being simply to park and lock the vehicle in a public area. The police chose to impound and search the vehicle instead. The dissent argued that this, in effect, gave the police discretion regarding whether to search.

■━■

Quicknotes

CONTRABAND Items that are illegal to have in one's possession or to trade or produce.

■━■

Terry v. Ohio

Armed suspect (D) v. State (P)

392 U.S. 1 (1968).

NATURE OF CASE: Certiorari from conviction for carrying a concealed weapon.

FACT SUMMARY: When Officer McFadden became suspicious of the behavior of three men in downtown Cleveland, he stopped them, identified himself, and, believing that they were armed and dangerous, frisked them (i.e., patted their outer clothing), finding a concealed weapon on Terry (D).

🏛 RULE OF LAW
Regardless of the existence of probable cause, where a police officer "reasonably" concludes in the light of his experience that criminal activity may be afoot and that the persons with whom he is dealing may be armed and dangerous, he may "stop" such persons; and, if after identifying himself and making reasonable inquiries, his fears are not dispelled, he may conduct a carefully limited search of the outer clothing of such persons for weapons.

FACTS: Officer McFadden, a Cleveland plainclothes detective, became suspicious of two men (one of whom was Terry (D)) who were repeatedly peering into a store down the street and then returning to a corner. When a third man joined these two suspects, Officer McFadden, surmising that the suspects were "casing" a stickup and, therefore, might be armed and dangerous, stopped them. Upon identifying himself as a policeman and receiving only mumbling replies to his questions, McFadden patted (i.e., "frisked") their outer clothing and, upon feeling a pistol under Terry's (D) clothing, removed it. Terry (D) was charged with carrying a concealed weapon. At his trial, Terry (D) moved to suppress the evidence, but the trial court denied his motion and Terry (D) was convicted. Upon affirmance of his conviction by the Ohio Court of Appeals, and dismissal of his appeal by the state supreme court, Terry (D) filed a petition for certiorari with this court.

ISSUE: Is it always unreasonable for a policeman, absent probable cause, to stop a person and subject him to a limited search of his outer clothing for weapons?

HOLDING AND DECISION: (Warren, C.J.) No. Regardless of the existence of probable cause, where a police officer "reasonably" concludes in the light of his experience that criminal activity may be afoot and that the persons with whom he is dealing may be armed and dangerous, he may "stop" such persons and, if after identifying himself and making reason-

able inquiries, his fears are not dispelled, he may conduct a carefully limited search of the outer clothing of such persons for weapons. Stop-and-frisk conduct, although covered by the Fourth Amendment, should not be subjected to the warrant requirement as well. The wide variety of street encounters found by the police requires "necessarily swift action upon on-the-spot observations of the officer on the beat," which historically has not, and practically cannot, be subjected to the warrant requirement. As such, the brief intrusion on the suspect's freedom is more properly tested under the Fourth Amendment's general proscription against "unreasonable" searches and seizures. Under this test of reasonableness, the need to search must be balanced against the invasion involved. In the stop-and-frisk situation, the government has a need to search to promote effective crime control and to protect the police officer's safety. Furthermore, if (1) the stop-and-frisk is based upon "specific inferences" (not on "unparticularized suspicion or hunches"), so that the officer's behavior can later be objectively reviewed, and if (2) the stop-and-frisk is limited to a frisk for weapons, the invasion is justified and reasonable. Here, Officer McFadden legitimately investigated suspicious behavior, acted under "reasonable suspicion" that the suspects might be armed and dangerous, and frisked only their outer garments. As such, the search was reasonable and the evidence is admissible. Judgment affirmed.

CONCURRENCE: (Harlan, J.) There are a few gaps in the decision of the court, although its ultimate conclusion is sound. If a frisk is to be justified in order to protect the officer, the officer must first have constitutional grounds to make a forcible "stop" (i.e., reasonable suspicion), but a limited frisk incident to such a lawful stop requires no additional justification. There is no reason why an officer should risk a bullet by first questioning the suspect.

CONCURRENCE: (White, J.) There is no need for interrogation during an investigative stop before the officer frisks the suspect. Although an officer may question the suspects briefly, when a temporary detention is justified by a fear for the officer's and others' safety, a protective frisk for weapons is justified regardless of whether or not any questions are asked.

DISSENT: (Douglas, J.) A search and seizure cannot be justified by Fourth Amendment standards unless there is "probable cause" to believe that a crime has been committed

Continued on next page.

or is about to be committed. Here, however, since there was no "probable cause" for the issuance of a warrant, the court's holding allows police greater freedom to search and seize than even a judge could authorize.

▶ *ANALYSIS*

This case illustrates the less stringent rule applicable to stop-and-frisk than that applicable to arrest and search. This rule was further clarified in *Sibron v. New York*, 392 U.S. 40 (1968), in which the court stated than an officer "must be able to point to particular facts from which he reasonably inferred that the individual was armed and dangerous." However, in *Adams v. Williams*, 407 U.S. 143 (1972), the Court stated that this "reasonable inference" need not be based upon the officer's personal observation. Rather, it may be based upon an unnamed informer's tip that "carries some indicia of reliability," even though the unverified tip is not so reliable as to constitute "probable cause" for an arrest or search warrant.

■══■

Quicknotes

REASONABLE SUSPICION   That which would cause an ordinary prudent person under the circumstances to suspect that a crime has been committed based on specific and articulable facts.

STOP AND FRISK   A brief, nonintrusive stop, requiring the police officer to have a reasonable suspicion that a crime has been committed based on specific and articulable facts, and involving a search for a concealed weapon that is conducted by patting down the clothes of the person.

■══■

Schneckloth v. Bustamonte

Court (P) v. Car passenger (D)

412 U.S. 218 (1973).

NATURE OF CASE: Petition for writ of habeas corpus, after conviction.

FACT SUMMARY: An officer stopped a car carrying Bustamonte (D) and five other men because it had a burned-out headlight. The one man who had identification said that the car belonged to his brother. When the officer asked if he could search it the man replied, "Sure." The officer found some stolen checks in the car.

🏛 RULE OF LAW
Whether a consent to a search was, in fact, voluntary is a question of fact to be determined from all of the circumstances, and while the person's knowledge of a right to refuse is a factor to be taken into account, the prosecution is not required to demonstrate such knowledge as a prerequisite to establishing a voluntary consent.

FACTS: Officer Rand stopped an automobile when he observed that its headlight and license plate light were burned out. There were six men, including Bustamonte (D), in the car. Only one of the men had identification, and he said that the car belonged to his brother. When Rand asked if he could search the car, the man replied, "Sure, go ahead," and helped Rand with the search. Rand found some stolen checks in the car. Bustamonte (D) was convicted on the basis of the checks and other evidence. The court of appeals granted Bustamonte's (D) petition for a writ of habeas corpus, holding that when a prosecutor relies upon consent to justify a search, it is an essential part of the state's burden to prove that the person knew of his/her right to refuse consent.

ISSUE: Must it be shown by the State that a person who consented to a search knew of his/her right to refuse consent in order for the consent (and the search) to be valid?

HOLDING AND DECISION: (Stewart, J.) No. A search conducted pursuant to a valid consent is constitutionally permissible. But when the State seeks to rely on a consent to justify a search, it has the burden of showing that the consent was freely and voluntarily given. Whether a consent to a search was voluntary or was the product of duress or coercion is a question of fact to be determined from the totality of all the circumstances. While knowledge of the right to refuse consent is one factor to be considered, the State need not prove such knowledge in order to prove consent. Searches authorized by consent are of unquestioned benefit to the police. However, such consent must not be coerced. "To approve such searches without the most careful scrutiny would sanction the possibility of official coercion; to place artificial restrictions upon such searches would jeopardize their basic validity; to require that proof that the person consenting to the search knew of his/her right to refuse consent would seriously impair such searches. In many cases where there was no evidence of coercion, the State would still be unable to show that the person knew of the right to refuse. Likewise, a person who consented to a search could prevent the use of the fruits of the search as evidence by failing to testify to having knowledge of the right to refuse consent. It is suggested that subjects of searches could be advised of their right to refuse. However, "It would be thoroughly impracticable to impose on the informal and unstructured conditions of the normal consent search the detailed requirements of an effecting warning." These conditions are far removed from the structured atmosphere of a trial or even "custodial interrogation." It is contended that a consent is a waiver of a person's Fourth and Fourteenth Amendment rights, and that only knowing and intelligent waivers are valid. However, the knowing and intelligent waiver requirement is almost always only applied to those rights guaranteed to a criminal defendant in order to preserve a fair trial, such as rights to counsel, to confrontation, to a jury trial, and to a speedy trial. These rights are aimed at promoting the fair ascertainment of truth at trial. Fourth Amendment rights are quite different and protect one's privacy against arbitrary police intrusion. It would be unrealistic to expect that in the informal, unstructured context of a consent search, an officer could make the detailed type of examination demanded by the intelligent and knowing waiver requirements. Also, a waiver approach to consent searches would be inconsistent with decisions approving third party consents. It is inconceivable that the Constitution could countenance the waiver of a defendant's right to counsel or to confrontation by a third party. Yet, such consents to searches by third parties have been held valid. Here, there was no evidence of any coercive tactics by the police, either from the nature of the police questioning or the environment in which it took place. The court of appeals decision is reversed.

DISSENT: (Marshall, J.) This case deals not with "coercion" but with "consent," a subtly different concept. Freedom from coercion is a substantive right, guaranteed by the Fifth and Fourteenth Amendments. Consent is a mechanism by

Continued on next page.

which substantive requirements are avoided. Consent searches are submitted not because such an exception to the requirements of probable cause and warrant is essential to law enforcement, but because citizens are permitted to choose whether or not they wish to exercise their constitutional rights. Our prior decisions do not support the view that a meaningful choice has been made simply because no coercion was used. Consent means a knowing choice. How can a decision made without knowledge of the available alternatives be called a choice? I would hold that the State may not rely on a purported consent to a search if the subject of the search did not know of his right to refuse consent. The subject's knowledge of this right could be shown by his demonstration of such knowledge at the time of the search, by having him testify under oath (if he is not the defendant), by the subject's prior experience or training, or if the police, at the time of the search, told the subject of his right to refuse consent. There is nothing impractical about this latter method, and the decision to employ it would lie with the officers. "I doubt that a simple statement by an officer of an individuals' right to refuse consent would do much to alter the informality of this exchange, except to alert the subject to a fact that he is entitled to know. For many years, FBI agents have routinely informed subjects of their right to refuse consent. I must conclude, with some reluctance, that when the court speaks of practicality, what it really is talking of is the continued ability of the police to capitalize on the ignorance of citizens so as to accomplish by subterfuge what they could not achieve by relying only on the knowing relinquishment of constitutional rights."

▶ *ANALYSIS*

A search based upon a valid consent may be conducted without a warrant and without probable cause. Most federal courts have applied the light standards normally applicable to the waiver of constitutional rights to determine the validity of a consent to a search. It is said that a consent, in order to be voluntary, must be unequivocal, specific, and intelligently given, uncontaminated by any duress or coercion, and is not lightly to be inferred. In *Bumper v. North Carolina*, 391 U.S. 543 (1968), consent for a search was given after the officer had stated that he had a search warrant. The Court held that the consent was not valid, since the officer's claim of authority was, in effect, an announcement that the occupant had no right to resist the search. Under such circumstances, acquiescence could not be construed as consent.

Quicknotes

CONSENT A voluntary and willful agreement by an individual possessing sufficient mental capacity to undertake an action suggested by another.

DURESS Unlawful threats or other coercive behavior by one person that causes another to commit acts that he would not otherwise do.

PROBABLE CAUSE A reasonable basis for believing that a crime has been committed.

Illinois v. Rodriguez

State (P) v. Drug possessor (D)

497 U.S. 177 (1990).

NATURE OF CASE: Appeal from acceptance of motion to suppress evidence.

FACT SUMMARY: In Illinois's (P) criminal action against Rodriguez (D) for possession of a controlled substance with intent to deliver, the trial court accepted Rodriquez's (D) motion to suppress evidence relating to his controlled substance possession.

🏛 RULE OF LAW
Where a third party agrees to allow officers to search certain premises over which the officers reasonably believe that the third party has common authority, their subsequent warrantless search of the premises is reasonable under the Fourth Amendment.

FACTS: Fischer, Rodriguez's (D) former girlfriend, authorized the police to conduct a warrantless search of Rodriguez's (D) apartment after he had apparently assaulted her. Prior to entering the apartment, Fischer had referred to it as "our" apartment, and she had told police that she had personal belongings there. Subsequently, after Fischer opened the apartment with a key and gave the police permission to search it, the police found drugs and related paraphernalia, whereupon Rodriguez (D) was arrested. At the criminal proceedings Illinois (P) brought against Rodriguez (D) for possession of a controlled substance with intent to deliver, Rodriguez (D) moved to suppress all evidence seized at the time of his arrest, claiming that Fischer had vacated the apartment several weeks earlier and had no authority to consent to the entry. On the other hand, Illinois (P) argued that even if Fischer had no authority to consent to the entry, since the police reasonably believed that she did, then their entry was permissible. Notwithstanding Illinois's (P) argument, the trial court granted Rodriguez's (D) motion, which was affirmed on appeal to the Illinois Supreme Court. Illinois (P) appealed.

ISSUE: Where a third party agrees to allow officers to search certain premises over which they reasonably believe that the former has common authority, is their subsequent warrantless search of the premises reasonable under the Fourth Amendment?

HOLDING AND DECISION: (Scalia, J.) Yes. When a third party agrees to allow officers to search certain premises over which they reasonably believe that the former has common authority, their subsequent warrantless search of the premises is reasonable under the Fourth Amendment.

This rule is derived from examining various common law requirements, such as warrant and probable cause requirements, which govern the execution of a government agent's constitutional authority to intrude on individual liberty. Although unapparent on their face, these requirements have a built-in reasonable standard that allows an agent to exercise reasonable judgment in determining the requirement's scope. Hence, if an agent, in view of the facts and circumstances, is reasonably mistaken as to an applicable requirement's scope, then even though the agent's intrusion on individual liberty is not constitutionally authorized, his conduct is deemed permissible. Since these requirements possess a built-in reasonable standard, then this standard should likewise be deemed applicable to facts bearing upon the authority of consent to a search. In the instant case, although the officers were mistaken as to the authority Fischer apparently had in authorizing the search of Rodriguez's (D) premises, since they, under the circumstances, reasonably believed that she possessed such authority, then evidence of the drugs and related paraphernalia was legitimately found. Hence, Rodriguez's (D) motion to suppress evidence of the drugs' seizure should have been denied. Reversed and remanded.

DISSENT: (Marshall, J.) Third-party searches are not based on an exigency and therefore serve no compelling social goal. Moreover, warrantless home intrusions in the absence of exigency are never reasonable since a warrant can be readily secured. As a result, since reasonable factual errors by law enforcement officers will not validate unreasonable searches, the reasonableness of the officers' mistaken belief that the third party had authority to consent is irrelevant.

▌ANALYSIS

In *State v. Leach*, 782 P.2d 1035 (Wash. 1989), the court ruled that the co-owner's prior consent to the search of a travel agency was not effective against the defendant, who was arrested there but remained present during the search. The court stated as where "the police have obtained consent to search from an individual possessing, at best, equal control over the premises, that consent remains valid against a cohabitant, who also possesses equal control, only while the cohabitant is absent," and "should the cohabitant be present and able to object, the police must also obtain the cohabitant's consent."

■━■

Wiretapping, Electronic Eavesdropping, the Use of Secret Agents to Obtain Incriminating Statements, and the Fourth Amendment

Quick Reference Rules of Law

United States v. White

Federal government (P) v. Wiretapped convict (D)

401 U.S. 745 (1971).

NATURE OF CASE: Appeal from criminal conviction for violation of narcotics laws.

FACT SUMMARY: A government informer carrying a concealed radio transmitter engaged in conversation with White (D), and those conversations were simultaneously transmitted to federal narcotic agents. Those agents testified at White's (D) trial as to the conversations they had heard.

RULE OF LAW

The Fourth Amendment does not protect a person from having his conversations with an associate recorded by that associate or transmitted to a recording or listening device located elsewhere.

FACTS: A government informer had engaged White (D) in numerous conversations in a restaurant, White's (D) home, the informer's car, and the informer's house. During these conversations, the informer carried a concealed radio transmitter which transmitted the conversations to federal agents who had a listening and recording device. Additionally, while the conversations were carried on in the informer's house, an agent, with the informer's consent, hid in the kitchen and overheard the conversations, but this agent did not testify at White's (D) trial. The federal agents did not obtain a warrant or a court order before engaging in this activity. At White's (D) trial, the informer did not testify, but the federal agents testified as to the conversations they had overheard by the use of the radio transmitter. White (D) was convicted, but the U.S. Court of Appeals overturned the conviction, holding that *Katz* prohibited testimony about the conversations.

ISSUE: Does the Fourth Amendment protect a person from having his conversations transmitted and recorded by the other party to a two-party conversation?

HOLDING AND DECISION: (White, J.) No. The Fourth Amendment does not protect a person from having his conversations electronically overheard if the other party to the conversation has consented to this action. Although *Katz v. United States*, 389 U.S. 347 (1967), stated that the Fourth Amendment protects a person's justifiable expectation of privacy, it did not hold that a person has a justifiable and constitutionally protected expectation that a person with whom he is talking will not reveal that conversation to the police. And under *Hoffa v. United States*, 385 U.S. 293 (1966), no matter how strongly a person trusts an associate, this expectation that the

associate will be faithful is not protected by the Fourth Amendment if it turns out that person is a government agent; when a person voluntarily engages in a conversation with another, he risks the chance that the other person will relate the conversation to the police. In a case with very similar facts as this case, *On Lee v. United States*, 343 U.S. 747 (1952), this Court held that electronic eavesdropping on a conversation with the cooperation of one of the parties is not a violation of the Fourth Amendment. Since the law does not protect a person when an associate testifies as to a conversation in which they engaged, there should not be a different result if that same associate, rather than testifying, transmits the conversation to another by use of electronic equipment. Since the associate could testify as to the conversation, the recording serves the same function but with increased reliability and accuracy. Additionally, with a recording, the informant/associate is less likely to later change his story. A different result is not required because the informant did not testify at the trial; the question of whether an act violates the Fourth Amendment is determined at the time of the act and is not changed by later events. Reversed.

DISSENT: (Douglas, J.) With the existence of electronic surveillance, a strict construction of the Fourth Amendment is necessary to preserve the concept of privacy. This case should follow the *Katz* statement that a search without a warrant is per se unreasonable. The essence of privacy within the First, Fourth, and Fifth Amendments is total freedom of discourse; this decision will cause everyone to live with the fear that his most minor statement will be recorded and replayed, producing an incredible chilling effect in all levels of society.

DISSENT: (Harlan, J.) The majority assumes that if a person can later testify to a conversation or record it, it is not a greater infringement of privacy if a third party is allowed simultaneously to overhear and record the conversation; this assumption is invalid because recording allows full and accurate disclosure of all aspects of the conversation. Electronic surveillance jeopardizes a person's sense of security in dealing with others which is guaranteed by the Fourth Amendment, so, at the least a warrant must be sought before third-party bugging is allowed. Otherwise, third-party surveillance of completely innocent people will be allowed, undermining everyone's sense of security.

Continued on next page.

DISSENT: (Marshall, J.) The correct view of the Fourth Amendment in the area of electronic surveillance is one that brings the safeguards of the warrant requirement to bear on the investigatory activity involved in the instant case. In short, *On Lee* cannot be considered viable in light of the constitutional principles articulated in *Katz* and other cases.

CONCURRENCE: (Brennan, J.) Current Fourth Amendment jurisprudence interposes a warrant requirement not only in cases of third-party electronic monitoring (the situation in *On Lee* and in this case), but also in cases of electronic recording by a government agent of a face-to-face conversation with a criminal suspect.

▶ *ANALYSIS*

Katz held that the Fourth Amendment protects a defendant's justifiable expectations of privacy; whatever a person knowingly exposes to the public is not protected, but whatever a person justifiably considers as private, and keeps from public view or hearing, is protected. *White*, however, holds that when a person engages in a conversation, he does not have a constitutionally protectable expectation that the other party to the conversation will not reveal the conversation to the authorities, either by testifying or by contemporaneously transmitting the conversation to third-party eavesdroppers. This appears to be a sharp limitation on *Katz*'s rather broad "expectation of privacy" approach. But, under *Katz*, unless the defendant knowingly exposes a conversation to the public (by speaking too loudly in a public place), the conversation cannot be subjected to electronic surveillance without a warrant or the cooperation of the other party to the conversation.

Quicknotes

EXPECTATION OF PRIVACY Requirement that in order to invoke the Fourth Amendment's protection against unreasonable searches and seizures, the individual must have a reasonable expectation of privacy in respect to the location searched or thing seized.

WIRETAP A means of acquiring the content of a communication through an electronic or other device.

Police "Encouragement" and the Defense of Entrapment

Quick Reference Rules of Law

United States v. Russell

Federal government (P) v. Narcotics manufacturer (D)

411 U.S. 423 (1973).

NATURE OF CASE: Appeal from conviction for manufacture of narcotics.

FACT SUMMARY: Russell (D) contended his conviction for narcotics manufacture should be overturned because the arresting officer's supplying of an essential ingredient in the illegal manufacture of methamphetamines constituted entrapment.

RULE OF LAW
Entrapment as a defense requires a showing the defendant was not predisposed to committing the offense.

FACTS: Russell (D) was under suspicion for the manufacture and sale of methamphetamines. Shapiro, an undercover government agent, approached Russell (D) and offered to supply phenyl-2-propanone, a legal substance essential to the manufacture of the narcotic. In return, Russell (D) showed Shapiro his laboratory where he had previously manufactured the drug. Russell (D) was subsequently tried and convicted of manufacturing and selling the drug. He appealed on the basis that because the Government (P) had supplied an essential ingredient to the manufacture of the drug, the entrapment defense shielded him from guilt. The court of appeals reversed, and the Supreme Court granted review.

ISSUE: Does the defense of entrapment require evidence of an absence of predisposition to commit the crime?

HOLDING AND DECISION: (Rehnquist, J.) Yes. The defense of entrapment requires a showing that the defendant was not predisposed to committing the crime. In this case substantial evidence was presented showing Russell (D) had manufactured the drug both before and after he received the ingredient from Shapiro. Thus, the Government's (P) role merely facilitated him in his preexisting plan to manufacture the drug. He clearly was predisposed to committing the crime, and his failure to rebut this precludes his assertion of the entrapment defense. Reversed.

DISSENT: (Stewart, J.) The key to the entrapment defense is the conduct of the government, not the predisposition of the defendant. When the government participates substantially in a criminal enterprise, such conduct is beyond the allowable scope of criminal investigation and allows application of the entrapment defense.

▶ ANALYSIS

Many courts have allowed application of the entrapment defense as a punitive measure against government overreaching. In such instances, the defense has little to do with a defendant's being drawn into a criminal enterprise. Rather, government action is reviewed as inappropriate and not worthy of supporting a conviction.

■■■

Quicknotes

ENTRAPMENT An act by public officers which induces a defendant into committing a criminal act.

PREDISPOSITION Defendant's inclination to engage in the illegal activity for which he has been charged.

■■■

United States v. Kelly

Federal government (P) v. Narcotics manufacturer (D)

707 F.2d 1460 (D.C. Cir. 1983).

NATURE OF CASE: Appeal from a dismissal of an indictment for bribery.

FACT SUMMARY: After Congressman Kelly (D) accepted a direct bribe for agreeing to help wealthy Arabs with their immigration problems, he was arrested as a result of this elaborate sting operation, called Abscam.

🏛 RULE OF LAW
A successful due process defense must be predicated on intolerable government conduct which reaches a demonstrable level of outrageousness.

FACTS: In an attempt to catch corrupt public officials accepting a bribe, the FBI designed an elaborate sting operation, known as Abscam, through which it spread the word that wealthy Arabs were willing to bribe members of Congress who could help them with their immigration difficulties. Included among the middlemen used by the FBI agents was a convicted confidence man. When an acquaintance asked Congressman Kelly (D) if he could help, Kelly (D) said he would be glad to. Although Kelly (D) first refused to accept a direct bribe, he later agreed to do so. He was then arrested and charged with bribery and other federal offenses. The jury found him guilty on all counts. However, the district court granted Kelly's (D) motion to dismiss, concluding that the FBI's actions in furtherance of Abscam were so outrageous that prosecution of Kelly (D) was barred by principles of due process. This appeal followed.

ISSUE: Must a successful due process defense be predicated on intolerable government conduct which reaches a demonstrable level of outrageousness?

HOLDING AND DECISION: (Per curiam) Yes. A successful due process defense must be predicated on intolerable government conduct which reaches a demonstrable level of outrageousness. Kelly (D) contends that the FBI operatives violated due process when they persisted in offering a bribe after what he characterizes as his initial rejection. However, the evidence clearly demonstrates that at no time did Kelly (D) reject Abscam's corrupt immigration proposal. Moreover, the employment of a convicted confidence man in Abscam is analogous to the entirely proper employment of a convicted seller of drugs to purchase drugs from a suspected distributor. Considering the genuine need to detect corrupt public officials, the FBI's conduct in furtherance of its Abscam operation, insofar as it involved Kelly (D), simply did not reach intolerable levels. Reversed.

▶ ANALYSIS

While Judge MacKinnon wrote the major portion of the opinion, Judge Ginsburg also filed an opinion, with Chief Judge Robinson concurring in both. Judge Ginsburg noted that under the level of outrageousness established by the Supreme Court, the broad "fundamental fairness" guarantee was not transgressed absent "coercion, violence, or brutality to the person." Although Ginsburg felt compelled to reverse, she shared the district court's grave concern that the Abscam drama unfolded as "an unwholesome spectacle."

Quicknotes

ENTRAPMENT An act by public officers which induces a defendant into committing a criminal act.

PROCEDURAL DUE PROCESS The constitutional mandate that if the state or federal government acts so as to deny a citizen of a life, liberty or property interest the individual is first entitled to notice and the right to be heard.

Jacobson v. United States

Pornography buyer (D) v. Federal government (P)

503 U.S. 540 (1992).

NATURE OF CASE: Appeal of conviction for receiving child pornography.

FACT SUMMARY: Jacobson (D) claimed the Government (P) had entrapped him into violating a child pornography law.

🏛 RULE OF LAW
Where government actions create a person's disposition to commit a crime, and then the government suggests the crime which that person commits, it is entrapment.

FACTS: At a time when it was legal, Jacobson (D) ordered from an adult bookstore two magazines picturing nude boys, though he later testified he thought he was ordering photos of young men over 17. Congress subsequently passed the Child Protection Act of 1984, criminalizing receipt by mail of sexually explicit depictions of children. The Postal Service found Jacobson's (D) name on the store's mailing list and began mailing Jacobson (D) letters and questionnaires from fictitious research and lobbying organizations and a fake pen pal. The mailings discussed and asked about Jacobson's (D) tastes in pornography and views on censorship. Each time he answered, the next mailing was fit more to his tastes. After two years, the Customs Service, through a fake company, sent Jacobson (D) a child pornography brochure. He placed an order, but it was never filled. The Postal Service, using a fake company, sent Jacobson (D) a letter decrying censorship and claiming the media and government were trying to keep its material out of the country. Jacobson (D) requested a catalogue, from which he later ordered child pornography. Jacobson (D) was arrested upon controlled delivery of the magazine. He unsuccessfully raised an entrapment defense and was convicted under the 1984 Act. The court of appeals affirmed, and Jacobson (D) appealed.

ISSUE: Where government actions create a person's disposition to commit a crime, and then the government suggests the crime which that person consents, is it entrapment?

HOLDING AND DECISION: (White, J.) Yes. Where government acts create a person's disposition to commit a crime, and then the government suggests the crime which that person commits, it is entrapment. Jacobson (D) had become predisposed to break the law by the time he ordered a magazine from the Government (P). However, the Government (P) did not prove this disposition was not the product of years of Government (P) targeting. The magazines Jacobson (D) ordered from the bookstore were legal when bought. Evidence of predisposition to do what was once legal is not sufficient to show predisposition to do what now is illegal, since most people obey laws they disagree with. Jacobson's (D) claim that he did not know he was ordering photos of minors from the bookstore was unchallenged. His answers to Government (P) mailings showed predisposition to view child pornography and to support a given agenda through lobbying groups but did not support an inference of predisposition to commit the alleged crime. The strong arguable inference is that by waving the banner of individual rights and disparaging efforts to restrict pornography, the Government (P) excited Jacobson's (D) interest in banned materials and exerted substantial pressure on him to fight censorship by obtaining such materials. The government may not play on an innocent man's weaknesses and beguile him into committing crimes he would not commit otherwise. Reversed.

DISSENT: (O'Connor, J.) Both times the Government (P) offered Jacobson (D) a chance to buy pornography he responded enthusiastically. Thus, a reasonable jury could find a predisposition to commit the crime. Predisposition should be assessed as of the time the government suggested the crime, not when the government first became involved; the government does not need a reasonable suspicion before it can investigate. Moreover, the two-year investigation of Jacobson (D) involved no threats, coercion, or "substantial pressure" to commit the crime. Finally, the Government (P) did not have to prove Jacobson (D) was predisposed to break the law, only that he was predisposed to receive child pornography. The 1984 Act does not require specific intent to break the law, only knowing receipt. Since the requirement of predisposition is designed to eliminate the entrapment defense for those who would have committed the crime absent government inducement, the elements of predisposition should track the elements of the crime.

▶ ANALYSIS

The Court follows the subjective test for entrapment, i.e., whether the defendant was predisposed to commit the crime, as opposed to the objective test, i.e., whether police conduct created a substantial risk that an innocent person would commit the crime. However, as the dissent points

Continued on next page.

out, the Court's main concern "is that the Government went too far and 'abused' the 'processes of detection and enforcement' by luring an innocent person to violate the law." *Jacobson* illustrates how the subjective and objective tests are blurred in application. In analyzing an entrapment claim, courts must look to the conduct of both the defendant and the police.

■═■

Quicknotes

ENTRAPMENT An act by public officers which induces a defendant into committing a criminal act.

PREDISPOSITION Defendant's inclination to engage in the illegal activity for which he has been charged.

■═■

Police Interrogation and Confessions

Quick Reference Rules of Law

Miranda v. Arizona (No. 759)
(Together with Vignera v. New York,
Westover v. U.S., and California v. Stewart)

Interrogated suspect (D) v. State (P)

384 U.S. 436 (1966).

NATURE OF CASE: Certiorari from various convictions, and from the reversal of one.

FACT SUMMARY: Convictions resulted in several cases from confessions obtained through incommunicado interrogation in a police-dominated atmosphere, without full warnings of constitutional rights.

🏛 RULE OF LAW
When a person has been taken into police custody or otherwise deprived of his freedom of action in any significant way, the following warnings must be given prior to questioning: (1) that he has the right to remain silent; (2) that any statement he does make may be used as evidence against him; (3) that he has the right to have an attorney present; and (4) that if he cannot afford an attorney, one will be appointed for him.

FACTS: Convictions in the cases of *Miranda v. Arizona*, *Vignera v. New York*, *Westover v. United States*, and *California v. Stewart* are brought before this Court through petitions of certiorari. In each of these cases, confessions resulted after incommunicado interrogation in a police-dominated atmosphere, without full warning of constitutional rights (or without any indication in the police records that such warnings were given). And in each of these cases, the confessions obtained from such interrogation were used as the basis for the resulting convictions. Only in the case of Stewart (D) was the conviction reversed by the Supreme Court of California, on the basis that he had not been informed of his rights. Because of the related nature of these cases, this Court granted certiorari to determine the central issue involved.

ISSUE: When a person is taken into custody, is it necessary that his constitutional rights to remain silent and to have an attorney present be explained to him before questioning?

HOLDING AND DECISION: (Warren, C.J.) Yes. "(T)he prosecution may not use statements, whether exculpatory or inculpatory, stemming from custodial interrogation of the defendant unless it demonstrates the use of procedural safeguards effective to secure the privilege against self-incrimination. By custodial interrogation, we mean questioning initiated by law enforcement officers after a person has been taken into custody or otherwise deprived of his freedom of action in any significant way. As for the procedural safeguards to be

employed, unless other full effective means are devised to inform accused persons of their right to silence and to assure a continuous opportunity to exercise it, the following measures are required. Prior to any questioning, the person must be warned that he has a right to remain silent, that any statement he does make may be used against him as evidence, and that he has the right to the presence of an attorney, either retained or appointed (if he cannot afford). The defendant may waive effectuation of these rights, provided the waiver is made voluntarily, knowingly, and intelligently. If, however, he indicates in any manner and at any stage of the process that he wishes to consult with an attorney before speaking, there can be no questioning. Likewise, if the individual is alone and indicates in any manner that he does not wish to be interrogated, the police may not question him. The mere fact that he may have answered some questions or volunteered some statements on his own does not deprive him of the right to refrain from answering any further inquiries until he has consulted with an attorney and thereafter consents to be questioned." The rationale for this decision is based upon the nature of custodial interrogation and its relationship to the Fifth Amendment's Self-Incrimination Clause. The true nature of custodial interrogation clearly is described in standard police manuals and texts, which teach "psychologically oriented coercive techniques" (e.g., incommunicado detention, prolonged questioning). Such practices are inherently contrary to the principle that an individual may not be compelled to incriminate himself. And freedom from self-incrimination is "one of our nation's most cherished principles," based upon our accusatory system of justice which protects the "dignity and integrity of its citizens" by requiring that government may only produce incriminating evidence "by its own independent labors." It is elementary that, unless there are sufficient safeguards (i.e., those announced in this decision) to ensure the right against self-incrimination in custodial interrogation, its recognition at trial is meaningless. Here, in each case, the accused was put through custodial interrogations without the appropriate safeguards, and the prosecution has not demonstrated any "knowing and intelligent waiver" of rights in any of the cases. It is true that Westover (D) was informed of his rights by the FBI before his statement, but he had been subjected to police interrogation for over 14 hours prior to that time (i.e., before

Continued on next page.

he was handed over to the FBI). Since the FBI questioning immediately followed the police interrogation, from Westover's (D) point of view, at least, there had, in fact, been one continuous period of questioning with the warning of his rights only at the end of the process. In conclusion, one of the convictions based upon confessions given without a full warning of rights can be upheld.

DISSENT in the cases of *Vignera, Westover,* and *Miranda,* and CONCURRENCE in the case of *Stewart:* (Clark, J.) The Court should have been more restrained in these cases. There is a decided lack of information and empirical data on the practical operation of requirements comparable to those announced today. Furthermore, custodial interrogation has long been recognized as a "essential tool in effective law enforcement," and the rule prior to today recognized this fact by judging the voluntariness from the "totality of all the circumstances" (including whether an accused had been advised of his rights). The rule today, however, is too rigid.

DISSENT: (Harlan, J.) The decision of the Court today in abandoning its historical case-by-case approach represents poor constitutional law. The Court's new rules are designed to "ultimately discourage any confession at all." Such an approach cannot be sustained by constitutional or policy considerations. First, constitutionally, there is no basis for extending the Fifth Amendment to the police station. Historically, the ban against self-incrimination has applied only in criminal proceedings, not in "extra-legal" situations, such as interrogations. Furthermore, even if it can be applied to custodial interrogations, it has never been held to forbid all pressures on an accused, as the Court today attempts to do. Similarly, there is no constitutional basis for applying the right to counsel to custodial interrogations. The danger of injustice by allowing an untrained person to defend himself in a technical court situation is the basis for this right, and that rationale is not applicable to custodial situations. Second, in considering policy issues, although it is true that police questioning will inherently entail some pressure on the suspect, until today the role of the Constitution has been to "sift out" only "undue pressure." The inflexible rules today, however, ignore this. Those who use coercive tactics may simply lie in court about having given the required warnings. Nothing is gained and many voluntary confessions will be lost. In conclusion, neither the constitutional interpretations nor the consequence of today's ruling are justifiable.

DISSENT: (White, J.) First, the Fifth Amendment forbids self-incrimination only if it is "compelled." Yet, the Court today has no factual basis for concluding that custodial interrogations are so inherently coercive, as to make any statements arising from them, if there is no warning of rights, compelled. In fact, the Court has not examined a single transcript of any

police interrogation. Furthermore, even if it is assumed that "all" such interrogations are coercive, the rule adopted today is irrational. If such interrogations are so "coercive," how can a suspect ever voluntarily waive his rights as the Court indicates he can? Second, and more importantly, the Court overlooks the ominous consequences of its decision. Although the Court states that the rule adopted is necessary to preserve the "integrity" of the individual, it overlooks the fact that without effective prevention of crime (or personal violence) there can be no human dignity. The most basic function of any government is to provide for the security of an individual and his property, but after today's decision, effective law enforcement will be impaired, both by the fact that more who are guilty may go free and many who could easily explain their innocence will waste police time while waiting for their attorneys.

▶ ANALYSIS

Miranda illustrates the rule applicable to evidence sought to be admitted against an accused as "part of the prosecution's case," but a statement obtained in violation of the *Miranda* rule "may be used to impeach" an accused's testimony if he takes the stand at trial and if the statement is otherwise "voluntary and trustworthy." *Miranda* also does not apply to mere on-the-scene questioning, general fact-finding inquiries of citizens, or spontaneous admissions volunteered before the police began interrogation. Furthermore, it must be noted that several issues or problems have been raised in the wake of *Miranda*. First, while a waiver of rights will not be inferred from silence, the type of expression required still remains open to question. However, the lower courts are in general agreement that a warning of rights need not be repeated at the beginning of each successive interrogation for a valid waiver to occur. Second, the Supreme Court has not addressed itself to the question of whether automatic reversal of a conviction, based upon a confession obtained in violation of *Miranda*, is required. Third, the Supreme Court has, also, left open the question of whether the "fruits" (Wong Sun) derived from statements obtained in violation of *Miranda* are admissible. Finally, fourth, although the Court in *Miranda* states that the warnings are necessary "unless other full effective means are devised to inform accused persons" of their rights, it is questionable what would be considered "effective." The Crime Control Act of 1968, applicable to federal criminal trials, seeks to substitute for the Miranda warnings a test of "voluntariness" based upon the totality of circumstances. However, the Court in *Miranda* does seem to indicate that something more than test of voluntariness is required, although the constitutionality of this legislation is presently undetermined.

Yarborough v. Alvarado

State (P) v. Alleged murderer (D)

541 U.S. 652 (2004).

NATURE OF CASE: Appeal by state from Federal circuit court's granting of a motion to exclude a murder suspect's incriminating statements.

FACT SUMMARY: When Michael Alvarado (D), aged 17½, was questioned for two hours by a detective in a sheriff station's interrogation room in regard to his role in a murder, without being given Miranda warnings, he moved to exclude his incriminating statements upon being charged with the murder.

🏛 RULE OF LAW
Police questioning is "custodial" requiring Miranda warnings only where there is a formal arrest or restraint on freedom of movement of the degree associated with a formal arrest.

FACTS: Michael Alvarado (D), aged 17½, helped another person try to steal a truck, which led to the shooting of the truck's owner. Shortly thereafter, a detective left word with Alvarado's (D) parents that she wanted to talk to him. Alvarado's (D) parents brought him to the sheriff's station during a lunchtime period, and remained in the lobby during the two-hour interrogation, which occurred in a small room where only the female detective and Alvarado (D) were present. Alvarado (D) was not given Miranda warnings. Alvarado (D) at first denied any involvement in the shooting, but by the end of the two hours had made major incriminating statements. He was charged with murder. The trial court rejected his Miranda motion to exclude the incriminating statements, finding that he had not been in "custody" when questioned by the detective, and the state appellate court agreed. The federal district court denied federal habeas relief; however the federal court of appeals reversed, holding that the state court erred in failing to take into account Alvarado's (D) youth and inexperience. California appealed.

ISSUE: Is police questioning "custodial" requiring Miranda warnings only where there is a formal arrest or restraint on freedom of movement of the degree associated with a formal arrest?

HOLDING AND DECISION: (Kennedy, J.) Yes. Police questioning is "custodial" requiring Miranda warnings only where there is a formal arrest or restraint on freedom of movement of the degree associated with a formal arrest. Here, the police did not transport Alvarado (D) to the police station or require him to appear at a particular time. They did not threaten him or suggest he would be placed under arrest. His

parents remained in the lobby during the interview, suggesting that the interview would be brief. Instead of pressuring Alvarado (D) with the threat of arrest and prosecution, the detective appealed to his interest in telling the truth and being helpful to a police officer. In addition, the detective twice asked Alvarado (D) if he wanted to take a break. At the end of the interview, Alvarado (D) went home. All of these objective facts are consistent with an interrogation environment in which a reasonable person would have felt free to terminate the interview and leave. While there are some factors that point in the other direction, such as the fact the interrogation lasted two hours, nevertheless, the state court's decision that Miranda "custody" had not occurred cannot be said to be objectively unreasonable. This Court cannot conduct its own independent inquiry into whether the state court was correct as a de novo matter. Relief is available only if the state court's decision is objectively unreasonable. Reversed.

CONCURRENCE: (O'Connor, J.) It is difficult to expect police to recognize that a suspect is a juvenile when, as here, he is so close to the age of majority. Even when police do know a suspect's age, it may be difficult for them to ascertain what bearing it has on the likelihood that the suspect would feel free to leave.

DISSENT: (Breyer, J.) Alvarado (D) clearly was "in custody" when the police questioned him. Certainly a "reasonable person" of Alvarado's (D) age and experience and in his "position" would not have felt he was at liberty to terminate the interrogation and leave.

▶ ANALYSIS

The Miranda custody inquiry is an objective test. Such test furthers the clarity of Miranda's rule, ensuring that the police do not need to make guesses as to the circumstances at issue before deciding how they may interrogate the suspect.

━━━

Quicknotes

CUSTODIAL INTERROGATION The questioning of a suspect by police while in custody.

MIRANDA WARNINGS Specified warnings that must be communicated to a person prior to a custodial interrogation; in the absence of the communication of such warnings, any communications made during the interrogation is inadmissible at trial.

━━━

Rhode Island v. Innis

State (P) v. Convict with a conscience (D)

446 U.S. 291 (1980).

NATURE OF CASE: Appeal from a murder conviction.

FACT SUMMARY: On the way to the police station in a police car after his arrest, Innis (D) overheard remarks between the officers expressing concern that handicapped children in the area might find the hidden shotgun, whereupon Innis (D) told them to turn around so he could show them where he had hidden it.

> ## 🏛 RULE OF LAW
> Any words or actions on the part of the police that they should know are reasonably likely to elicit an incriminating response from the suspect constitute "interrogation" under *Miranda* and bring the *Miranda* safeguards into play.

FACTS: After being arrested for murder, Innis (D) received the Miranda warnings and said he wanted to speak with an attorney. While being taken to the station in a police car, he overheard a conversation between the officers. "God forbid," one officer said, "that one of the students at the school for the handicapped find a gun and hurt himself." At that point, Innis (D) told the officers to turn the car around so that he could show them where he had hidden the gun used in the murder. The gun that was thus found was used in evidence when Innis (D) was later convicted of murder. The Rhode Island Supreme Court reversed the conviction, holding that the officers had engaged in "interrogation" in violation of *Miranda*.

ISSUE: If the police should know that their words or actions are reasonably likely to elicit an incriminating response from the suspect, do such words or actions constitute "interrogation"?

HOLDING AND DECISION: (Stewart, J.) Yes. Any words or actions on the part of the police that the police should know are reasonably likely to elicit an incriminating response from the suspect constitute "interrogation" under *Miranda*. That is, the term "interrogation" as used in *Miranda* covers express questioning or its functional equivalent. In this particular case, the facts are that the officers engaged in an entire conversation that consisted of no more than a few off-hand remarks. The Court cannot say, on that basis, that the officers should have known that it was reasonably likely that Innis (D) would suddenly be moved to make a self-incriminating response to this overheard conversation. Therefore, whatever "subtle compulsion" Innis (D) experienced cannot be equated with "interrogation" bringing Miranda into play. Reversed and remanded.

CONCURRENCE: (Burger, C.J.) The test adopted in this case introduces new elements of uncertainty. It requires a police officer, in the brief time available, to evaluate the suggestibility and susceptibility of an accused. Even psychiatrists would normally have to employ extensive questioning and observation to make the judgment now charged to police officers. However, I concur in the result in this case because it is not inconsistent with *Miranda*.

DISSENT: (Marshall, J.) As I read the Court's definition of "interrogation" for *Miranda* purposes, I find it equivalent, for practical purpose, to my own formulation. I view the *Miranda* safeguards as applying whenever police conduct is intended or likely to produce a response from a suspect in custody. I am, however, utterly at a loss to understand how the objective standard adopted by the Court, when applied to this case, can rationally lead to the conclusion that there was no interrogation. One can scarcely imagine a stronger appeal to the conscience of a suspect than the assertion that if the weapon is not found an innocent, handicapped child will be hurt or killed.

DISSENT: (Stevens, J.) In my view, any statement that would normally be understood by the average listener as calling for a response is the functional equivalent of a direct question, whether or not it is punctuated by a question mark. The Court takes a narrower view in defining "interrogation" for *Miranda* purposes in a holding which represents a plain departure from the principles set forth in *Miranda*. It prohibits only those relatively few statements or actions that a police officer should know are likely to elicit an incriminating response, when statements that appear to call for a response from the suspect, as well as those that are designed to do so, should be considered interrogation. What the Court does in this decision is to narrow the scope of protection afforded a suspect. However, even if the Court's definition of "interrogation" is assumed to be the proper standard, the officers should have known that their appeal to the conscience of the suspect was likely to elicit an incriminating response. Thus, under either definition of the term, "interrogation" occurred in violation of *Miranda*.

Continued on next page.

ANALYSIS

In *Harryman v. Estelle*, 616 F.2d 879 (5th Cir. 1980), Harryman was arrested as a burglary suspect. A search of his person revealed a condom containing white powder tucked under the waistband of his trousers. The officer, who later claimed he spoke out of shock and surprise, asked, "What is this?"— to which Harryman answered: "Oh, you know what it is. It is heroin." Noting that the rigidity of the *Miranda* rules and the way they are to be applied is recognized as the decision's greatest strength, the court of appeals found *Miranda* had been violated by this interchange between officer and suspect. In its opinion, the court stated "it is enough to decide that what the officer said could reasonably have had the force of a question on the accused."

Quicknotes

CUSTODIAL INTERROGATION The questioning of a suspect by police while in custody.

PRIVILEGE AGAINST SELF-INCRIMINATION A privilege guaranteed by the Fifth Amendment to the federal Constitution in a criminal proceeding for communications made by an accused and protecting an accused or witness from having to give testimony that may incriminate himself.

Minnick v. Mississippi

Accused murderer (D) v. State (P)

498 U.S. 146 (1990).

NATURE OF CASE: Appeal from denial of motion to suppress evidence.

FACT SUMMARY: In Mississippi's (P) criminal action against Minnick (D) for murder, the trial court denied Minnick's (D) motion to suppress incriminating statements he made to Denham, a Mississippi sheriff, out of the presence of and after several consultations with his attorney.

> ## 🏛 RULE OF LAW
> When an accused requests counsel, interrogation must cease, and officials may not reinstate interrogation without counsel present, whether or not the accused has consulted with him.

FACTS: Denham, a Mississippi sheriff, requested that Minnick (D), an accused murderer, speak with him regarding the facts surrounding the murders, shortly after Minnick (D) had spoken with his requested-for attorney on several previous occasions subsequent to his arrest. After Denham advised Minnick (D) of his rights and Minnick (D) refused to sign a rights waiver form, Minnick (D) agreed to answer some questions and made a number of incriminating statements. However, at no time during this interrogation was Minnick's (D) attorney present. Subsequently, Minnick (D) was tried for murder in Mississippi. During this trial, Minnick (D) moved to suppress the statements made to Denham, arguing that they were taken in violation of his rights to counsel under the Fifth and Sixth Amendments. Despite Minnick's (D) argument, the trial court denied his motion, which was affirmed on appeal to the Mississippi Supreme Court. Minnick (D) appealed.

ISSUE: Where an accused requests counsel and interrogation ceases, may officials reinitiate interrogation without counsel present after the accused has consulted with him?

HOLDING AND DECISION: (Kennedy, J.) No. When an accused requests counsel, interrogation must cease, and officials may not reinitiate without counsel present, whether or not the accused has consulted with him. This rule logically follows from *Edwards*, 451 U.S. 477 (1981), whereby it was held that a defendant's waiver of his Miranda rights to counsel, made in the course of a police-initiated encounter after he had required counsel but before counsel had been provided, was an involuntary waiver per se. The irrebuttable assumption in Edwards is that a police officer who obtained an accused waiver of Miranda rights under the case's circumstances probably did so illegitimately, i.e., through coercion.

Hence, *Edwards*, as well as other cases dealing with the same subject, emphasized the necessity of an attorney's presence to presumably deter such illegitimate behavior. Consequently, extending *Edwards* to include the circumstances where, as here, an attorney has been consulted but is not present during a subsequent police-initiated interrogation will presumably, as in *Edwards*, deter such coercive tactics since these tactics are just as likely to occur after consultation as they would before. Since the incriminating statements made by Minnick (D) to Denham were made out of his attorney's presence and were not the result of his initiation, then they were involuntarily made. As a result, Minnick's (D) motion to suppress these statements is granted. Reversed and remanded.

DISSENT: (Scalia, J.) Under the circumstances in Edwards, an irrebuttable presumption that any police-prompted confession is the result of, for example, coercion has no genuine basis in fact. Moreover, the Constitution's proscription of compelled testimony does not remotely authorize this incursion upon the state's practices.

▶ ANALYSIS

In *McNeil v. Wisconsin*, 501 U.S. 171 (1991), a 6–3 majority held that a suspect's assertion of his Sixth Amendment right to counsel, by his appearance with counsel at a bail hearing concerning an offense with which he had been charged, does not serve as an invocation of the Fifth Amendment–based *Miranda-Edwards-Roberson* right to have counsel present during custodial interrogation. Thus, assertion of the Sixth Amendment right does not prevent the police from initiating counselless interrogation about unrelated and uncharged crimes.

■▬■

Quicknotes

CUSTODIAL INTERROGATION The questioning of a suspect by police while in custody.

FIFTH AMENDMENT Provides that no person shall be compelled to serve as a witness against himself, or be subject to trial for the same offense twice, or be deprived of life, liberty, or property without due process of law.

SIXTH AMENDMENT Provides the right to a speedy trial by impartial jury, the right to be informed of the accusation, to confront witnesses and to have the assistance of counsel in all criminal prosecutions.

■▬■

Moran v. Burbine

Court (P) v. Murder convict (D)

475 U.S. 412 (1986).

NATURE OF CASE: Appeal from reversal of denial of habeas corpus in state criminal proceeding.

FACT SUMMARY: While being interrogated by police, an attorney wishing to represent Burbine (D) called the police, a fact not conveyed to Burbine (D) by the police.

RULE OF LAW

A voluntary confession obtained by police, who fail to inform a defendant that an attorney attempted to contact him, is not an invalid intrusion upon the defendant's Miranda rights.

FACTS: Burbine (D) was arrested on suspicion of breaking and entering, and murder. Burbine (D) did not request an attorney. His sister obtained one to represent him, and the attorney called the police station, informing the police that she wished to represent him. The police informed the attorney that Burbine (D) was not to be further questioned that night. Nonetheless, Burbine (D) was later interrogated, after having expressly waived his Miranda rights following a proper warning. Burbine (D) confessed to the murder. The confession was admitted at trial, and Burbine (D) was convicted. After exhausting state appeals, Burbine (D) petitioned for federal habeas corpus. The district court declined to grant habeas corpus, but the court of appeals reversed.

ISSUE: Is a voluntary confession obtained by police, who fail to inform a defendant that an attorney attempted to contact him, an invalid intrusion upon the defendant's Miranda rights?

HOLDING AND DECISION: (O'Connor, J.) No. A voluntary confession obtained by police, who fail to inform a defendant that an attorney attempted to contact him, is not an invalid intrusion upon the defendant's Miranda rights. A Miranda waiver is valid if it is voluntary and intelligently made. A failure to be informed of an attorney's attempts at contact in no way diminishes one's ability to knowingly waive a right which Burbine (D) did. Had Burbine (D) requested an attorney, matters would be different, but Burbine (D) never did so. Police are not under a duty to provide a defendant with a steady stream of information not asked for. The benefits of burdening the police with such a duty would be minimal and would come at the cost of making it much harder to obtain confessions, something in which society has a strong interest. Since no constitutional right was violated, the conduct of the police, while not exemplary, did not call for reversal of the conviction. Reversed.

DISSENT: (Stevens, J.) As the attorney was, in effect, an agent of Burbine (D), the deception practiced upon her was in fact a deception upon Burbine (D), which necessarily invalidated the "intelligent" and "knowing" aspect of the waiver of his rights.

ANALYSIS

Besides the Fifth Amendment issue, the Court also discussed Sixth and Fourteenth Amendment concerns. The Sixth Amendment argument was dismissed because Burbine (D) had not yet been formally charged. With regard to the Fourteenth Amendment, the Court concluded that the police conduct was not fundamentally unfair, a conclusion with which the dissent took issue.

Quicknotes

MIRANDA RULE A required warning given before any questioning by law enforcement authorities can take place. Individuals receive warnings regarding their privilege against self-incrimination, right to remain silent, and right to be represented by an attorney.

SIXTH AMENDMENT Provides the right to a speedy trial by impartial jury, the right to be informed of the accusation, to confront witnesses and to have the assistance of counsel in all criminal prosecutions.

Dickerson v. United States

Bank robber (D) v. Federal government (P)

530 U.S. 428 (2000).

NATURE OF CASE: Appeal from denial of motion to suppress statement based on Miranda violation.

FACT SUMMARY: Dickerson (D) sought to suppress a statement he made while in an FBI field office prior to being given his Miranda warnings.

🏛 RULE OF LAW
When a decision of the court involves interpretation and application of the Constitution, Congress may not legislatively supercede such decision.

FACTS: Dickerson (D) was indicted for bank robbery and conspiracy to commit bank robbery. Before trial he moved to suppress a statement he made at an FBI field office, on the grounds that he had not received Miranda warnings before being interrogated. The district court granted the motion, and the government (P) took an interlocutory appeal to the court of appeals, which reversed, stating that § 3501 was satisfied since the statement was made voluntarily. Dickerson (D) appealed.

ISSUE: Where a decision of the court involves interpretation and application of the Constitution, may Congress legislatively supercede such decision?

HOLDING AND DECISION: (Rehnquist, C.J.) Where a decision of the court involves interpretation and application of the Constitution, Congress may not legislatively supercede such decision. Miranda and its progeny govern the admissibility of statements made during custodial interrogation in both state and federal courts. Section 3501 provides that the admissibility of a custodial suspect's statements should depend on whether they are voluntarily made. Prior to Miranda, the admissibility of a suspect's confession was evaluated under a voluntariness test. The requirement of voluntariness was based on the Fifth Amendment right against self-incrimination and the Due Process Clause of the Fourteenth Amendment. The Court's decisions in *Miranda* and *Malloy* changed the focus of the due process inquiry. In *Malloy* [*Malloy v. Hogan*, 378 U.S. 1 (1964)], the Court held that the Fifth Amendment's Self-incrimination clause is incorporated into the Due Process Clause of the Fourteenth Amendment and this applies to the states. In *Miranda*, the Court recognized that the coercion inherent in custodial interrogation makes it difficult to determine whether a statement is voluntary or involuntary and heightens the risk of self-incrimination. Section 3501 was enacted two years after the decision in *Miranda*

and was intended by Congress to overrule the Court's decision in that case. The issue is whether Congress has the constitutional authority to do so. While Congress retains the ultimate authority to modify or set aside any judicially created rules of evidence and procedure that are not required by the Constitution, it may not legislatively supercede the Court's decisions that interpret and apply the Constitution. *Miranda* is a constitutional decision. The Court specifically stated that it was intended "to explore some facets of the problems of applying the privilege against self-incrimination to in-custody interrogation and to give concrete constitutional guidelines for law enforcement agencies and courts to follow." The decision is otherwise replete with references to constitutional rules and standards. *Miranda* announced a constitutional rule that Congress may not supercede legislatively.

DISSENT: (Scalia, J.) *Marbury v. Madison*, 1 Cranch 137 (1803), held that an Act of Congress will not be enforced if what it prescribes violated the Constitution. The majority opinion fails to state, however, that what § 3501 prescribes, the use of a voluntary confession at trial, violates the Constitution.

▌ANALYSIS

The Court also relies on the principle of stare decisis as weighing heavily against overruling *Miranda*, since Miranda warnings have become "embedded in routine police practice to the point where the warnings have become part of our national culture." Justice Scalia rejects such rationale on the basis that the court rules are both "mutable and modifiable" and that they "must make sense."

▬═▬

Chavez v. Martinez

Police officer (D) v. Initiator of § 1983 suit (P)

538 U.S. 760 (2003).

NATURE OF CASE: Appeal from refusal of federal court of appeals to grant qualified immunity to police officer in a § 1983 suit against him.

FACT SUMMARY: Martinez (P) brought a § 1983 suit against Chavez (D), a police officer, for interrogating him in the hospital during emergency medical treatment for life-threatening gunshot wounds, arguing that such conduct violated his Fifth Amendment protection against self-incrimination.

RULE OF LAW
The Fifth Amendment protection against self-incrimination applies only in criminal cases.

FACTS: During a police altercation, an officer shot Martinez (P) five times, causing life-endangering injuries. Chavez (D), a police officer, arrived on the scene and accompanied Martinez (P) to the hospital where he continuously interrogated Martinez (P) during medical treatment, despite Martinez's (P) statements to the officer, "I don't know," "I am choking," "I am dying, please," and "I don't want to die." Although Martinez (P) was never charged with a crime and his answers were never used against him in any criminal prosecution, he brought a § 1983 suit, arguing, inter alia, that Chavez (D) had violated his Fifth Amendment privilege against self-incrimination. The federal court of appeals held that Chavez (D) was not entitled to a defense of qualified immunity because he violated Martinez's (P) clearly established constitutional rights. Chavez (D) appealed.

ISSUE: Does the Fifth Amendment protection against self-incrimination apply only in criminal cases?

HOLDING AND DECISION: (Thomas, J.) Yes. The Fifth Amendment protection against self-incrimination applies only in criminal cases. The Fifth Amendment requires that no person shall be compelled "in any criminal case" to be a witness against himself. This Court fails to see how Martinez (P) can allege a violation of this right since he was never prosecuted for a crime, let alone compelled to be a witness in a criminal case. A "criminal case" at the very least requires the initiation of criminal proceedings. Although conduct by law enforcement officials prior to trial may ultimately impair that right, a *constitutional violation* occurs only at trial. Here, Martinez (P) was never made to be a "witness" against himself because his statements were never admitted as testimony against him in a criminal case. Nor was he ever placed under oath and exposed to the cruel trilemma of self-accusation,

perjury, or contempt. Rules designed to safeguard a constitutional right do not extend the scope of the constitutional right itself, just as violations of judicially crafted prophylactic rules do not violate the constitutional rights of any person. Even assuming, arguendo, that the persistent questioning of Martinez (P) somehow deprived him of a liberty interest, this Court cannot agree with Martinez's (P) characterization of Chavez's (D) behavior as "egregious" or "conscience shocking" since medical personnel were able to treat Martinez (P) throughout the interrogation and Chavez (D) did not interfere with the medical treatment. Reversed.

CONCURRENCE: (Souter, J.) Martinez (P) has not here been able to make the "powerful showing," subject to a realistic assessment of costs and risks, necessary to expand protection of the privilege against compelled self-incrimination to the point of the civil liability he asks this Court to recognize.

CONCURRENCE: (Scalia, J.) Without a violation of the actual right protected by the text of the Self-Incrimination Clause, the § 1983 action is doomed.

DISSENT IN PART: (Stevens, J.) The interrogation was the functional equivalent of an attempt to obtain an involuntary confession from a prisoner by torturous methods. As a matter of law, that type of brutal police conduct constitutes an immediate deprivation of the prisoner's constitutionally protected interest in liberty.

DISSENT IN PART: (Kennedy, J.) A constitutional right arises the moment torture or its close equivalents are brought to bear. Constitutional protection for a tortured suspect is not held in abeyance until some later criminal proceeding takes place.

DISSENT IN PART: (Ginsburg, J.) The Self-Incrimination Clause applies at the time and place police use severe compulsion to extract a statement from a suspect.

ANALYSIS

As the *Chavez* decision makes clear, the text of the Self-Incrimination Clause cannot support a view that the mere use of compulsive questioning, without more, violates the Constitution.

■■■

Quicknotes

LIBERTY INTEREST A right conferred by the Due Process Clauses of the state and federal constitutions.

■■■

United States v. Patane

Federal government (P) v. Possessor of illegal firearm (D)

124 S. Ct. 2620 (2004).

NATURE OF CASE: Appeal from suppression of physical evidence in criminal case.

FACT SUMMARY: When a police officer seized Samuel Patane's (D) pistol from his bedroom during an arrest, after being given Patane's (D) permission to do so, Patane (D) was subsequently indicted for possession of an illegal firearm. Pantane (D) argued that since he was not given full Miranda warnings, the pistol should be suppressed as a "physical fruit" of the poisonous tree.

RULE OF LAW
The Self-Incrimination Clause is not violated by the admission into evidence of the physical fruit of a voluntary statement.

FACTS: Upon arresting Samuel Patane (D) at his residence for violating a restraining order, a police officer attempted to advise Patane (D) of his Miranda rights but got no further than the right to remain silent. At that point, Patane (D) interrupted, asserting that he knew his rights, whereupon the warnings were not completed. The police officer asked Patane (D) about an illegal Glock pistol he believed Patane (D) possessed. Pantane (D) told the police officer the pistol was in his bedroom and gave permission to seize it. Pantane (D) was indicted for possession of the pistol. The court of appeals affirmed the district court's suppression of the pistol, and the Government (P) appealed.

ISSUE: Is the Self-Incrimination Clause violated by the admission into evidence of the physical fruit of a voluntary statement?

HOLDING AND DECISION: (Thomas, J.) No. The Self-Incrimination Clause is not violated by the admission into evidence of the physical fruit of a voluntary statement. The police do not necessarily violate Miranda rights by negligent or even deliberate failures to provide a suspect with the full panoply of Miranda warnings. Potential violations occur, if at all, only upon the admission of unwarned statements into evidence at trial. At that point, the exclusion of unwarned statements is a complete and sufficient remedy for any perceived Miranda violation. Thus, unlike unreasonable searches under the Fourth Amendment or actual violations of the Due Process Clause or the Self-Incrimination Clause, there is, with respect to mere failures to warn, nothing to deter. There is therefore no reason to apply the "fruit of the poisonous tree" doctrine. It is not for this Court to impose its preferred police practices on either federal law enforcement officials or their state counterparts. Characterization of *Miranda* as a constitutional rule does not lessen the need to maintain the closest possible fit between the Self-Incrimination Clause and any judge-made rule designed to protect it. Here, there is no such fit because the introduction of the nontestimonial fruit of a voluntary statement (the pistol) does not implicate the Self-Incrimination Clause. The admission of such fruit presents no risk that a defendant's coerced statements will be used against him or her at a criminal trial. There is simply no need to extend (and therefore no justification for extending) the prophylactic rule of *Miranda* to this context. Reversed.

CONCURRENCE: (Kennedy, J.) In light of the important probative value of reliable physical evidence, it is doubtful that exclusion can be justified by a deterrence rationale sensitive to both law enforcement interests and a suspect's rights during an in-custody interrogation.

DISSENT: (Souter, J.) In closing their eyes to the consequences of giving an evidentiary advantage to those who ignore *Miranda*, the majority adds an important inducement for interrogators to ignore the rule in that case. While there is a price for excluding evidence, the Fifth Amendment is worth a price.

DISSENT: (Breyer, J.) The "fruit of the poisonous tree" should be extended to cases such as this.

ANALYSIS

As *Patane* makes clear, the Miranda rule is not a code of police conduct, and police do not necessarily violate the Constitution (or even the Miranda rule, for that matter) by mere failures to warn. Because various prophylactic rules (including the Miranda rule) necessarily sweep beyond the actual protections of the Self-Incrimination Clause, the Supreme Court has consistently taken the position that any further extension of these rules must be justified by its necessity for the protection of the actual right against compelled self-incrimination. It is for this reason, for example, that statements taken without Miranda warnings (though not actually compelled) can be used to impeach a defendant's testimony at trial.

Continued on next page.

explained the Court, to treat two bouts of integrated and proximately conducted questioning as independent interrogations subject to independent evaluation simply because Miranda warnings formally punctuate them in the middle.

■═■

Quicknotes

CUSTODIAL INTERROGATION   The questioning of a suspect by police while in custody.

MIRANDA RULE   A required warning given before any questioning by law enforcement authorities can take place. Individuals in custody receive warnings regarding their privilege against self-incrimination, right to remain silent, and right to be represented by an attorney.

MIRANDA WARNINGS   Specified warnings that must be communicated to a person prior to a custodial interrogation; in the absence of the communication of such warnings, any communications made during the interrogation are inadmissible at trial.

■═■

Missouri v. Seibert

State (P) v. Murder suspect (D)

124 S. Ct. 2601 (2004).

NATURE OF CASE: Appeal from reversal of a murder conviction.

FACT SUMMARY: Patrice Seibert (D) argued that since her murder confession was obtained by the police technique of interrogating in successive, unwarned and warned phases, known as "question-first," the requirements of *Miranda* were violated.

🏛 RULE OF LAW
The police technique of interrogating in successive, unwarned and warned phases violates the requirements of *Miranda*.

FACTS: In questioning Patrice Seibert (D), a murder suspect, the police interrogator employed a widely used interrogation technique known as "question-first" in which the interrogator questions the suspect first, then gives the Miranda warnings, and then repeats the questioning until the interrogator obtains the confession or incriminating statement which the suspect has already previously provided. After employing this technique of interrogating in successive, unwarned and warned phases, Seibert (D) confessed to murder prior to her warnings and then again after being given the warnings. The trial court suppressed Seibert's (D) pre-warning confession but admitted her post-warning confession. She was convicted of murder. The Missouri Supreme Court reversed, holding that here where the interrogation was "nearly continuous," the second statement was clearly "the product of the invalid first statement" and should have been suppressed. Missouri (P) appealed.

ISSUE: Does the police technique of interrogating in successive, unwarned and warned phases violate the requirements of *Miranda*?

HOLDING AND DECISION: (Souter, J.) Yes. The police technique of interrogating in successive, unwarned and warned phases violates the requirements of *Miranda*. *Miranda* addressed interrogation practices likely to disable an individual from making a free and rational choice about speaking and held that a suspect must be "adequately and effectively" advised of the choice the Constitution guarantees. The object of the "question-first" technique here utilized against Seibert (D) was to render Miranda warnings ineffective by waiting for a particularly opportune time to give them, after the suspect had already confessed. Just as no talismanic incantation is required to satisfy *Miranda*'s strictures, it would be absurd to think that mere recitation of the litany suffices to satisfy *Miranda* in every conceivable circumstance. The issue when interrogators question first and warn later is thus whether the warnings reasonably convey to a suspect his Miranda rights. Unless the warnings could place a suspect who has just been interrogated in a position to make an informed choice as to whether to speak, there is no practical justification for accepting the formal warnings as compliance with *Miranda*, or for treating the second stage of interrogation as distinct from the first, unwarned and inadmissible segment. By any objective measure, applied to circumstances exemplified here, it is likely that if the interrogators employ the technique of withholding warnings until after interrogation succeeds in eliciting a confession, the warnings will be ineffective in preparing the suspect for successive interrogation, close in time and similar in content. Accordingly, the question-first tactic effectively threatens to thwart *Miranda*'s purpose of reducing the risk that a coerced confession would be admitted. Affirmed.

CONCURRENCE: (Breyer, J.) Courts should exclude the "fruits" of the initial unwarned questioning unless the failure to warn was in good faith.

CONCURRENCE: (Kennedy, J.) Not every violation of *Miranda* requires suppression of the evidence obtained. The scope of the *Miranda* suppression remedy depends on a consideration of whether admission of the evidence under the circumstances would frustrate *Miranda*'s "central concerns and objectives."

DISSENT: (O'Connor, J.) Because here the isolated fact of the interrogating officer's intent could not have had any bearing on Seibert's (D) capacity to comprehend and knowingly relinquish her right to remain silent, it could not by itself affect the voluntariness of her confession.

▶ ANALYSIS

As the Supreme Court makes clear in *Seibert*, the reason for the increased popularity of the question-first method of interrogation is to obtain a confession the suspect would not make if he understood his rights at the outset. The underlying police assumption, which is accurate, is that with one confession in hand before the warnings, the interrogator can usually count on getting a duplicate. It is unrealistic,

Continued on next page.

explained the Court, to treat two bouts of integrated and proximately conducted questioning as independent interrogations subject to independent evaluation simply because Miranda warnings formally punctuate them in the middle.

■■■■

Quicknotes

CUSTODIAL INTERROGATION The questioning of a suspect by police while in custody.

MIRANDA RULE A required warning given before any questioning by law enforcement authorities can take place. Individuals in custody receive warnings regarding their privilege against self-incrimination, right to remain silent, and right to be represented by an attorney.

MIRANDA WARNINGS Specified warnings that must be communicated to a person prior to a custodial interrogation; in the absence of the communication of such warnings, any communications made during the interrogation are inadmissible at trial.

■■■■

Brewer v. Williams (Williams I)

Court (P) v. Mental patient (D)

430 U.S. 387 (1977).

NATURE OF CASE: Appeal from a conviction of murder.

FACT SUMMARY: Williams (D) was convicted of murder based on a confession obtained during a custodial trip.

RULE OF LAW

The police cannot interrogate a defendant represented by known counsel after a refusal to speak without the presence of his attorney.

FACTS: Williams (D), an escaped mental patient, killed a 10-year-old girl. Williams (D) subsequently contacted a lawyer in Des Moines, informed him that he was in Davenport, and was willing to surrender to the police in Des Moines who were searching for him. The attorney informed the police and they sent a car to Waterloo to return him to Des Moines under a warrant issued for his arrest. The attorney informed both the police and his client that under no circumstances was Williams (D) to say anything. Williams (D), in the meantime, had been arrested in Davenport and hired counsel there to represent him at the arraignment on the murder charge. His attorney requested permission to accompany Williams (D) on the trip to Des Moines, but was refused. The attorney warned both Williams (D) and the police that there was to be no conversation during the trip concerning the crime as Williams (D) was represented by counsel who had informed him to remain silent. During the first part of the trip, Williams (D) repeatedly refused to speak unless counsel were present. One of the detectives then began to play on Williams's (D) religious beliefs, pleading with him to reveal the dead girl's whereabouts so that she could obtain a Christian burial. Williams (D) finally revealed the whereabouts of the body after confessing to the crime. Williams (D) appealed the admissibility of his confession after conviction. Williams (D) alleged, among other things, that the tactics used to obtain the confession violated his right to counsel.

ISSUE: Is questioning without the presence of known counsel during a critical stage of the proceedings violative of the Sixth and Fourteenth Amendments?

HOLDING AND DECISION: (Stewart, J.) Yes. The Sixth and Fourteenth Amendments grant an accused the right to the presence of counsel during all critical stages of proceedings. First, this was a critical stage. Williams (D) had a warrant issued for his arrest and had already been arraigned in Daven-

port on the charge. The police officers knew he was represented by counsel; that he had been informed not to speak; that Williams (D) told them he would not speak without counsel present. Williams (D) had pleaded not guilty to the charge. There are no grounds present herein that establish that Williams (D) knowingly, intelligently and voluntarily waived his rights. The state bears the heavy burden of establishing that once rights have been invoked by the defendant/accused, that they have been waived. No clear and convincing evidence of such a waiver is present herein. While the crime is abhorrent, we must reverse the conviction and remand for a new trial. The judgment of the court of appeals is affirmed.

DISSENT: (Burger, J.) After at least five warnings from two attorneys, Williams (D) voluntarily lead the police to where the body was buried. There was no coercion or threats. Williams (D) was prompted solely on the simple statement by the detective. In my mind, this would constitute a voluntary waiver of known rights. The exclusionary rule should not be arbitrarily applied to nonegregious police conduct.

DISSENT: (Blackmun, J.) I feel that the voluntary confession of Williams (D), made without threats or coercions, of a known right is conclusive evidence of a waiver.

DISSENT: (Blackmun, J.) This was not an example of purposeful police conduct. The trip was necessary to transport Williams (D) to Des Moines. Merely making a Christian plea on behalf of the family seems to me not unreasonable and is simply not the type of coercion for which a reversal should be granted.

ANALYSIS

The Brewer decision follows the rationale of *Rhode Island v. Innis,* 446 U.D. 291 (1980), in which the Court "focuses primarily on the perceptions of the suspect" as to whether the suspect is being held for custodial interrogation. Brewer added that any information the officer has regarding the suspect's peculiar susceptibilities to a certain kind of persuasion is relevant in determining what the officer should have known was likely to occur. Brewer could probably have been reversed on Miranda grounds on a showing that the confession was involuntary, due to the suspect's known susceptibility to religion-based questioning.

Texas v. Cobb

State (P) v. Convicted murderer (D)

532 U.S. 162 (2001).

NATURE OF CASE: Murder case.

FACT SUMMARY: Cobb (D) argued that his conviction for capital murder should be reversed on the basis that his confession should have been suppressed since it was elicited in violation of his Sixth Amendment right to counsel.

🏛 RULE OF LAW
The Sixth Amendment right to counsel does not extend to crimes that are "factually related" to those that have actually been charged.

FACTS: Cobb (D) gave a written statement confessing to the burglary of his neighbor's house and was indicted. He later confessed to the killing of his neighbor's wife and daughter, which he had previously denied. He was convicted of capital murder for the murder of more than one person in the course of a criminal transaction and sentenced to death. He appealed, contending that his confession should be suppressed because it was obtained in violation of his Sixth Amendment right to counsel. The court of criminal appeals reversed and remanded, concluding that the right to counsel had attached on the capital murder charge when Cobb (D) was charged with the burglary because the two crimes were "factually interwoven," even though he had not yet been charged with murder.

ISSUE: Does the Sixth Amendment right to counsel extend to crimes that are "factually related" to those that have actually been charged?

HOLDING AND DECISION: (Rehnquist, C.J.) No. The Sixth Amendment right to counsel does not extend to crimes that are "factually related" to those that have actually been charged. The Sixth Amendment right of counsel is offense specific and cannot be invoked once for all future prosecutions since it does not attach until a prosecution has been commenced. This Court has held that a defendant's statements regarding offenses for which he had not been charged were admissible notwithstanding the attachment of his Sixth Amendment right to counsel on other charged offenses. Some courts, however, had craved an exception for crimes that are "factually related" to a charged offense. We decline to support this view. However, we do hold that the Sixth Amendment right to counsel, when it attaches, does encompass offenses that even if not formally charged would be considered the same offense under the Blockburger test (*Blockburger v. United States*, 284 U.S. 299 [1932]). The test to be applied to determine whether there is more than one offense is whether each provision requires proof of a fact that the other does not. As defined by Texas law, capital murder and burglary are not the same offense under Blockburger. Thus, the police were not barred from interrogating Cobb (D) regarding the murders and his confession was admissible. Reversed.

CONCURRENCE: (Kennedy, J.) Note that the court reached its conclusion without approving of the decision in *Michigan v. Jackson*, 475 U.S. 625 (1986). This is wise since I believe the reasoning in that case was questionable. It is difficult to see the utility of a rule that invalidates a confession obtained after a voluntary waiver of the suspect's Miranda rights.

DISSENT: (Breyer, J.) This case focuses on the meaning of the word "offense." The Court's definition undermines Sixth Amendment protections while doing nothing to further effective law enforcement. The majority's rule permits law enforcement to question those charged with a crime without first approaching counsel, by asking questions about any other related crime not charged in the indictment.

▌ *ANALYSIS*

The Blockburger test adopted here has also been applied to determine the scope of the Fifth Amendment's double jeopardy clause, prohibiting multiple or successive prosecutions for the same "offense." The Court extends such test to the Sixth Amendment's "offense" reasoning that there is no constitutional difference between the meanings of the term in either context.

Quicknotes

BURGLARY Unlawful entry of a building at night with the intent to commit a felony therein.

MIRANDA RULE A required warning given before any questioning by law enforcement authorities can take place. Individuals receive warnings regarding their privilege against self-incrimination, right to remain silent, and right to be represented by an attorney.

MURDER Unlawful killing of another person either with deliberation and premeditation or by conduct demonstrating a reckless disregard for human life.

SIXTH AMENDMENT Provides the right to a speedy trial by impartial jury, the right to be informed of the accusation, to confront witnesses, and to have the assistance of counsel in all criminal prosecutions.

Lineups, Showups, and Other Pre-Trial Identification Procedures

Quick Reference Rules of Law

United States v. Wade

Federal government (P) v. Convicted robber (D)

388 U.S. 218 (1967).

NATURE OF CASE: Appeal from conviction for robbery and conspiracy to commit robbery.

FACT SUMMARY: The police arranged a lineup where two witnesses recognized Wade (D) as the robber. Wade's (D) appointed counsel was not present at the lineup.

RULE OF LAW
Once the accused is formally charged in an indictment, information, preliminary hearing, or arraignment, the accused is entitled to have counsel present at a lineup where witnesses seek to identify the crime perpetrator.

FACTS: Wade (D) and an accomplice were charged in an indictment with robbing a federally insured bank. Two witnesses told police that a man with a small strip of tape on each side of his face entered the bank and ordered at gunpoint that the witnesses fill a pillowcase with money. The perpetrator drove away with an accomplice who was waiting in a stolen car. Pursuant to the indictment, Wade (D) was arrested on April 2, and counsel was appointed to represent him on April 26. Fifteen days after counsel was appointed, the FBI arranged to have the two witnesses observe a lineup made up of Wade (D) and five or six other prisoners which was conducted in a courtroom of the local county courthouse. Each participant wore tape and said, "Put the money in the bag." Both witnesses identified Wade (D) as the robber. Wade's (D) appointed counsel was not notified of the lineup, nor was he present at the lineup. At the trial, the witnesses identified Wade (D), and on cross-examination the prior lineup was exposed. Wade (D) moved for an acquittal, or alternatively, to strike the witness' identification, on the grounds that the lineup without presence of counsel violated Wade's (D) Fifth Amendment privilege against self-incrimination and his Sixth Amendment right to counsel. The motions were denied and Wade (D) was convicted. The court of appeals reversed the conviction and ordered a new trial at which the in-court identification evidence was excluded on Sixth Amendment grounds.

ISSUE: Is a post-indictment lineup a critical stage of criminal proceedings so as to require the presence of counsel?

HOLDING AND DECISION: (Brennan, J.) Yes. The confrontation of the accused with witnesses in order to elicit identification evidence is particularly susceptible to innumerable dangers which might deny the accused a fair trial. The lineup is therefore a critical stage of the criminal proceedings. The right of the accused to a meaningful cross-examination is indispensable to a fair trial. There can be a high degree of suggestion inherent in the manner which the accused is presented to the witnesses and it would be difficult for the defense to reconstruct the way in which the lineup was conducted. Thus, the issue of identification may be permanently settled at the lineup. As a result, there may be a denial of the right to cross-examination because the conviction may rest on a courtroom identification which is, in fact, the fruit of a suspect pretrial identification, and which the accused is helpless to subject to effective scrutiny at trial. As a result, the lineup is a critical stage of the criminal proceedings because of the prejudice which may not be capable of reconstruction at trial, and because counsel's presence can often avert prejudice and assure a meaningful confrontation. Because the accused and his counsel should have been notified and because counsel's presence is a prerequisite to the conduct of the lineup absent intelligent waiver, the conviction is vacated and the case remanded to the district court to determine whether the in-court identifications had an independent source or whether the identifications were harmless error. The Court rejects any assertion of a Fifth Amendment violation. Self-incrimination applies only against being compelled to testify against himself or otherwise provide the State with testimonial or communicative evidence. The lineup does not force the accused to be a source of real or physical evidence.

DISSENT AND CONCURRENCE: (Black, J.) Wade's (D) Fifth Amendment rights were violated when the State forced him to supply proof of his own crime by forcing him to utter certain words and to wear tape. The Court is correct as to its rule requiring the presence of counsel at the lineup. However, the conviction should not be reversed because the State made no use of the pre-trial identification at the trial but relied solely on the witness' trial identification of the accused.

DISSENT AND CONCURRENCE: (White, J.) The Court is mistakenly propounding a per se rule based on assumptions of improper police practices and pressures which has a derogatory impact on the right to a fair trial. There is no basis for these assumptions. The mistakes which have occurred in criminal trials are as much the consequence of eyewitness testimony problems as of police misconduct. The states should not be impaired in their conduct of the criminal process by per se constitutional rules.

Continued on next page.

▶ *ANALYSIS*

Under *Wade*, a post-indictment lineup requires notice both to the defendant and his counsel, and a lineup cannot be held until counsel is present. The rationale for this decision is the defendant's right of confrontation; by being present at the lineup, counsel will be aware of any prejudicial factors at the lineup and will be able to more effectively attack the credibility of later courtroom identification. The Court also expressly holds that a lineup, and requiring a defendant to speak or wear certain items, is not a denial of the Fifth Amendment privileges against self-incrimination. Although the opinion does not address itself to the issue, a later case held that the Wade protection extends only to post-indictment lineups, and the accused does not have a right to counsel at lineups held before he is arrested or charged with a crime.

■■■

Quicknotes

CRITICAL STAGE OF PROCEEDINGS That stage in criminal proceedings, when an accused's right to counsel arises, at which some action may be taken that will prejudice later proceedings.

PRETRIAL LINEUP Procedure whereby police officers place an alleged perpetrator of a crime in a line with several other persons for purposes of identification by a witness or victim.

RIGHT TO COUNSEL Right conferred by the Sixth Amendment that the accused shall be provided effective legal assistance in a criminal proceeding.

■■■

Kirby v. Illinois

Convicted robber (D) v. State (P)

406 U.S. 682 (1972).

NATURE OF CASE: Appeal from conviction for robbery.

FACT SUMMARY: A robbery victim was brought to police headquarters. Later, two men were brought into headquarters and the victim identified them as the robbers prior to the robbers being charged or having the right to counsel.

RULE OF LAW

There is no right to counsel at police lineups held before the accused is arrested or charged with a crime.

FACTS: A robbery victim reported to the police that two men had robbed him on the street. The next day, the police stopped Kirby (D) and Bean while investigating an unrelated crime. The officer brought the two men to headquarters, but only after arriving and checking the records did the officer learn of the robbery. The robbery victim was picked up and brought to the station by the police. Immediately upon entering the room where Kirby (D) and Bean were seated, the victim positively identified them as the robbers. No lawyer was present and neither suspect had asked for or been advised of any right to the presence of counsel. At the trial, the victim described his identification of the two suspects at the station and identified them again in the courtroom.

ISSUE: Should the *Wade-Gilbert* exclusionary rule of pretrial identifications at lineups without presence of counsel be extended to identification testimony based upon a confrontation that took place prior to the accused being indicted or otherwise formally charged with a criminal offense?

HOLDING AND DECISION: (Stewart, J.) No. The *Wade-Gilbert* line of cases stand for the proposition that the accused's right to counsel attaches only after adversary judicial proceedings have been instituted and, therefore, there is no right to counsel at a confrontation held prior to the accused being formally charged. It is only after formal charges have been instituted and the State has decided to prosecute, and only then, that the adverse positions of government and the accused have solidified. It is only then that the accused is faced with prosecution and the intricacies of the law. The *Wade-Gilbert* rule is that the accused is entitled to counsel at any critical stage of the criminal proceeding and a post-indictment lineup is a critical stage. This Court will not depart from the rationale in those cases. If an accused wishes to attack a preindictment confrontation, he must use the Due Process

Clause. If the lineup is unnecessarily suggestive and conducive to irreparable mistaken identification, then it can be voided. The rule in *Stovall* states that one must balance the accused's right to be protected from prejudicial procedures against the interests of society in the prompt and purposeful investigation of crime. The judgment is affirmed.

DISSENT: (Brennan, J.) There exists in a confrontation for identification conducted after arrest the identical hazards to a fair trial that inhere in such a confrontation conducted after the onset of formal prosecutorial proceedings. The point at which proceedings are formally initiated is relevant to the *Wade-Gilbert* rule. The majority does not consider an arrest to be the start of the criminal process. A post-arrest confrontation is as much a critical stage as is a post-charge confrontation.

DISSENT: (White, J.) *Wade* and *Gilbert* govern and compel the reversal of the judgment below.

ANALYSIS

Kirby reflects a new majority which has crystallized in the Burger Court. *Kirby* can be used to undermine the force and scope of *Wade* and *Gilbert*. All the police need do is not formally charge a suspect after they arrest him until they have an opportunity to conduct a lineup. Counsel would not be required in those circumstances.

Quicknotes

CRITICAL STAGE OF PROCEEDINGS That stage in criminal proceedings, when an accused's right to counsel arises, at which some action may be taken that will prejudice later proceedings.

PRETRIAL LINEUP Procedure whereby police officers place an alleged perpetrator of a crime in a line with several other persons for purposes of identification by a witness or victim.

United States v. Ash

Federal government (P) v. Convicted robber (D)

413 U.S. 300 (1973).

NATURE OF CASE: Appeal from conviction for robbery.

FACT SUMMARY: Shortly before Ash's (D) trial, the prosecutor showed color photographs to four witnesses. Three of them selected Ash's (D) picture. Neither Ash (D) nor his attorney were present at the photograph identification.

🏛 RULE OF LAW
Critical stages of the prosecution at which the defendant has the right to counsel are only those stages involving the physical presence of the defendant, at a trial-like confrontation, with the government, at which the accused requires the assistance of counsel.

FACTS: In preparing for Ash's (D) trial, the prosecutor decided to use a photographic display to determine whether the witnesses would be able to make in-court identifications. Shortly before the trial (and two years after Ash's [D] indictment), the prosecutor showed five color photographs to four witnesses. Three of them selected Ash's (D) picture. Neither Ash (D) nor his attorney were present at the photograph identification. Ash (D) contended, and the court of appeals agreed, that his Sixth Amendment right to counsel was violated when his attorney was not given the opportunity to be present at the post-indictment photographic displays.

ISSUE: Does the Sixth Amendment require that defense counsel be given the opportunity to be present at pretrial, post-indictment photographic identifications by government witnesses?

HOLDING AND DECISION: (Blackmun, J.) No. The test to determine whether the Sixth Amendment guarantees the defendant's right of counsel at a particular event is whether the defendant required aid at that event in coping with legal problems or meeting the adversary. In Wade, it was decided that the lineup constituted a trial-like confrontation requiring the assistance of counsel to preserve the adversary process by compensating for advantages of the prosecutor. Counsel was seen as being more sensitive to, and aware of, suggestive influences than the defendant would be, and more able to reconstruct these events at trial. Lack of scientific precision and inability to reconstruct an event (without the presence of counsel) are the tests to determine whether counsel's presence at trial can substitute for counsel's presence at the pretrial confrontation. Wade held that counsel's presence at trial would

not substitute for such presence at a lineup. At a photographic display, the defendant is not present and asserts no right to be present. Hence, there is no possibility that the defendant might be misled by lack of legal knowledge or overpowered by the professional adversary. Nor is the situation a trial-like confrontation. Further, the defense counsel has equal access to the use of photographic displays. The Sixth Amendment does not grant the right to counsel to the defendant at photograph identifications by government witnesses as that situation does not involve the physical presence of the defendant in a trial-like confrontation at which the defendant required the assistance of counsel. The court of appeals' decision is reversed and remanded.

CONCURRENCE: (Stewart, J.) Pretrial proceedings are "critical" and so require the presence of defense counsel, if such presence is essential to protect the fairness of the trial itself. Wade held that the hazard of unfair suggestive influence at a lineup, which, because of the nature of the proceeding, could seldom be reconstructed at trial made the post-indictment lineup a critical stage. A photographic identification is quite different from a lineup because there are much fewer possibilities of impermissible suggestion, and any unfair influences can be reconstructed at trial. If a defendant's picture is marked differently, this unfairness can be demonstrated at trial. Likewise, a witness can testify if the photographs were arranged in a suggestive manner or if the defendant's picture was singled out by the prosecutor's comments or gestures.

DISSENT: (Brennan, J.) This Court has recognized that a corporeal identification is normally more accurate than a photographic identification. Hence, the dangers of misidentification are even greater at a photographic identification than at a lineup. Further, the possibility for impermissible suggestion in the context of a photographic display are great, because of either the photographs themselves, the manner in which they are presented, or comments or gestures by the prosecutor. As with lineups, the defense can seldom reconstruct at trial the mode and manner of the photographic identification. While the photographs used can be retained, retention cannot reveal subtle suggestions which might derive from the manner in which the display was conducted. The majority seeks to justify its result by engrafting a wholly unprecedented and insupportable limitation on the Sixth Amendment right to counsel in holding that critical stages are only those involving the

Continued on next page.

physical presence of the accused at a trial-like confrontation at which the accused requires the guiding hand of counsel. These requirements are not consistent with the established rule that stage must be deemed critical if it is one at which the presence of counsel is necessary to protect the fairness of the trial itself. None of the requirements were present in Powell, the seminal decision in this area, in which counsel for the defendants was not appointed until the eve of trial. It cannot be said that a preparation period of research and investigation involves the physical presence of the accused at a trial-like confrontation, but such a period is necessary to preserve the defendant's right to a fair trial. Nor did the conclusion in Wade turn on the fact that a lineup involves the confrontation requiring the assistance of counsel. Rather, *Wade* (388 U.S. 218 [1967]) envisioned counsel's function at the lineup to be that of a trained observer, able to detect any suggestive influences and capable of understanding the legal implications of what might transpire. "There is something ironic about the Court's conclusion today, that a pretrial lineup is a 'critical stage' because counsel's presence can help to compensate for the accused deficiencies as an observer, but that a pretrial photographic identification is not a 'critical stage' because the accused is not able to observe at all."

▌ *ANALYSIS*

Both the majority and concurring opinions in Ash indicated concern that granting a right to counsel at photographic displays might lead to the extension of the right to all pretrial interviews of prospective witnesses. However, under the traditional analysis, the right to counsel does not apply unless the lack of counsel at the stage in question might make the right to counsel at trial meaningless. One commentator notes that "the fact that photographic identifications were found to be 'critical' would not necessarily lead to a finding that other interviews between the prosecutor and witnesses were critical. The basis for extending the right to counsel to the identification context was that identification by eyewitnesses—like confessions—are such damning evidence that they may completely decide the guilt or innocence of the accused. Routine interviews between the prosecutor and witnesses, on the other hand, do not have the potential for such damaging results." Note, 26 Stan. L. Rev. 399, 416–7 (1974).

■■■

Quicknotes

RIGHT TO COUNSEL   Right conferred by the Sixth Amendment that the accused shall be provided effective legal assistance in a criminal proceeding.

ROBBERY   The unlawful taking of property from the person of another through the use of force or fear.

SIXTH AMENDMENT   Provides the right to a speedy trial by impartial jury, the right to be informed of the accusation, to confront witnesses, and to have the assistance of counsel in all criminal prosecutions.

■■■

Manson v. Brathwaite

Court (P) v. Heroin dealer (D)

432 U.S. 98 (1977).

NATURE OF CASE: Appeal from the reversal of a conviction for the sale of narcotics.

FACT SUMMARY: Glover, a police officer, after describing the man who had sold him heroin, was given a photograph of the suspect for identification purposes.

RULE OF LAW

If an identification is independently reliable, it will not be excluded solely because police identification techniques were suggestive.

FACTS: Glover, an undercover policeman, purchased heroin from Brathwaite (D). During the purchase, which took several minutes, Glover was no more than 2 or 3 feet from him. Glover returned to headquarters and described the individual whom he had seen in greater detail. From the description, another officer pulled a picture of Brathwaite (D) from their files. Glover saw the photograph 2 days later and promptly identified Brathwaite (D) as the seller. The photograph and identification were subsequently admitted at trial without objection. Brathwaite (D) was found guilty and was sentenced to prison. Fourteen months later, Brathwaite (D) challenged the photographic identification on the grounds that it was too suggestive, thereby rendering the identification itself per se excludable. The court of appeals reversed the conviction on the basis, holding that independent indicia of reliability could not overcome the suggestibility of the identification technique.

ISSUE: Will independent indicia of reliability allow admissibility of a witness whose original police identification was based on suggestive identification techniques?

HOLDING AND DECISION: (Blackmun, J.) Yes. The circuits have split over whether or not a per se rule should apply to excluding identification based on suggestive identification procedures. Some favor per se exclusion. Others take each case separately in order to determine if the identification would be otherwise reliable, and, if so, allowing it in evidence. We think the latter theory is correct. To hold otherwise would exclude relevant information from the jury merely because of improper police procedure. The case-by-case approach will be a deterrent to the police and will prevent the guilty from being freed. The lynch-pin in this area is the independent reliability of the identification. Here, we have a trained police officer who viewed Brathwaite (D) closely for 2 to 3 minutes from a short distance. Glover then described Brathwaite (D)

in detail shortly thereafter. The pictorial identification was 2 days later. All of this indicates independent reliability based on a trained observer, a prompt identification, and a reasonable opportunity to view the suspect. Independently reliable identifications need not be excluded to satisfy due process requirements. Reversed.

DISSENT: (Marshall, J.) In this case, the Court disregards distinctions in analysis developed in previous decisions and fashions a rule which is not supported by precedent. The use of a single picture on the presentation of a single suspect is inherently suggestive.

▶ *ANALYSIS*

The per se rule is used to discourage police abuses. The majority appears to indicate that nonpolice witnesses will be less likely to survive an ad hoc, case-by-case, approach because they are more prone to misidentification since they are not trained observers. The stress on them is also deemed greater which may cause faulty identifications. No hard and fast rules can be developed in this area, but the Court apparently focuses on (1) the length of time in which the accused was viewed; (2) the nature of the witness; (3) the circumstances; (4) the length of time between the incident and the identification; (5) the ability to give an initial description of the accused.

Quicknotes

PRIVILEGE AGAINST SELF-INCRIMINATION A privilege guaranteed by the Fifth Amendment to the federal Constitution in a criminal proceeding for communications made by an accused and protecting an accused or witness from having to give testimony that may incriminate himself.

PROCEDURAL DUE PROCESS The constitutional mandate that if the state or federal government acts so as to deny a citizen of a life, liberty or property interest the individual is first entitled to notice and the right to be heard.

Grand Jury Investigations

Quick Reference Rules of Law

Boyd v. United States

Illegal importer (D) v. Federal government (P)

116 U.S. 616 (1886).

NATURE OF CASE: Appeal of forfeiture action.

FACT SUMMARY: Using evidence secured per force from Boyd (D), the Government (P) seized property illegally imported.

RULE OF LAW
A defendant cannot be compelled to produce incriminating documents.

FACTS: Using a statute validating the practice, a government attorney obtained an order mandating that Boyd (D) produce an invoice covering certain imported glass, which the Government (P) suspected had been illegally imported. Using the invoice as evidence, the Government (P) seized the glass and confiscated it. Boyd (D) appealed, contending the production order was unconstitutional.

ISSUE: Can a defendant be compelled to produce incriminating documents?

HOLDING AND DECISION: (Bradley, J.) No. A defendant cannot be compelled to produce incriminating documents. The Fourth Amendment protects citizens against unreasonable searches and seizures. The forcible production of one's papers is much like forced testimony, which is clearly prohibited by the Fifth Amendment. In either case, such governmental conduct constitutes an excessive intrusion of the Government (P) into an individual's realm of protected liberty and cannot be permitted. Reversed.

CONCURRENCE: (Miller, J.) The Fourth Amendment is not involved here, as no search or seizure occurs. However, forced document production is tantamount of self-incrimination.

► ANALYSIS

Both in its application of the Fourth and Fifth Amendments, *Boyd* is no longer good law. Compelled document production has long since ceased to be considered a Fourth Amendment issue. As far as the Fifth Amendment is concerned, document production is no longer equated with compelled testimony.

■■■

Quicknotes

PRIVILEGE AGAINST SELF-INCRIMINATION A privilege guaranteed by the Fifth Amendment to the federal Constitution in a criminal proceeding for communications made by an accused and protecting an accused or witness from having to give testimony that may incriminate himself.

■■■

United States v. Dionisio

Federal government (P) v. Subpoenaed defendant (D)

410 U.S. 1 (1973).

NATURE OF CASE: Appeal from judgment for civil contempt.

FACT SUMMARY: Dionisio (D) refused to give voice exemplars to the grand jury.

> ## 🏛 RULE OF LAW
> Both the initial compulsion of a person to appear before a grand jury and a subsequent directive to make a voice recording are not unreasonable seizures within the meaning of the Fourth Amendment.

FACTS: Approximately 20 persons, including Dionisio (D), were subpoenaed before the grand jury to give voice exemplars for comparison with recorded conversations taken pursuant to a court-ordered surveillance. Dionisio (D) refused to give a voice exemplar, claiming protection under the Fourth and Fifth Amendments. The district judge ordered Dionisio (D) to give a voice exemplar. When Dionisio (D) refused, he was held in civil contempt and was committed to custody until he obeyed the order or until the expiration of 18 months.

ISSUE: Do voice exemplars, required to be given to a grand jury to be used for comparison with recorded conversations, violate a defendant's Fourth Amendment rights?

HOLDING AND DECISION: (Stewart, J.) No. First, a subpoena to appear before a grand jury is not a seizure of the person. It is the obligation of every person to appear and give evidence before the grand jury. It is an orderly, lawful process without social stigma and under the supervision of a judge. The fact that 20 persons were subpoenaed for the same reason is constitutionally irrelevant. Second, the order to give a voice exemplar was not a seizure under the meaning of the Fourth Amendment. What a person knowingly exposes to the public is not protected. Physical characteristics of voice, as opposed to content of conversations, are not reasonably expected to be private. Therefore, there is no need for the grand jury to determine reasonableness prior to ordering the exemplar where there is no other Fourth Amendment violation. To so require would impede the grand jury's proper function. Reversed.

DISSENT: (Marshall, J.) The only recognized exception in prior cases from Fourth Amendment coverage involved grand jury subpoenas requiring individuals to appear and testify. There is no basis for extending that exception when we move beyond the realm of grand jury investigations limited to testimonial inquiries, as in this case. The danger that law enforcement officials may seek to usurp the grand jury process to secure incriminating evidence from a suspect through the simple expedient of a subpoena arises and would, if the Fourth Amendment was held inapplicable here, allow law enforcement to accomplish indirectly what it would not be able to constitutionally accomplish directly.

▶ ANALYSIS

In *Davis v. Mississippi*, 394 U.S. 721 (1969), the Court held that an unlawful seizure could not be used to obtain fingerprints to be used to determine whether a person is the suspected criminal. *Dionisio* allows the grand jury to do exactly that on the rationale that subpoena is not a seizure and that voice prints are not a seizure. The grand jury is thus in a position to gain real evidence from a potential defendant prior to any finding of probable cause.

■==■

Quicknotes

EXPECTATION OF PRIVACY Requirement that in order to invoke the Fourth Amendment's protection against unreasonable searches and seizures, the individual must have a reasonable expectation of privacy in respect to the location searched or thing seized.

GRAND JURY A group summoned to investigate, inform, and accuse persons of crimes when sufficient evidence exists to do so.

SUBPOENA A mandate issued by court to compel a witness to appear at trial.

■==■

United States v. R. Enterprises, Inc.

Federal government (P) v. Pornography company (D)

498 U.S. 292 (1991).

NATURE OF CASE: Appeal from a partial grant of motions to quash subpoenas by a grand jury investigating interstate transportation of obscene materials.

FACT SUMMARY: After R. Enterprises, Inc. (D) and two other companies were served with subpoenas duces tecum in connection with a grand jury investigation, they moved to quash the subpoenas on the grounds that the materials sought were irrelevant to the grand jury's investigation.

🏛 **RULE OF LAW**
Where a subpoena is challenged on relevancy grounds, a motion to quash must be denied unless there is no reasonable possibility that the materials being sought will produce information relevant to the general subject of the grand jury's investigation.

FACTS: Three companies, including R. Enterprises, Inc. (D), that distributed adult and sexually oriented materials were served with subpoenas duces tecum in connection with a grand jury investigation into allegations of interstate transportation of obscene materials. The grand jury sought a variety of corporate books and records and, from one company, videotapes which had been shipped to retailers. All three companies moved to quash the subpoenas, arguing that the materials requested were irrelevant to the investigation. The district court denied the motions. The court of appeals, however, quashed the business records subpoenas issued to R. Enterprises (D) and one other company. The Government (P) appealed.

ISSUE: Where a subpoena is challenged on relevancy grounds, must a motion to quash be denied unless there is no reasonable possibility that the materials being sought will produce information relevant to the general subject of the grand jury's investigation?

HOLDING AND DECISION: (O'Connor, J.) Yes. Where a subpoena is challenged on relevancy grounds, a motion to quash must be denied unless there is no reasonable possibility that the materials being sought will produce information relevant to the general subject of the grand jury's investigation. The burden of showing unreasonableness must be on the recipient who seeks to avoid compliance. Where a challenging party does not know the general subject of the investigation, a court may be justified in requiring the Government (P) to reveal that information before requiring the party to carry its burden of persuasion. Here, however, there is no

doubt that R. Enterprises (D) knew the subject of the grand jury investigation. Because the district court could have concluded on the facts that there was a reasonable possibility that the information requested was relevant to the investigation, it correctly denied the motions to quash. Thus, the judgment of the court of appeals is reversed.

CONCURRENCE: (Stevens, J.) The trial court need only inquire into the relevance of subpoenaed materials after the moving party has initially demonstrated to the court that he has some valid objection to compliance. In the grand jury context, the law enforcement interest will almost always prevail, and the documents must be produced. However, it should not be suggested that the deferential relevance standard formulated here will govern decisions in every case, no matter how intrusive or burdensome the request.

▶ **ANALYSIS**

Many of the rules and restrictions that apply at a trial do not apply in grand jury proceedings. This is especially true of evidentiary restrictions. The Court rejected the use of the standard applied by the court of appeals, set out by the Supreme Court in *United States v. Nixon*, 418 U.S. 683 (1974), since that standard of relevancy, admissibility, and specificity was established in the trial context. In announcing the instant rule, the Court referred to Federal Rule of Criminal Procedure 17(c), which governs subpoenas duces tecum issued in federal criminal proceedings.

■=■

Quicknotes

GRAND JURY A group summoned to investigate, inform, and accuse persons of crimes when sufficient evidence exists to do so.

MOTION TO QUASH To vacate, annul, void.

SUBPOENA DUCES TECUM A subpoena compelling a witness to bring specified documents to court or to deposition.

■=■

Fisher v. United States

Income tax violator (D) v. Federal government (P)

425 U.S. 391 (1976).

NATURE OF CASE: Action to enforce an IRS summons.

FACT SUMMARY: The IRS sought to compel Fisher's (D) attorney to turn over accountants' worksheets, tax returns, and accountant-client correspondence Fisher (D) had obtained from his accountant and turned over to his attorney when it looked as if an income tax case against Fisher (D) might arise.

RULE OF LAW
The Fifth Amendment does not protect against compelled production of a taxpayer's papers if such production would not involve testimonial self-incrimination.

FACTS: The IRS was investigating Fisher (D) for possible civil or criminal liability under the federal income tax laws. Thus, Fisher (D) went to his accountant and recovered the accountant's worksheets, retained copies of the tax returns, and the accountant's copies of correspondence between the accounting firm and Fisher (D). He turned them over to his attorney, but the IRS issued a summons directing the attorney to produce those documents. The attorney refused, and the United States (P) began enforcement actions. Fisher's (D) attorney basically argued that the Fifth Amendment's protection against self-incrimination precluded forced production of these documents.

ISSUE: Does the Fifth Amendment protect against compelled production of a taxpayer's papers if such production would not involve testimonial self-incrimination?

HOLDING AND DECISION: (White, J.) No. The Fifth Amendment protects against compelled production of a taxpayer's papers only if such production would involve testimonial self-incrimination, which it would not under the circumstances of this particular case. It protects against "compelled self-incrimination," not the disclosure of private information. The attorney-client privilege applies only to documents in the hands of an attorney which would have been privileged in the hands of the client by reason of the Fifth Amendment, and the documents sought would not have been privileged in Fisher's (D) hands under the Fifth Amendment. Thus, they must be produced.

CONCURRENCE: (Brennan, J.) While I agree the privilege against compelled self-incrimination did not protect the papers in this case, I feel the court's opinion does not adequately stress the protection secured by the privilege against compelled production of one's private books and papers.

CONCURRENCE: (Marshall, J.) The proper focus is, in cases like this, upon the private nature of the papers subpoenaed and not whether the act of production involves testimonial self-incrimination.

▶ ANALYSIS

One law review note takes a similar position to that expressed by Justice Marshall. It argues that this case and another similar one mean that "no zone of privacy now exists that the government cannot enter to take an individual's property for the purpose of obtaining criminal information." Note, 76 Mich. L. Rev. 184, 209-11 (1977).

■━■

Quicknotes

ATTORNEY-CLIENT PRIVILEGE   A doctrine precluding the admission into evidence of confidential communications between an attorney and his client made in the course of obtaining professional assistance.

PRIVILEGE AGAINST SELF-INCRIMINATION   A privilege guaranteed by the Fifth Amendment to the federal Constitution in a criminal proceeding for communications made by an accused and protecting an accused or witness from having to give testimony that may incriminate himself.

■━■

United States v. Hubbell

Federal government (P) v. Criminal (D)

520 U.S. 27 (2000).

NATURE OF CASE: Grant of writ of certiorari to review conditional plea agreement and court of appeals decision.

FACT SUMMARY: Pursuant to a subpoena and a grant of immunity from prosecution, Hubbell (D) produced documents to the Independent Counsel (P). A grand jury later returned an indictment against Hubbell (D) after the government (P) presented evidence based on the same documents Hubbell (D) produced.

RULE OF LAW

The Fifth Amendment prevents the government from compelling a suspect to produce incriminating documents under a grant of immunity and then prosecuting that suspect using information gained from those incriminating documents.

FACTS: Hubbell (D) pled guilty and was sentenced to prison. In the plea agreement, Hubbell (D) agreed to provide information about matters related to the Whitewater investigation. While Hubbell (D) was serving his sentence, the Independent Counsel (P) served him (D) with a subpoena requesting the production of certain documents. Hubbell (D) refused, invoking his Fifth Amendment right against self-incrimination. The Government (P) obtained a court order directing Hubbell (D) to produce the documents under a grant of immunity. The documents were then produced. A second prosecution arose out of information gained from these documents. The district court dismissed the indictment, holding that the evidence was derived from the testimonial aspects of the immunized act of producing documents. The court of appeals vacated that judgment and remanded for the lower court to hold a hearing to establish the extent of the Government's (P) independent knowledge of the documents. On remand, the Government (P) entered into a conditional plea bargain with Hubbell (D) and the United States Supreme Court granted the Government's (P) request for a writ of certiorari.

ISSUE: Does the Fifth Amendment protect a witness from being compelled to disclose the existence of incriminating documents that the government is unable to describe with reasonable particularity and can the government prosecute that witness if he or she produces such documents under a grant of immunity?

HOLDING AND DECISION: (Stevens, J.) No. There is a difference between the use of compulsion to extort communications from a defendant and compelling a person to engage in conduct that may be incriminating. Thus, criminal suspects may be compelled to provide blood or handwriting samples. This act of exhibiting physical characteristics is not the same as a sworn communication by a witness that relates either express or implied assertions of fact or belief. Thus, although a person may be compelled to provide documents, even though they may contain incriminating evidence, the Fifth Amendment protects a witness from prosecution using this incriminating information, whether it was derived directly or indirectly from the compelled production of documents. Hubbell's (D) action of producing hundreds of documents was a first step in a chain of evidence that led to his own prosecution. The documents were produced only under a grant of immunity and a district court order. Compliance under these circumstances cannot then be turned against him (D). The indictment against Hubbell (D) must be dismissed. Affirmed.

CONCURRENCE: (Thomas, J.) This decision involves the act-of-production doctrine that provides that those who are compelled to produce incriminating physical evidence pursuant to a subpoena may invoke the Fifth Amendment privilege as a bar to production when the act of producing the evidence would contain testimonial features. The Fifth Amendment may be broader than this doctrine, however, and protect against compelled production of any incriminating evidence. The Fifth Amendment provides that no person shall be compelled in any criminal case to be a witness against himself. *Witness* has been defined as "a person who provides testimony." This definition restricts the Fifth Amendment. *Witness* also means a person who gives or furnishes evidence. Therefore, a person who responds to a subpoena by producing documentation is also a witness. I remain open to a reconsideration of this definition.

ANALYSIS

In its holding, the court of appeals likened the use of the contents of the produced documents to the use of data drawn from a forced blood draw or compelled handwriting exemplar. The difference, however, may be that the forced blood draws or the giving of handwriting samples are usually not done under grants of immunity.

Doe v. United States

Bank signatory (D) v. Federal government (P)

487 U.S. 201 (1988).

NATURE OF CASE: Appeal from contempt order.

FACT SUMMARY: Doe (D) contended that he could not be compelled to authorize the release of banking records as such would be self-incrimination.

🏛 RULE OF LAW
Written consent to release information, if in existence, is not testimonial and thus can be compelled without violating the freedom against self-incrimination.

FACTS: Doe (D), the object of a grand jury investigation, was served with a motion to compel his signature authorizing the release of banking information. The banks, headquartered in foreign countries, had refused to honor a subpoena and insisted upon Doe's (D) authorization. The authorization allowed the disclosure of information, if any existed. Doe (D) refused to sign, contending such would violate his right against self-incrimination. He was held in contempt, and the court of appeals affirmed.

ISSUE: Can written consent to release to release information be compelled without violating the right against self-incrimination?

HOLDING AND DECISION: (Blackmun, J.) Yes. Written consent to release information, if in existence, is not testimonial in nature and thus can be compelled without violating the right against self-incrimination. The release does not acknowledge the existence of any records. It does not acknowledge that the defendant possesses any records, and it does not authenticate any records. Thus, the act of consent does not equate with testimonial evidence and is not subject to the self-incrimination analysis. Thus, the contempt citation was proper. Affirmed.

▶ ANALYSIS

The dissent drew an analogy between a situation wherein a defendant can lawfully be compelled to open a safe deposit box containing evidence and this case. Justice Stevens indicated that the defendant's mind cannot be used against him. Requiring him to consent is tantamount to requiring him to reveal a combination to a locked safe containing evidence, and, thus, such could not be compelled.

Quicknotes

GRAND JURY A group summoned to investigate, inform, and accuse persons of crimes when sufficient evidence exists to do so.

PRIVILEGE AGAINST SELF-INCRIMINATION A privilege guaranteed by the Fifth Amendment to the federal Constitution in a criminal proceeding for communications made by an accused and protecting an accused or witness from having to give testimony that may incriminate himself.

SUBPOENA A mandate issued by court to compel a witness to appear at trial.

The Scope of the Exclusionary Rules

Quick Reference Rules of Law

Minnesota v. Carter

State (P) v. Accused (D)

525 U.S. 83 (1998).

NATURE OF CASE: Appeal from an order holding that an illegal search had occurred.

FACT SUMMARY: When a police officer saw people packaging cocaine through a window and later arrested the occupants of the apartment, they alleged that their Fourth Amendment rights had been violated, and sought to have the evidence excluded.

RULE OF LAW
An overnight guest in a home may claim the protection of the Fourth Amendment, but one who is merely present with the consent of the householder may not.

FACTS: A confidential informant told the police that when walking by the window of a ground floor apartment, he had seen people putting a white powder into bags. The police officer looked through the same window and saw the men, and notified headquarters to prepare affidavits for a search warrant. When Carter (D) and Johns (D) left the building, they were arrested while in a motor vehicle, and cocaine was later found in the vehicle and in the apartment. Carter (D) and Johns (D) had never been in that apartment before and had been there for 2½ hours to package the cocaine. Carter (D) and Johns (D) were convicted of state drug offenses. The trial court held that since they were only temporary out-of-state visitors, they could not challenge the legality of the government intrusion into the apartment, and that the police officer's observation through the window was not a "search" within the meaning of the Fourth Amendment. The state supreme court reversed, holding that Carter (D) and Johns (D) did have "standing" because they had a legitimate expectation of privacy in the invaded place, and that the officer's observation constituted an unreasonable "search" of the apartment. Minnesota (P) appealed.

ISSUE: If an overnight guest in a home may claim the protection of the Fourth Amendment, may one who is merely present with the consent of the householder also do so?

HOLDING AND DECISION: (Rehnquist, C.J.) No. An overnight guest in a home may claim the protection of the Fourth Amendment, but one who is merely present with the consent of the householder may not. The purely commercial nature of the transaction engaged in here, the relatively short time on the premises, and the lack of any previous connection between Carter (D) and the householder, all lead to the conclusion that their situation is closer to that of one simply permitted on the premises, rather than that of an overnight guest. Therefore, any search that may have occurred did not violate their Fourth Amendment rights. Reversed.

CONCURRENCE: (Scalia, J.) Whereas it is plausible to regard a person's overnight lodging as at least his "temporary" residence, it is entirely impossible to give that characterization to an apartment that he uses to package cocaine.

CONCURRENCE: (Kennedy, J.) Almost all social guests have a legitimate expectation of privacy, and hence protection against unreasonable searches, in their host's home. In this case, Carter (D) and Johns (D) have established nothing more than a fleeting and insubstantial connection with Thompson's home.

DISSENT: (Ginsburg, J.) The court's decision undermines not only the security of short-term guests, but also the security of the home resident herself. When a homeowner chooses to share the privacy of her home and her company with a short-term guest, both host and guest have exhibited an actual (subjective) expectation of privacy, and that expectation is one that our society is prepared to recognize as reasonable.

ANALYSIS

Property used for commercial purposes is treated differently for Fourth Amendment purposes than residential property. While Carter (D) and Johns (D) were present in a "home," it was not their home. Only the Dissent argued that a short-term guest in a home should share his host's shelter against unreasonable searches and seizures. Since there was no violation of the Fourth Amendment, the evidence seized by the police was used against Carter (D) and Johns (D).

Quicknotes

EXPECTATION OF PRIVACY Requirement that in order to invoke the Fourth Amendment's protection against unreasonable searches and seizures, the individual must have a reasonable expectation of privacy in respect to the location searched or thing seized.

FOURTH AMENDMENT Provides that persons be secure as to their person and private belongings against unreasonable searches and seizures.

SEARCH An inspection conducted in order to obtain evidence to be utilized for the prosecution of a crime.

SEIZURE The removal of property from one's possession due to unlawful activity or in satisfaction of a judgment entered by the court.

Nix v. Williams (Williams II)

Court (P) v. Convicted child murderer (D)

476 U.S. 431 (1984).

NATURE OF CASE: Appeal from denial of writ of habeas corpus.

FACT SUMMARY: The district court held that evidence illegally obtained against Williams (D) need not be suppressed because the police would have inevitably discovered it legally.

🏛 RULE OF LAW
Evidence obtained as the result of the denial of a defendant's rights need not be suppressed if it is shown that the police inevitably would have discovered it legally.

FACTS: A child disappeared from a shopping mall, and volunteers began to search for her. At the time of the search, Williams (D) was arrested and was interrogated while in custody, outside the presence of his attorney, and revealed the location of the child's body. He was convicted and appealed, contending the evidence gained from his statements should have been suppressed as the fruit of illegal interrogation. The Supreme Court of Iowa affirmed the conviction on the basis that the body would have been discovered by the volunteers regardless of Williams's (D) statements. The district court denied Williams (D) petition for habeas corpus relief on the same grounds. The court of appeals reversed, and the Supreme Court granted certiorari.

ISSUE: Is there an inevitable discovery exception to the Sixth Amendment exclusionary rule?

HOLDING AND DECISION: (Burger, C.J.) Yes. Evidence obtained as a result of the denial of constitutional rights to counsel need not be suppressed if it would have inevitably been discovered legally. The exclusionary rule requires suppression of evidence which is, in some sense, the product of illegal governmental activity. If it is established that the evidence would have been discovered anyway, the evidence is in no way produced by illegal conduct. In this case, the body would have been found by the volunteers. Therefore, its location need not have been suppressed. Reversed.

CONCURRENCE: (Stevens, J.) The rule announced today is not ad hoc in nature and is strongly supported by precedent.

DISSENT: (Brennan, J.) The government should be required to prove that inevitable discovery would have occurred by clear and convincing evidence, rather than merely by a preponderance, as stated by the Court.

▶ ANALYSIS

The court of appeals in this case suggested that the government be required to show a lack of bad faith before it could use the inevitable discovery exception. The Court rejected this argument on the basis that it would require courts to withhold relevant truthful evidence from juries that would have been available absent any unlawful police conduct. This would put police in a worse position and undercut the exception for inevitable discovery.

Quicknotes

CUSTODIAL INTERROGATION The questioning of a suspect by police while in custody.

FRUIT OF POISONOUS TREE Doctrine that evidence obtained as a result of illegal procedures is inadmissible at trial.

INEVITABLE DISCOVERY If the government can show that discovery of evidence by lawful means was inevitable, it can use unlawfully obtained evidence in a criminal case as an exception to the exclusionary rule.

People v. Berrios

State (P) v. Heroin possessors (D)

N.Y. Ct. App., 270 N.E. 2d 709, 28 N.Y. 2d 361 (1971).

NATURE OF CASE: Appeals from conviction for possession of narcotics and from denial of motions to suppress in actions for the possession of narcotics.

FACT SUMMARY: Arresting officers testified that Berrios (D), Oritz (D), and Tate (D) each dropped glassine envelopes containing heroin as the officers approached them. Berrios (D), Oritz (D), and Tate (D) maintain that the envelopes were taken from them in an unlawful search.

🏛 RULE OF LAW
Where defendants challenge the admissibility of physical evidence or make a motion to suppress, they bear the ultimate burden of proving that the evidence should not be used against them.

FACTS: In *People v. Berrios*, an officer testified that Berrios (D) dropped a glassine envelope as the officer approached him. At the trial, Berrios (D) and another man testified that the officer had searched him. In *People v. Oritz*, officers testified that they instructed a group of men, including Oritz (D), to stop walking and Oritz (D) dropped nine glassine envelopes. In *People v. Tate*, officers testified that Tate (D) walked away as they approached him, and he dropped 25 glassine envelopes. Berrios (D), Oritz (D), and Tate (D) contend that the burden of proof as to the admissibility of physical evidence seized in warrantless crimes should be shifted from the defendant to the People. They assert that the change is necessary to alleviate the problem of perjured police testimony. They contend that since *Mapp v. Ohio*, 367 U.S. 643, there has been a great incidence of "dropsy" testimony by officers. The New York County District Attorney also suggests that the burden of proof be imposed upon the People (P) rather than the defendant.

ISSUE: Should the burden of proving the admissibility of physical evidence seized in warrantless searches be imposed upon the people in order to alleviate the problem of perjured police testimony?

HOLDING AND DECISION: (Scileppi, J.) No. Where defendants challenge the admissibility of physical evidence or make motions to suppress, they bear the ultimate burden of proving that the evidence should not be used against them. The words of the motion to suppress statute suggest no other rational conclusion. Since the defendant claims he was wronged and asks the court to give redress, it is most reasonable that he should bear the burden of proof. The people, of course, bear the burden of showing the legality of the police conduct. It is contended that the change is needed to cope with the problem of perjured police testimony. This court is asked to infer that the police are systematically evading the mandate of *Mapp* by fabricating their testimony. "We reject this frontal attack on the integrity of our law enforcement system." Further, the proposed change is no more effective in preventing perjury than the present burden of proof. Under either the change or the present rule, the defendant must still refute the testimony of the police officer. Lastly there are more appropriate methods for dealing with these abuses. The police departments can formulate procedures and policies to eliminate these problems. Berrios's (D) conviction and the denial of Oritz's (D) and Tate's (D) motions to suppress are affirmed.

DISSENT: (Fuld, C.J.) I agree with the majority that there is no valid proof that all police are perjurers. However, the district attorney does inform us that he and many others believe that in a substantial number of dropsy cases, officers' testimony is tailored to meet the search and seizure requirements and it is very difficult to tell fact from fiction. Underlying the Fourth and Fifth Amendments is the basic proposition that "No person is to be convicted on unconstitutional evidence." The present burden of proof rule subverts this principle by making it possible for some defendants to be convicted on evidence obtained illegally. A trial judge who is unsure whether the officer's testimony is true must, nevertheless, resolve her doubt in favor of the people and admit the evidence. The federal courts and California courts hold that the prosecution bears the burden of justifying a warrantless seizure of evidence. Even our court requires the people to bear the burden of proof of the voluntariness of consents to searches.

▶ ANALYSIS

Aside from the justification of a search on the basis of consent (where the burden universally is placed on the prosecution), states vary considerably in the allocation of both the burden of going forward and the ultimate burden of proof on the admissibility of evidence. There are four general categories. Under the New York approach described in Berrios, the prosecution has the burden of going forward to establish the legality of the search. The ultimate burden of proof is then upon the defendant to rebut this evidence and prove that the search is invalid. A larger group of states puts

Continued on next page.

both the initial burden of going forward and the ultimate burden upon the defendant. Many states follow the federal court pattern of allocation which places the burden on the prosecution. But the defendant must first show that he has standing. In at least two jurisdictions, the prosecution has both the burden of going forward and the burden of proof on all Fourth Amendment objections. Lower courts are generally agreed, however, that the burden of establishing a confession's admissibility rests upon the prosecution.

■■■

Quicknotes

BURDEN OF PERSUASION The duty of a party to introduce evidence to support a fact that is in dispute in an action.

PERJURY The making of false statements under oath.

■■■

CHAPTER 13

Pretrial Release

Quick Reference Rules of Law

United States v. Salerno

Federal government (P) v. RICO violator (D)

481 U.S. 739 (1987).

NATURE OF CASE: Appeal from denial of bail.

FACT SUMMARY: Salerno (D) contended the Bail Reform Act violated his constitutional rights by allowing a denial of bail based on his potentially dangerous activities.

🏛 RULE OF LAW
The Bail Reform Act, allowing for the denial of bail upon a showing that the defendant presents a risk of danger, is constitutional.

FACTS: Salerno (D) was charged with violation of the criminal RICO statute. He was denied bail after a hearing resulted in a finding that no release conditions would reasonably assure the safety of any person and the community. He appealed, contending the statute allowing for such denial violated due process and excessive bail prohibitions, and was thus unconstitutional on its face. The court of appeals reversed, and the Supreme Court granted certiorari.

ISSUE: Is the Bail Reform Act constitutional?

HOLDING AND DECISION: (Rehnquist, C.J.) Yes. The Bail Reform act is constitutional. Detention is not punishment. This Act is regulatory, not punitive. The regulatory goal was to protect the public and people close to the trial from potentially harmful individuals. Thus, the regulatory goal was directly related to its means. The Government's (P) interest in preserving safety may outweigh an individual's right to freedom. Thus, some circumstances exist wherein application of the Act is constitutional. Thus, it is not invalid on its face. Reversed.

DISSENT: (Marshall, J.) This statute punishes a person for the commission of a perceived future crime. Incarceration is punishment. Thus, the statute is unconstitutional.

DISSENT: (Stevens, J.) Pretrial commission for future dangerousness is unconstitutional.

▶ ANALYSIS

The traditional basis for determining if bail is available is whether there is a risk of flight. That is, whether there is a risk the defendant will not show up for court proceedings. The higher the possibility for flight, usually based on the severity of the crime, the higher the bail. A person is considered innocent until proven guilty; thus, pretrial detention walks a thin constitutional line.

Quicknotes

PROCEDURAL DUE PROCESS The constitutional mandate that if the state or federal government acts so as to deny a citizen of a life, liberty or property interest the individual is first entitled to notice and the right to be heard.

The Decision Whether to Prosecute

Quick Reference Rules of Law

United States v. Armstrong

Federal government (P) v. Federal law violator (D)

517 U.S. 456 (1996).

NATURE OF CASE: Review of dismissal of an indictment for possession of crack cocaine and federal firearms offenses.

FACT SUMMARY: After charges were brought against him for violating federal drug laws, Armstrong (D), alleging that he was selected for prosecution because he was black, brought a motion for discovery in support of his selective-prosecution claim or for dismissal of the indictment.

RULE OF LAW
A criminal defendant bringing a selective-prosecution claim must make a credible showing of different treatment of similarly situated persons in order to obtain discovery in support of the claim.

FACTS: Armstrong (D) was arrested for violation of federal drug and firearms laws. Armstrong (D) alleged that he had been selected for prosecution because he was black, and filed a motion for dismissal of the charges or for discovery of government (P) documents regarding their prosecution of similar defendants. The district court granted the discovery motion and dismissed the indictment when the government (P) would not comply with discovery. The court of appeals reversed but then, upon hearing the case en banc, affirmed the district court's order of dismissal. The Supreme Court granted certiorari.

ISSUE: Must a criminal defendant bringing a selective-prosecution claim make a credible showing of different treatment of similarly situated persons in order to obtain discovery in support of the claim?

HOLDING AND DECISION: (Rehnquist, C.J.) Yes. A criminal defendant bringing a selective-prosecution claim must make a credible showing of different treatment of similarly situated persons in order to obtain discovery in support of the claim. Under Federal Rule of Civil Procedure 16, which controls discovery in a criminal case, a defendant must show some evidence of disparate treatment—similar to the requirement under equal protection claims. Here, Armstrong (D) did not make such a showing. Thus, the district court's dismissal of the case was improper. Reversed and remanded.

DISSENT: (Stevens, J.) While the defendant did not make a strong enough showing to merit discovery, the district court did not abuse its discretion in requiring some response from the United States (P) Attorney's Office.

▶ ANALYSIS

The Court notes that the test for obtaining discovery for a selective-prosecution claim should be similar to that of an equal protection claim. Recall that to successfully pursue an equal protection claim, the claimant must show both a discriminatory effect and a discriminatory purpose. In order to show a discriminatory effect, the claimant must also show that similarly situated persons (but of a different race or religion) were not prosecuted. From this equal protection language, the Court developed the test in this case.

Quicknotes

DISCOVERY Pretrial procedure during which one party makes certain information available to the other.

EN BANC The hearing of a matter by all the judges of the court, rather than only the necessary quorum.

EQUAL PROTECTION A constitutional guarantee that no person shall be denied the same protection of the laws enjoyed by other persons in life circumstances.

The Preliminary Hearing

Quick Reference Rules of Law

State v. Clark

State (P) v. Alleged forgers (D)

Utah Sup. Ct., 20 P.3d 300 (2001).

NATURE OF CASE: State's appeal from the quashing of a bindover for trial.

FACT SUMMARY: When Clark (D) and Smith (D) were bound over for trial, the district court quashed the bindover.

🏛 RULE OF LAW

To support a bindover for trial, the prosecution must present sufficient evidence only to support a reasonable belief that an offense has been committed and that the defendant committed it.

FACTS: Clark (D) and Smith (D) were charged with forgery and bound over for trial by a magistrate. The bindover was quashed by the district court on grounds the state failed to meet its evidentiary burden at the preliminary hearing, and the state appealed.

ISSUE: To support a bindover for trial, must the prosecution present sufficient evidence only to support a reasonable belief that an offense has been committed and that the defendant committed it?

HOLDING AND DECISION: (Durrant, J.) Yes. To support a bindover for trial, the prosecution must present sufficient evidence only to support a reasonable belief that an offense has been committed and that the defendant committed it. Unlike a motion for a directed verdict, this evidence need not be capable of supporting a finding of guilt beyond a reasonable doubt. Instead, the quantum of evidence necessary to support a bindover is less than that necessary to survive a directed verdict motion. Specifically, there is no principled basis for attempting to maintain a distinction between the arrest warrant probable cause standard and the preliminary hearing probable cause standard. The "reasonable belief" standard has the advantage of being more easily understood while still allowing magistrates to fulfill the primary purpose of the preliminary hearing, namely, ferreting out groundless and improvident prosecutions. Here, the district court, by dismissing the forgery charges because the state failed to demonstrate the defendants had acted with the requisite intent, wrongly applied the directed verdict standard. Viewed in the light most favorable to the prosecution, the facts presented here were sufficient to meet the reasonable belief standard since the facts revealed that the defendants attempted to cash a forged check at local banks mere hours after the check was reported stolen. When cashiers told defendants they were seeking approval to cash the check, defendants abandoned the forged check and left the bank. Reversed.

▶ ANALYSIS

As the *Clark* decision notes, notwithstanding that the evidence to bindover will be viewed in the light most favorable to the prosecution, to prevail at a preliminary hearing the prosecution must still produce believable evidence of all the elements of the crime charged.

■══■

Quicknotes

DIRECTED VERDICT A verdict ordered by the court in a jury trial.

PROBABLE CAUSE A reasonable basis for believing that a crime has been committed.

QUANTUM An essential amount; a modicum of the required degree.

REASONABLE BELIEF A reasonable basis for believing that a crime is being or has been committed.

REASONABLE DOUBT Enough doubt on the part of jurors to acquit a defendant based on the absence of evidence.

■══■

Grand Jury Review

Quick Reference Rules of Law

Costello v. United States

Grand jury indictee (D) v. Federal government (P)

350 U.S. 359 (1956).

NATURE OF CASE: Petition for certiorari after conviction of income tax invasion.

FACT SUMMARY: Three investigating officers were the only witnesses before the grand jury who indicted Costello (D). They had no firsthand knowledge of the transactions upon which their computations were based. Hence, the indictment was based solely on hearsay.

🏛 **RULE OF LAW**
An indictment returned by a legally constituted and unbiased grand jury, if valid on its face, is enough to call for trial of the charge on the merits, regardless of the fact that the only evidence before the grand jury was hearsay.

FACTS: At Costello's (D) trial, the government called 144 witnesses and introduced 368 exhibits, all of which related to business transactions and expenditures by the Costellos (D). Three government agents, whose investigations had produced the evidence used against Costello (D) at trial, summarized the evidence already introduced, and introduced computations showing, if correct, that the Costellos (D) had received far greater income than they had reported. The three agents were the only witnesses before the grand jury. Costello (D) moved to dismiss the indictment on the ground that the only evidence before the grand jury was hearsay since the officers had no firsthand knowledge of the transactions upon which their computations were based.

ISSUE: May a defendant be required to stand trial and a conviction be sustained where only hearsay evidence was presented to the grand jury?

HOLDING AND DECISION: (Black, J.) Yes. Neither the Fifth Amendment nor any other constitutional provision prescribes the kind of evidence upon which grand juries must act. The grand jury convenes as a body of lay people, free from technical rules. If indictments could be challenged on the ground that there was inadequate or incompetent evidence before the grand jury, a great delay would result, since before a trial on the merits, an accused could insist on a kind of preliminary trial to determine the adequacy and competency of the evidence before the grand jury. Perhaps most importantly, such a change would run as a body not hampered by rigid procedural or evidential rules. An indictment returned by a legally constituted and unbiased grand jury, if valid on its face, is enough to call for trial of the charge of the merits.

The Fifth Amendment requires nothing more. Costello's (D) conviction is affirmed.

CONCURRENCE: (Burton, J.) In this case, substantial and rationally persuasive evidence apparently was presented to the grand jury. Hence, the indictment should be sustained. However, if it is shown that the grand jury had before it no such evidence upon which to base its indictment, that indictment should be quashed.

▶ **ANALYSIS**

Depending upon its scope, Costello may (or may not) reflect the majority position among those states that regularly prosecute by indictment. In many, courts will dismiss an indictment upon a showing that there was no sworn witness or legal documentary evidence before the grand jury. In several, courts have held an indictment is also subject to attack where based solely on the testimony of an incompetent witness. Most indictment states, however, will go no further. An indictment will not be dismissed even if issued solely upon hearsay testimony, and in some jurisdictions, indictments regularly are based entirely upon a summary of investigative reports presented by a single officer or the prosecuting attorney.

Quicknotes

GRAND JURY A group summoned to investigate, inform, and accuse persons of crimes when sufficient evidence exists to do so.

HEARSAY An out-of-court statement made by a person other than the witness testifying at trial that is offered in order to prove the truth of the matter asserted.

TRIAL ON THE MERITS A judicial determination of the facts or issues brought before it pursuant to its jurisdictional authorities.

United States v. Williams

Federal government (P) v. Federal statute violator (D)

504 U.S. 36 (1992).

NATURE OF CASE: Appeal from dismissal of an indictment.

FACT SUMMARY: The court of appeals, agreeing with the district court, dismissed an indictment against Williams (D) since the Government (P) failed to disclose substantial exculpatory evidence in its possession to the grand jury.

🏛 RULE OF LAW
A federal court may not dismiss an otherwise valid indictment for failure of the prosecution to disclose substantial exculpatory evidence to the grand jury.

FACTS: After a federal grand jury indicted Williams (D) for violating a federal statute, the Tenth Circuit Court of Appeals, agreeing with the district court, granted Williams's (D) motion to dismiss the indictment on the grounds that the Government (P) failed to disclose to the grand jury substantial exculpatory evidence in its possession. The Government (P) appealed.

ISSUE: May a federal court dismiss an otherwise valid indictment for failure of the prosecution to disclose substantial exculpatory evidence to the grand jury?

HOLDING AND DECISION: (Scalia, J.) No. A federal court may not dismiss an otherwise valid indictment for failure of the prosecution to disclose substantial exculpatory evidence to the grand jury. Federal courts "may, within limits, formulate procedural rules not specifically required by the Constitution or . . . Congress" which deal strictly with their power to control their "own" procedures [see *U.S. v. Hasting*, 461 U.S. 499, 505 (1983)]. Moreover, this "supervisory power" may be used in the grand jury context, but only to proscribe misconduct before the grand jury, which amounts to a violation of one of those carefully drafted and approved rules that ensure the integrity of the grand jury's functions. In the instant case, since failure of the Government (P) to disclose substantial exculpatory evidence before the grand jury does not amount to a violation of one of the above rules, its indictment may not be dismissed. Reversed and remanded.

DISSENT: (Stevens, J.) A United States Attorney is the representative not of an ordinary party but of a sovereign whose obligation to govern impartially is compelling and whose interest in a criminal prosecution is not that it shall win a case, but that justice shall be done. It is as much such attorney's duty to refrain from improper methods calculated to produce a wrongful conviction as it is to use every legitimate means to bring about a just one. A federal prosecutor has this exact same duty to protect fundamental fairness when presenting evidence to a grand jury.

▶ *ANALYSIS*

In *U.S. v. John Doe, Inc. I,* 481 U.S. 102 (1987), the Supreme Court held that a government attorney who was involved in a grand jury proceeding may use information obtained during that proceeding in a subsequent civil proceeding in which he is involved, without a disclosure order under Rule 6(e). The Court also upheld a disclosure order. Discussing the requirement of "particularized need," it said generally that "the question that must be asked is whether the public benefits of the disclosure . . . outweigh the dangers created by the limited disclosure requested." 481 U.S. at 113.1.

Quicknotes

EXCULPATORY EVIDENCE A statement or other evidence which tends to excuse, justify, or absolve the defendant from alleged fault or guilt.

GRAND JURY A group summoned to investigate, inform, and accuse persons of crimes when sufficient evidence exists to do so.

CHAPTER 7

The Charging Instrument

Quick Reference Rules of Law

Russell v. United States

Grand jury indictee (D) v. Federal government (P)

369 U.S. 749 (1962).

NATURE OF CASE: Appeal from conviction under federal law of refusing to answer questions when summoned before a congressional subcommittee.

FACT SUMMARY: A grand jury indictment failed to identify the subject under congressional inquiry at the time Russell (D), a witness, was interrogated.

RULE OF LAW

The sufficiency of an indictment is to be measured by two criteria: (1) whether the indictment contains the elements of the offense intended to be charged so as to sufficiently apprise the defendant of what he must be prepared to defend against, and (2) in case any other proceedings are taken against him for a second offense, whether the record shows with accuracy to what extent he may plead a former conviction or acquittal.

FACTS: Russell (D) and other witnesses, were indicted by a grand jury for refusing to answer certain questions when summoned before a congressional subcommittee. The indictments stated only that the questions to which answers were refused "were pertinent to the question then under inquiry" by the subcommittee. Motions to quash the indictments, on the ground they failed to state the subject under investigation, were denied. Russell (D) and the other defendants, were convicted under a federal law which stated that prosecutions under it could be initiated only by grand jury indictment.

ISSUE: Where witnesses have been indicted, under federal law, for failure to answer questions when summoned by a congressional investigatory body, must the indictment identify the subject which was under inquiry at the time of the defendant's alleged default or refusal to answer?

HOLDING AND DECISION: (Stewart, J.) Yes. By invoking the aid of the federal courts in dealing with reluctant witnesses, Congress conferred upon the courts the duty to provide individuals prosecuted for this statutory offense every safeguard accorded other types of criminal defendants. There can be criminality here only if (1) the witness refused to answer a question which pertained to the subject then under investigation by the body; and (2) the pleadings so showed this. Although convictions will not be overturned because of minor, technical deficiencies in an indictment which does not prejudice the accused, care must still be taken. The indictments involved here satisfied the requirement that Russell (D) and the other defendants would not be reindicted for the same offense

since the precise questions asked them were given. However, the indictments are fatally defective for failing to sufficiently apprise them of what they must be prepared to meet. An indictment must do more than simply repeat the language of the criminal statute. It must, in precise terms, inform the accused with reasonable certainty, of the nature of the accusation against him. A corollary purpose of requiring specificity in the indictment is to inform a court of the facts alleged so as to enable it to decide whether they are sufficient in law to suppose a conviction. A court, or prosecutor, should not have to guess what was in the mind of the grand jury at the time it returned the indictment. Reversed.

DISSENT: (Harlan, J.) It is inconceivable how the indictments here can be deemed insufficient to apprise these defendants of the charges against them. The subject matter of the hearings were told them at the time they appeared before the subcommittee and a copy of the hearing's transcripts were either in their possession or available to them. The court's reasoning with respect to the "pertinency" requirement would also require a first-degree murder indictment to particularize "premeditation." As for the argument that the court's holding is necessary to prevent the prosecution from switching, on appeal, to a different theory of delinquency from that on which the conviction may have rested, the prosecution may not go beyond the confines of the trial record, of which the defendant has full knowledge. A defendant has ample safeguards: he may object at the hearing to the pertinency of any question asked him so as to "freeze" this issue, or, if he does not do so, he may seek, at trial, particularization through a bill of particulars. As for protecting the defendant from being convicted at trial on a theory of delinquency based upon a different subject of investigation than that actually found by the grand jury, this would prevent the prosecutor from presenting, at trial, evidence or theories, however relevant to the charge, that he had not presented to the grand jury. The impact of this decision will be to encourage witnesses appearing before subcommittees to refuse to answer questions.

ANALYSIS

It has been generally held that a charging instrument—indictment, or information—must fulfill three functions: (1) notice, to enable the defendant to adequately mount a defense; (2) protection against additional prosecutions

Continued on next page.

stemming from the same defense (double jeopardy); and (3) enable a court to judge whether the government's case is based upon a valid interpretation of the offense charged (judicial review). A court satisfies the judicial review function when it determines that the charging instrument sets out the essential elements of the offense. When the instrument has been found to be defective in not setting out all the requisite elements, the ruling is said to be based on the notice function. Russell suggests, perhaps, a fourth function—that the defendant not be tried upon a theory or evidence different than the one embraced in the charging instrument.

■━━■

Quicknotes

GRAND JURY   A group summoned to investigate, inform, and accuse persons of crimes when sufficient evidence exists to do so.

INDICTMENT   A formal written accusation made by the prosecution to the grand jury under oath, charging an individual with a criminal offense.

MOTION TO QUASH   To vacate, annul, void.

■━━■

United States v. Cotton

Government (P) v. Drug dealer (D)

535 U.S. 625 (2002).

NATURE OF CASE: Government's (D) appeal from the reversal of an enhanced drug sentence.

FACT SUMMARY: Cotton (D) argued that since the indictment against him failed to charge any of the threshold levels of drug quantity that lead to statutorily enhanced penalties, the court was without jurisdiction to impose an enhanced sentence.

 RULE OF LAW
Indictment omissions do not deprive a court of jurisdiction.

FACTS: Cotton (D), among others, was involved in a "vast drug organization" and was indicted for conspiracy to distribute and to possess with intent to distribute a "detectable amount" of cocaine. The indictment failed to charge any of the threshold levels of drug quantity that lead to statutorily enhanced penalties. Cotton (D) was found guilty and received a statutorily enhanced sentence based on an amount of drug quantity not alleged in the indictment. The federal court of appeals vacated Cotton's (D) sentence on the grounds that an indictment setting forth all the essential elements of an offense is both mandatory and jurisdictional hence that a court is without jurisdiction to impose a sentence for an offense not charged in the indictment. The Government (P) appealed.

ISSUE: Do indictment omissions deprive a court of jurisdiction?

HOLDING AND DECISION: (Rehnquist, C.J.) No. Indictment omissions do not deprive a court of jurisdiction. This court some time ago departed from its view in *Ex parte Bain*, 121 U.S. 1 (1887), that indictment defects are jurisdictional. Insofar as it held that a defective indictment deprives a court of jurisdiction, *Bain* is overruled. *Bain* was the product of an era in which the Supreme Court's authority to review criminal convictions was greatly circumscribed. At the time it was decided, a defendant could not obtain direct review of a criminal conviction in the Supreme Court. The Court's authority to issue a writ of habeas corpus was limited to cases in which the convening court had no jurisdiction to render the judgment which it gave. In 1887, therefore, the Supreme Court could examine constitutional errors in a criminal trial only on a writ of habeas corpus, and only then if it deemed the error "jurisdictional." The Court's desire to correct obvious constitutional violations led to a somewhat expansive notion of "jurisdiction." However, *Bain*'s elastic concept of jurisdic-

tion is not what the term "jurisdiction" means today, namely, "the courts' statutory or constitutional *power* to adjudicate the case." This latter concept of subject-matter jurisdiction, because it involves a court's power to hear a case, can never be forfeited or waived. Freed from the view that indictment omissions deprive a court of jurisdiction, we proceed to apply the plain error test and hold that the failure to include the amount of drugs in the indictment was not plain error because there was substantial evidence of the amount of drugs presented at trial so that Cotton (D) was not substantially prejudiced. Reversed.

▶ *ANALYSIS*

As the Supreme Court notes in the *Cotton* decision, defects in subject matter jurisdiction require correction regardless of whether the error was raised in district court.

United States v. Miller

Federal government (P) v. Fraudulent insurance claimant (D)

471 U.S. 130 (1985).

NATURE OF CASE: Appeal from reversal of fraud conviction.

FACT SUMMARY: Although Miller (D) was indicted for setting up a burglary of his own office and for subsequent exaggeration of his fraudulent insurance claim, he was convicted only of fraud.

RULE OF LAW
The Fifth Amendment grand jury guarantee is not violated when a defendant is convicted on a charge more narrow, although included, in the indictment.

FACTS: Miller (D) was charged with arranging a burglary of his own office, and then exaggerating the fraudulent insurance claim. At trial, proof was only offered regarding the latter offense, and a conviction was had. Miller appealed the conviction, claiming that it was unconstitutional for a conviction to be based on grounds narrower than the indictment's charges. The Third Circuit reversed the conviction, and the Government (P) appealed.

ISSUE: Is the Fifth Amendment grand jury guarantee violated when a defendant is convicted on a charge more narrow, although included, in the indictment?

HOLDING AND DECISION: (Marshall, J.) No. The Fifth Amendment's grand jury guarantee is not violated when a defendant is convicted on a charge more narrow, although included, in the indictment. The purpose of the indictment requirement is to give the accused notice of that with which he is charged. As long as the offense upon which the conviction is made is included in the indictment, the accused has such notice. Allegations not proved at trial constitute mere surplusage. Reversed.

▶ ANALYSIS

The Third Circuit based its decision upon *Stirone v. United States*, 361 U.S. 212 (1980). What occurred there was that a defendant was convicted of a charge broader than that found in the indictment. As the Court pointed out, the situation in this action was the opposite of that found in *Stirone*.

Quicknotes

FRAUD A false representation of facts with the intent that another will rely on the misrepresentation to his detriment.

GRAND JURY A group summoned to investigate, inform, and accuse persons of crimes when sufficient evidence exists to do so.

INDICTMENT A formal written accusation made by the prosecution to the grand jury under oath, charging an individual with a criminal offense.

The Location of the Prosecution

Quick Reference Rules of Law

United States v. Rodriguez-Moreno

Federal government (P) v. Kidnapper (D)

526 U.S. 275 (1999).

NATURE OF CASE: Appeal from conviction of kidnapping and carrying a firearm during and in relation to a crime of violence under 18 U.S.C. § 924(c)(1).

FACT SUMMARY: The government appealed from the reversal of a kidnapping conviction by the court of appeals on the basis that § 924(c)(1) was not violated since the defendant only used a firearm in Maryland and the kidnapping occurred in New Jersey.

RULE OF LAW
Venue in a prosecution for using or carrying a firearm during and in relation to any crime of violence in violation of 18 U.S.C. § 924(c)(1) is proper in any district in which the crime was committed, even if the firearm was only carried in a single district.

FACTS: During a drug transaction taking place in Houston, a New York drug dealer stole 30 kilograms of Texas drug distributor's cocaine. The distributor hired Rodriguez-Moreno (D) and others to find the dealer and to hold captive the middleman in the transaction, Avendano. Rodriguez-Moreno (D) and his codefendants were tried jointly and charged with conspiring to kidnap Avendano, kidnapping Avendano, and using a firearm in relation to kidnapping Avendano, in violation of 18 U.S.C. § 924(c)(1). Rodriguez-Moreno (D) moved to dismiss for lack of venue, contending that venue was proper only in Maryland, the only place where the Government (P) had proved that he actually used the gun. The district court denied the motion and convicted defendants and the court of appeals reversed.

ISSUE: Is venue in a prosecution for using or carrying a firearm during and in relation to any crime of violence in violation of 18 U.S.C. § 924(c)(1) proper in any district in which the crime was committed, even if the firearm was only carried in a single district?

HOLDING AND DECISION: (Thomas, J.) Yes. Venue in a prosecution for using or carrying a firearm during and in relation to any crime of violence in violation of 18 U.S.C. § 924(c)(1) is proper in any district in which the crime was committed, even if the firearm was only carried in a single district. Here the statute provides that "Whoever, during and in relation to any crime of violence . . . for which he may be prosecuted in a court of the United States, uses or carries a firearm, shall, in addition to the punishment provided for such crime of violence . . . be sentenced to imprisonment for five

years. . . ." The court of appeals looked to the verbs of the statute to determine the nature of the substantive offense. While the verb test has value as an investigative tool, it cannot be applied to the exclusion of other relevant statutory language. To prove the § 924(c)(1) violation the Government (P) was required to show the defendants used a firearm, committed all acts necessary to be subject to punishment for kidnapping in a court of the United States, and used the gun "during and in relation to" the kidnapping of Avendano. Defendants argue that for venue purposes the New Jersey kidnapping was irrelevant to the Maryland firearm crime since a gun was not used during the New Jersey crime. Several circuits have defined kidnapping as a unitary crime which once began does not end until the victim is free. Section 924(c)(1) does not define a "point-in-time" offense when a firearm is used during and in relation to a continuing crime of violence. Reversed.

DISSENT: (Scalia, J.) The issue here is whether the defendant's alleged act of using a firearm during and in relation to a kidnapping occurred; since it occurred only in Maryland, then venue is only proper there.

ANALYSIS

"The locus delicti of the charged offense must be determined from the nature of the crime alleged and the location of the acts constituting the crime." *United States v. Cabrales,* 524 U.S. 1 (1998). First the court must identify the conduct constituting the offense and then discern the location of the commission of the criminal acts.

The Scope of the Prosecution: Joinder and Severance of Offenses and Defendants

Quick Reference Rules of Law

Cross v. United States

Robbery convict (D) v. Federal government (P)

335 F.2d 987 (D.C. Cir. 1964).

NATURE OF CASE: Appeal after conviction of robbery.

FACT SUMMARY: Cross (D) and Jackson (D) were charged in Count I with robbery of a church and in Count II with robbery of a tourist home. Their motions for severance of the counts were denied. Cross (D) claims that he wanted to testify on Count II, and remain silent on Count I.

RULE OF LAW

Where a defendant wishes to testify on one but not the other of two joined offenses, he is prejudiced within the meaning of Federal Rule of Criminal Procedure 14 and the counts should be separated.

FACTS: Cross (D) and Jackson (D) were charged in Count I with robbery of a church and in Count II with robbery of a tourist home. Their pretrial motions for severance of the charges were denied. Cross's (D) testimony as to Count II was that he was a victim, rather than a cohort, of the tourist home robbery. The jury acquitted on Count II. On Count I, he denied participation in the robbery, testifying that he had been drinking heavily and did not know his whereabouts at the time of the robbery. On cross-examination, he was open to questioning concerning his generally tawdry way of life and his prior conviction. He was found guilty as to Count I.

ISSUE: Where a defendant wishes to testify on one but not the other of two joined offenses, is he sufficiently prejudiced so that the counts should be separated?

HOLDING AND DECISION: (Bazelon, C.J.) Yes. Federal Rule of Criminal Procedure 14 provides that if it appears that a defendant is prejudiced by a joinder of offenses, the court may order an election or separation of the counts or provide whatever relief justice requires. A defendant's decision whether to testify involves the balancing of several factors, such as the evidence against him, the plausibility of his testimony, etc. If two counts are joined for trial, it is not possible for him to weigh these factors separately as to each count. Moreover, a defendant's silence on one count would be damaging in the face of his express denial of the other. Thus, he may be coerced into testifying on the count upon which he remained silent. This constitutes prejudice within the meaning of Rule 14. Here, the evidence supposes Cross's (D) claim that he wished to testify on Count II, but not on Count I. His testimony on Count II was so convincing that the jury believed him and ac-

quitted. His denial on Count I, however, was plainly evasive and unconvincing. Thus, it appears that Cross (D) had reason not to testify on Count I and would not have done so at a separate trial. Nor would the jury at a separate trial hear his admissions of prior convictions and unsavory activities. Since the joinder embarrassed and confounded Cross (D) in making his defense, the joinder was prejudicial within the meaning of Rule 14. The judgment on Count I is vacated, and the case is remanded for a new trial.

DISSENT: (Bastian, J.) As a general rule, acquittal on one of several counts in an indictment cures any defect of misjoinder under Rule 14. In this case, the trial judge specifically charged the jury that the counts must be considered separately. He then summarized the evidence with regard to each defendant on each count. Moreover, a typewritten form was given to the jury on which to record its verdict. The form set out the name of each defendant and required separate notations by the jury as to its decision on each of the two counts. The form was a constant reminder to the jury that each count was to be considered separately.

ANALYSIS

If a defendant requests a severance of offenses or defendants, and the motion is denied by the trial judge, on appeal the appellate court reviews this decision only on the standard of abuse of discretion. There are four doctrines which are commonly relied upon by appellate courts to support a finding that the defendant was not prejudiced by the joinder. They are: (1) that a jury is capable of following the judge's instructions to ignore certain evidence or to consider certain evidence only as to some of the charges; (2) that if the jury has acquitted the defendant on any count, this shows that the jury has been selective and has kept the evidence separate; (3) that the defendant has no ground for complaint if he was convicted of several counts but was sentenced concurrently; and (4) that any prejudice from the joinder is cured by overwhelming evidence of guilt.

Quicknotes

INDICTMENT A formal written accusation made by the prosecution to the grand jury under oath, charging an individual with a criminal offense.

JOINDER The joining of claims or parties in one lawsuit.

Drew v. United States

Robbery suspect (D) v. Federal government (P)

331 F.2d 85 (D.C. Cir. 1964).

NATURE OF CASE: Appeal from conviction on one count of robbery and one count of attempted robbery.

FACT SUMMARY: Drew's (D) motion to have the counts of robbery and attempted robbery against him severed were denied. Both of the crimes had been committed in a similar way.

🏛 RULE OF LAW
Where evidence of two joined offenses would not be admissible in a separate trial of the other and where the evidence of each offense is not simple and distinct, the offenses should be tried separately.

FACTS: A robbery was committed at High's Neighborhood store. A sales clerk testified that a Negro male, wearing sunglasses, entered the store. When approached by the clerk, he said, "This is a holdup; I want your money, all of it." When the clerk hesitated, he said, "Get it," and pulled a gun partially out of his pocket. The clerk gave him the money and he left. An attempted robbery occurred at another High's store. The sales clerks testified that a Negro male, wearing a coat, cap, and sunglasses, entered the store. When the clerk asked to help him, he asked for some peanuts. When the clerk asked which size bag he wanted, he replied, "Give me all the money." The clerk replied, "If you want it, come and get it." He repeated his statement several times and each time the clerk repeated his. Finally, he said, "You are not going to give me the money?" The clerk replied he was not. A customer entered, and the attempted robber left. The clerk testified that he was not threatened in any way. The police apprehended Drew (D) near the store 25 minutes later and returned him to the store where the clerk identified him. Drew (D) was tried for both offenses at the same trial.

ISSUE: When a defendant is being charged with two offenses at the same trial, should the joined offenses be severed where the jury might use the evidence of one crime to convict for the other or cumulate the evidence to find guilt as to both charges?

HOLDING AND DECISION: (McGowan, J.) Yes. Evidence of one crime is inadmissible to prove disposition to commit crime, from which the jury may infer that the defendant committed the crime charged. Since the likelihood that juries will make such an improper inference is high, courts presume prejudice and exclude evidence of other crimes unless that evidence can be admitted for some legitimate purpose. The same principles apply when two crimes are joined for trial. Evidence of the other crimes is admissible when relevant to motive, intent, the absence of mistake or accident, a common scheme or plan embracing two or more crimes so related to each other that proof of one tends to establish the other, and the identity of the person charged. If, then, under the rules relating to other crimes, the evidence of each of the joined crimes on trial would be admissible in a separate trial for the other, the possibility of "criminal propensity" prejudice would not be enlarged by joinder. Also, the federal courts have found no prejudicial effect from joinder when the evidence of each crime is simple and distinct, even though such evidence might not have been admissible in separate trial under the above rules. Turning to the facts of this case, there is not such a close similarity in the manner of committing the crimes as would make them admissible in separate trials. Nor did the two offenses arise out of the same transaction, series of transactions, or continuing state of affairs so that the evidence would have come in under the exception stated above. We cannot find absence of prejudice on the ground that the evidence would have been admissible in separate trials. Nor were the two crimes "simple and distinct," since there was a superficial similarity in the way they were committed. Drew's (D) conviction is reversed and the case is remanded.

▶ ANALYSIS

Existing statutes and court rules on severance afford little guidance as to what criteria the trial judge should apply in deciding such a motion. Some assert that a severance may be ordered in the discretion of the court. Others say that severance is called for if it appears that a defendant is prejudiced by a joinder. Still others say a severance may be ordered in the interest of justice and for good cause shown. Most of the cases are not based upon the rationale of *Cross*, 335 F.2d 987 (1964), or *Drew*. Rather, the usual inquiry is whether in view of the number of offenses charged and the complexity of the evidence to be offered, the trier of fact will be able to distinguish the evidence and apply the law intelligently as to each offense.

Quicknotes

JOINDER The joining of claims or parties in one lawsuit.

RELEVANT EVIDENCE Evidence having any tendency to prove or disprove a disputed fact.

United States v. Dixon

Federal government (P) v. Double jeopardy appellant (D)

509 U.S. 688 (1993).

NATURE OF CASE: Consolidated appeals cases from ruling barring subsequent criminal prosecution in one and allowing it in the other.

FACT SUMMARY: Both Dixon (D) and Foster (D), who were convicted of criminal contempt in connection with alleged underlying criminal conduct, argued that the Double Jeopardy Clause barred any subsequent criminal prosecution on charges arising out of the same criminal conduct.

🏛 RULE OF LAW
The Double Jeopardy Clause does not permit subsequent prosecution of an offense which has already been the basis of criminal contempt proceedings.

FACTS: Dixon (D) had been arrested for second-degree murder. The form by which he was released on bond specified that he was not to commit "any criminal offense," and warned that any violation of the conditions of release would subject him "to revocation of release, an order of detention, and prosecution for contempt of court." While awaiting trial, Dixon (D) was arrested and indicted for possession of cocaine with intent to distribute. He was found guilty of criminal contempt and sentenced to 180 days in jail. The trial court later granted Dixon's (D) motion to dismiss the cocaine indictment on double jeopardy grounds. Foster (D) violated a civil protection order (CPO), requiring that he not "molest, assault, or in any manner threaten or physically abuse" his wife. He was held in contempt for numerous violations of the CPO. The court found Foster (D) guilty beyond a reasonable doubt of four counts of criminal contempt, acquitted him on other counts, and sentenced him to 600 days imprisonment. The U.S. Attorney's office later obtained an indictment charging Foster (D) with simple assault, threatening to injure another, and assault with intent to kill. Foster (D) moved to dismiss, claiming a double jeopardy bar to all counts. The trial court denied the double jeopardy claim. The Government (P) appealed in Dixon (D), while Foster (D) appealed the trial court's denial of his motion. After consolidating the two cases, the court of appeals ruled that both subsequent prosecutions were barred by the Double Jeopardy Clause. The Government (P) appealed.

ISSUE: Does the Double Jeopardy Clause permit subsequent prosecution of an offense which has already been the basis of criminal contempt proceedings?

HOLDING AND DECISION: (Scalia, J.) No. The Double Jeopardy Clause does not permit subsequent prosecution of an offense which has already been the basis of criminal contempt proceedings. This protection applies both to successive punishments and to successive prosecutions for the same criminal offense. This Court has concluded that where the two offenses for which the defendant is punished or tried cannot survive the "same-elements" test, the double jeopardy bar applies. The same-elements test inquires whether each offense contains only elements contained in the other; if so, they are the "same offense" and double jeopardy bars additional punishment and successive prosecution. If not, they are not the same offense, and there is no double jeopardy bar. Dixon's (D) cocaine possession, although an offense under the D.C. Code, was not an offense under the contempt statute until a judge incorporated the statutory drug offense into his release order. Here, where the contempt sanction was imposed for violating the order through commission of the incorporated drug offense, the later attempt to prosecute Dixon (D) for the drug offense resembles the double jeopardy situation. Criminal contempt, at least in its nonsummary form, "is a crime in every fundamental respect." Because Dixon's (D) drug offense did not include any element not contained in his previous contempt offense, his subsequent prosecution violated the double jeopardy clause. The foregoing analysis obviously applies to the indictment against charging Foster (D), with assault, based on the same event that was the subject of his prior contempt conviction for violating the provision of the CPO forbidding him to commit simple assault. Thus the subsequent prosecution for assault is barred. However, the remaining four counts of assault with intent to kill and threats to injure or kidnap are not barred. Each of those offenses contained a separate element, and the test for double jeopardy was not met. Thus, Dixon's (D) subsequent prosecution for cocaine possession, as well as Foster's (D) subsequent prosecution for simple assault violate the Double Jeopardy Clause and are barred. Affirmed [as to Dixon (D)]. Affirmed in part; reversed in part [as to Foster (D)].

CONCURRENCE AND DISSENT: (Rehnquist, C.J.) A defendant who is guilty of possession with intent to distribute cocaine or of assault has not necessarily satisfied any statutory element of criminal contempt. Nor can it be said that a defendant who is held in criminal contempt has necessarily satisfied any element of those substantive crimes. The offenses for which Dixon (D) and Foster (D) were prosecuted in this case cannot be analogized to greater and lesser

Continued on next page.

included offenses; hence, they are separate and distinct for double jeopardy purposes.

CONCURRENCE AND DISSENT: (White, J.) The Double Jeopardy Clause bars prosecution for an offense if the defendant already has been held in contempt for its commission. Thus, the subsequent prosecutions in both Dixon (D) and Foster (D) were impermissible as to all counts.

CONCURRENCE AND DISSENT: (Blackmun, J.) If this were a case involving successive prosecutions under the substantive criminal law, the Double Jeopardy Clause could bar the subsequent prosecution. But the concern here was with contempt of court, a special situation. To consider the contempt litigator and the criminal prosecutor as one and the same would be to adopt an absurd fiction.

CONCURRENCE AND DISSENT: (Souter, J.) Both the prosecution of Dixon (D) and the prosecution of Foster (D) on all counts against him should be barred by the Double Jeopardy Clause.

▶ ANALYSIS

The same-elements test was first enunciated by the Court in *Blockburger v. United States*, 284 U.S. 299 (1932), and is commonly referred to as the Blockburger test. In arriving at its ruling in the instant case, the majority overruled its recent decision in *Grady v. Corbin*, 495 U.S. 508 (1990), which held that in addition to passing the Blockburger test, a subsequent prosecution must satisfy a "same-conduct" test to avoid the double jeopardy bar. The Grady test provided that if, to establish an essential element of an offense charged in that prosecution, the government would prove conduct that constituted an offense for which the defendant had already been prosecuted, a second prosecution may not be had. In the majority's view, *Grady* was not only wrong in principle, but had already proved inconsistent in application.

Quicknotes

CONTEMPT An act of omission that interferes with a court's proper administration of justice.

DOUBLE JEOPARDY A prohibition against a second prosecution for the same offense after an acquittal or conviction for that offense in a prior proceeding or against multiple punishments for the same offense.

Ashe v. Swenson

Robbery convict (D) v. Court (P)

397 U.S. 436 (1970).

NATURE OF CASE: Petition for writ of habeas corpus after conviction of robbery.

FACT SUMMARY: Three or four men robbed six men and stole one of the victims' cars. Each alleged robber was charged with seven separate offenses. Ashe (D) was acquitted on the robbery charge as to one of the victims. At that trial, the State's proof that the robbery had occurred and that the alleged victim was one of the victims was unassailable. The evidence that Ashe (D) was one of the robbers was weak. At a second trial for the robbery of a second victim, Ashe (D) was convicted.

RULE OF LAW

The doctrine of collateral estoppel is embodied in the Fifth Amendment guarantee against double jeopardy, and, accordingly, an acquittal based on a factual issue that is also presented as an essential element of a second charge bars trial on that charge.

FACTS: Three or four men robbed six men who were playing poker and stole one of the victims' cars. (It was never clear whether there were three or four robbers.) Three men were arrested near the abandoned stolen car. Ashe (D) was arrested separately some distance away. Each of the four was charged with six robbery counts and the theft of the car. At Ashe's (D) trial for the robbery of Knight, the proof that the armed robbery had occurred and that Knight had been a victim was unassailable. The State's evidence that Ashe (D) had been one of the robbers was weak. The jury found Ashe (D) not guilty. Six weeks later, Ashe (D) was brought to trial for the robbery of Roberts. The witnesses were the same but their testimony on Ashe's (D) identification was much stronger. One of the victims whose identification testimony had been negative at the first trial was not called at the second. The jury found Ashe (D) guilty, and he was sentenced to 35 years.

ISSUE: Is collateral estoppel a part of the Fifth Amendment's guarantee against double jeopardy?

HOLDING AND DECISION: (Stewart, J.) Yes. Collateral estoppel means that when an issue of ultimate facts has once been determined by a valid and final judgment, that issue cannot be litigated again between the same parties in any future lawsuit. Although first developed in civil litigation, the doctrine has long been held applicable in criminal cases. Where a previous judgment of acquittal was based upon a general verdict, as is usually the case, the court must examine the records of the prior proceedings to determine whether a rational jury could have grounded its verdict upon any issue other than the one which the defendant seeks to foreclose from consideration. Looking to the record here, there is no indication that the first jury could have rationally based its verdict on a finding that the robbery did not occur or that Knight had not been a victim. The only rationally conceivable issue in dispute before the jury was whether Ashe (D) had been one of the robbers. The jury, by its verdict, found that he had not. We hold that the doctrine of collateral estoppel is embodied in the Fifth Amendment guarantee against double jeopardy; a state could not constitutionally bring Ashe (D) before a second jury to decide whether he was one of the robbers after a first jury had already held that he was not. Reversed and remanded.

CONCURRENCE: (Brennan, J.) I agree with the majority's holding. However, even if collateral estoppel were not applicable here, the Double Jeopardy Clause bars the second trial, since the two prosecutions grew out of one criminal episode. The Double Jeopardy Clause requires the prosecution, except in most limited circumstances, to join at one trial all the charges against a defendant which grow out of a single criminal act, occurrence, episode, or transaction. This "same transaction" test enforces the ancient prohibition against multiple prosecutions and also promotes the justice, economy and convenience that results from consolidation in one lawsuit of all issues arising out of a single transaction or occurrence.

DISSENT: (Burger, C.J.) Nothing in the language or any of the gloss previously placed on the Double Jeopardy Clause remotely justifies the majority's treatment of the collateral estoppel doctrine. The essence of the concurring opinion is that all that occurred in this case was one transaction or episode. "For me it demeans the dignity of the human personality and individuality to talk of a 'single transaction' in the context of six separate assaults on six individuals."

▶ ANALYSIS

Ashe deprives the prosecution of a major tactical advantage in trying separately, closely related offenses arising from a single transaction. The effect of the collateral estoppel doctrine is to prevent the prosecutor from "treating the first trial as no more than a dry run for a second prosecution" on a second charge. With this tactic eliminated, the pros-

Continued on next page.

ecutor may find less advantage in separate prosecutions in such situations. In *Harris v. Washington*, 404 U.S. 55 (1971), the Court held that the constitutional guarantee applies, irrespective of whether the jury considered all relevant evidence, and irrespective of the State's good faith in bringing successive prosecutions. There a bomb sent through the mails killed Burdick and the defendant's son. After his acquittal on a charge of murdering Burdick, the defendant was charged with murdering his son. It was contended that the issue of identity had not been fully litigated because the trial judge had wrongly excluded a threatening letter written by the defendant.

■━━■

Quicknotes

COLLATERAL ESTOPPEL A doctrine whereby issues litigated and determined in a prior proceeding are binding upon all subsequent litigation between the parties regarding that issue.

DOUBLE JEOPARDY A prohibition against a second prosecution for the same offense after an acquittal or conviction for that offense in a prior proceeding or against multiple punishments for the same offense.

ULTIMATE FACT A fact upon which a judicial determination is made and which is inferred from the evidence presented at trial.

■━━■

Schaffer v. United States

Prejudiced conspirator (D) v. Federal government (P)

362 U.S. 511 (1960).

NATURE OF CASE: Appeal from criminal conviction.

FACT SUMMARY: The defendants were charged with conspiracy and with individual substantive crimes. At the close of the prosecution's case, the defendants moved successfully for dismissal of the conspiracy charge. They now contend that continued joinder of the individual cases was unduly prejudiced.

RULE OF LAW
Where the joinder of trials of multiple defendants is based on a charge of conspiracy, the failure of the conspiracy charge does not automatically mandate severance of the trials on the remaining substantive counts.

FACTS: The Schaffers (D) were charged with transporting stolen property across state lines along with three others named Stracuzzas. The Stracuzzas were also charged with separate interstate shipments involving two other individuals at separate times. All seven were also charged with conspiracy to commit the individual crimes charged and were tried in a joint trial. At the close of the prosecution's case, the seven moved for an acquittal on the conspiracy charge. The motion was granted on the basis that no connection, other than the common participation of the Stracuzzas, was shown between the Schaffers (D) and the other individual defendants. However, the motion for acquittal on the substantive crimes was denied along with a motion to sever the trials of the defendants.

ISSUE: Where the trial of multiple defendants is joined on the basis of a charge of conspiracy, must their trials thereafter be severed as to the substantive crimes charged if the conspiracy charge fails?

HOLDING AND DECISION: (Clark, J.) No. The trial was properly joined at the outset under Rule 8(b) of the Federal Rules of Criminal Procedure and any severance thereafter was controlled by Rule 14 which provides for separate trials where it appears that a defendant is prejudiced by such joinder. The remaining substantive charges involved an almost identical outline with only the names of the particular defendants and the destination of the stolen goods being different in each count. The trial court was meticulously fair in pointing out to the jurors that evidence against one defendant could in no way be considered against another. This caveat was repeated in the charge to the jury. The trial judge did not abuse the discretion vested in him as to severance, since no preju-dice can be shown by the trial record. While the trial judge must be particularly sensitive to the possibility of prejudice in cases such as these, we cannot hold as a hard and fast rule that the failure of a conspiracy charge that forms the basis for joinder must automatically result in severance of the trial on the remaining charges.

DISSENT: (Douglas, J.) While the initial charge of conspiracy was a proper foundation for joinder under Rule 8(b), the failure of proof of that charge removes the basis for joinder. This Court has previously held that joinder is not proper where the only connection between multiple defendants charged with similar offenses is the participation of one defendant in all the charged crimes. The possibility of prejudice by transferred inference of guilt is too strong to allow a joint trial. The showing of prejudice in such an instance is difficult, no matter how strong the possibility. The only sure way to protect against the subtle bond of guilt, and attendant prejudice, is to sever the trials. This circumstance is distinguishable from the case where both the conspiracy and substantive charges go to the jury and acquittal is rendered on the conspiracy charge but not on the substantive charge.

ANALYSIS

Two critical views were expressed toward this decision. In one, the commentator found that an unscrupulous prosecutor might frame a totally groundless conspiracy charge to support joinder to save the time and expense of separate trials. Since bad faith on the part of the prosecutor is difficult to prove, actual misjoinder may be allowed to persist. Another commentator found that the dissent's view might very well be self-defeating. Since the trial judge may be very reluctant to dismiss and sever after failure of the conspiracy charge, he might very well refuse such dismissal and submit that charge to the jury, confident of an acquittal on that charge.

Quicknotes

ACQUITTAL The discharge of an accused individual from suspicion of guilt for a particular crime and from further prosecution for that offense.

CONSPIRACY Concerted action by two or more persons to accomplish some unlawful purpose.

JOINDER The joining of claims or parties in one lawsuit.

Gray v. Maryland

State (P) v. Accused murderer (D)

523 U.S. 185 (1998).

NATURE OF CASE: Appeal of a criminal conviction for murder.

FACT SUMMARY: When a jury convicted Gray (D) of murder following a trial at which a co-defendant's redacted confession had been introduced, Gray (D) appealed, claiming that his constitutional rights had been violated.

🏛 RULE OF LAW
Redacted confessions that replace the proper name with an obvious blank, the word "delete," a symbol, or similarly notify the jury that a name has been deleted, violate a defendant's Sixth Amendment rights if introduced into evidence insulated from cross examination.

FACTS: Gray (D) and a co-defendant were both indicted for murder. Gray's (D) motion for a separate trial was denied, and Gray (D) was convicted after the co-defendant's redacted confession incriminating Gray (D) was introduced at the joint trial with a limiting instruction. Gray (D) appealed the verdict, claiming that under *Bruton v. United States*, 391 U.S. 123 (1968), his Sixth Amendment rights had been violated.

ISSUE: Do redacted confessions that replace the proper name with an obvious blank, the word "delete," a symbol or similarly notify the jury that a name has been deleted, violate a defendant's Sixth Amendment rights if introduced into evidence insulated from cross examination?

HOLDING AND DECISION: (Breyer, J.) Yes. Redacted confessions that replace the proper name with an obvious blank, the word "delete," a symbol or similarly notify the jury that a name has been deleted, violate a defendant's Sixth Amendment rights if introduced into evidence insulated from cross examination. Under *Bruton*, the introduction at trial of the powerfully incriminating extrajudicial statements of a codefendant who does not testify and cannot be cross examined violates a defendant's Sixth Amendment rights. The introduction of the redacted confession of Gray's (D) codefendant with the blank prominent on its face, "facially incriminated" Gray (D). There were no questions of policy to be considered here, since the connection of the defendant to the confession did not depend on the introduction of other evidence later in the trial. This case was not like *Richardson v. Marsh*, 481 U.S. 200 (1987), where the confession of the codefendant had been redacted, eliminating all reference to his codefendant and any indication that anyone else at all was implicated in the crime, and becoming incriminating only when linked to other evidence. The powerfully incriminating effect of an out-of-court accusation creates a special, and vital, need for cross-examination. Redactions that simply replace a name with a blank leave statements that, considered as a class, so closely resemble Bruton's unredacted statements that, in our view, the law must require the same result. Reversed.

DISSENT: (Scalia, J.) The Court's extension of *Bruton* to name-related confessions "as a class" will seriously compromise society's compelling interest in finding, convicting, and punishing those who violate the law. The Court's analogizing of "deleted" to a physical description that clearly identifies the defendant does not survive scrutiny. By "facially incriminating," we have meant incriminating independent of other evidence introduced at trial. The issue is not whether the confession incriminated Gray (D), but whether the incrimination was so "powerful" that we must depart from the normal presumption that the jury follows its instructions. It was not, and the line for departing from the ordinary rule at the facial identification of the defendant makes more sense than drawing it anywhere else.

▶ ANALYSIS

Since the redacted confession in this case referred directly to the "existence" of the nonconfessing codefendant, the court found more similarities with *Bruton* than with *Richardson*. In *Bruton*, the confession was held to be "incriminating on its face," while in *Richardson*, the confession became incriminating only by inference, and only when "linked" to other evidence. This "linkage" has proved problematic in other cases where the effect of a confession cannot be predicted until after the introduction of all the evidence.

■══■

Quicknotes

CROSS EXAMINATION The interrogation of a witness by an adverse party either to further inquire as to the subject matter of the direct examination or to call into question the witness' credibility.

LIMITING INSTRUCTION Directions given to a judge or jury prior to deliberation.

REDACTION Alteration of a confession to remove any reference by one joint defendant to any codefendant.

SIXTH AMENDMENT Provides the right to a speedy trial by impartial jury, the right to be informed of the accusation, to confront witnesses and to have the assistance of counsel in all criminal prosecutions.

■══■

The Right to Speedy Trial and Other Speedy Disposition

Quick Reference Rules of Law

Barker v. Wingo

Murder convict (D) v. Court (P)

407 U.S. 514 (1972).

NATURE OF CASE: Petition for certiorari of a murder conviction.

FACT SUMMARY: Although Barker (D) made no objections during the first four years of a five-year delay between his arrest and conviction for murder, he subsequently claimed that his right to a speedy trial had been violated.

🏛 RULE OF LAW
The determination of whether a defendant has been deprived of his Sixth Amendment right to a speedy trial must be made on a case-by-case basis by balancing the following four factors: (1) length of delay, (2) reason for delay, (3) the defendant's assertion of his right, and (4) prejudice to the defendant.

FACTS: On July 20, 1958, an elderly couple was murdered. Shortly afterwards, Silas Manning and Willie Barker (D) were arrested as suspects. On September 15, they were indicted, counsel was appointed on September 17, and Barker's (D) trial was set for October 21. However, Barker (D) was not brought to trial for more than five years after his arrest due to numerous continuances by the prosecution. Initially, the continuances were for the purpose of first convicting Manning, against whom the Commonwealth had a stronger case, to assure his testimony at Barker's (D) trial (i.e., to eliminate problems of self-incrimination). However, Manning was not convicted until 1962. Afterwards, Barker's (D) trial was delayed another seven months due to the illness of the chief investigating officer in the case. During these continuances, Barker (D) was free for all but ten months in jail, and he made no objections during the first four years of delay. However, Barker (D) objected to the last few continuances, and, at his trial, he moved for dismissal on the basis that his Sixth Amendment right to a speedy trial had been violated. This motion was denied and Barker (D) was convicted of murder. Upon appeal to the Kentucky Court of Appeals, the conviction was affirmed. Barker (D) then petitioned for habeas corpus in the United States District Court. Upon denial of that petition, he appealed to the Court of Appeals for the Sixth Circuit. Upon affirmance of his conviction, Barker (D) brought a petition for certiorari.

ISSUE: Is a delay of five years between the arrest and trial of a defendant a violation per se of his Sixth Amendment right to a speedy trial?

HOLDING AND DECISION: (Powell, J.) No. The determination of whether a defendant has been deprived of his Sixth Amendment right to a speedy trial must be made on a case-by-case basis by balancing the following four facts: (1) length of delay, (2) reason for delay, (3) the defendant's assertion of his right, and (4) prejudice to the defendant. Since the deprivation of the right to a speedy trial does not per se prejudice the ability of an accused to defend himself, it is impossible to state "with precision" when the right has been denied. Each factor, therefore, must be separately analyzed. First, it is true that a long delay before trial is more likely to be justified for a serious, complex crime (e.g., murder) than for a simple one. Here, however, the delay of over five years was extreme by any standard. Second, it is true that a delay in bringing an accused to trial may be justified by a showing of some strong reason for it. Here, however, there was a strong reason for delay (i.e., illness of the chief investigator) for only seven months of the five-year delay. Although some additional delay might also have been necessary to acquire Manning as a witness, over four years was clearly unreasonable. Third, it is true that failure to assert the right to a speedy trial will not constitute a waiver of that right, unless it is found to be an "intentional relinquishment or abandonment of a known right." Here, however, it is obvious that Barker (D) did not want a trial at all, hoping, rather, that the delays would ultimately result in dismissal of the charges against him. Fourth, it is true that the prejudice which results from a delay of a defendant's trial must be evaluated in the light of those interests which a speedy trial was designed to protect (i.e., prevention of "oppressive pre-trial incarceration," minimization of anxiety and concern of the accused, and limitation on the possibility that the defense will be "impaired"). Here, however, prejudice was minimal. Although Barker (D) was prejudiced to some extent by spending some time in jail and by living for years under "a cloud of suspicion," none of his witnesses died or became unavailable. In conclusion, the facts that Barker (D) did not want a trial and was not prejudiced by the delay outweigh the unjustified length of delay. Judgment affirmed.

CONCURRENCE: (White, J.) The concurrence emphasizes that a delay, whether the defendant is free or not, may "disrupt his employment, drain his financial resources, curtail his associations, subject him to public obloquy and create

Continued on next page.

anxiety in him." For these reasons, any defendant who "desires" a speedy trial should have it within a "reasonable" time, regardless of whether or not delay would prejudice his defense at trial, unless there are "special considerations."

▶ ANALYSIS

This case illustrates the discretion available (through the balancing test) to the courts in determining when the right to a speedy trial has been violated, and the emphasis on the desire of an accused to have a speedy trial. Note, that an accused "waives" the right to a speedy trial if he flees the state after arraignment or request postponement of his trial. Note, also, that the right to a speedy trial attaches only after a person is accused (i.e., indicted or arrested), so that it is not violated by a police delay in filing charges. However, if such a delay was purposeful, due process requires dismissal of the charges.

■━■

Quicknotes

PRIVILEGE AGAINST SELF-INCRIMINATION A privilege guaranteed by the Fifth Amendment to the federal Constitution in a criminal proceeding for communications made by an accused and protecting an accused or witness from having to give testimony that may incriminate himself.

PROCEDURAL DUE PROCESS The constitutional mandate that if the state or federal government acts so as to deny a citizen of a life, liberty or property interest the individual is first entitled to notice and the right to be heard.

■━■

United States v. Lovasco

Federal government (P) v. Subsequent indictee (D)

431 U.S. 783 (1977).

NATURE OF CASE: Appeal from dismissal of a criminal indictment.

FACT SUMMARY: The district court dismissed the criminal indictment against Lovasco (D) due to the delay between the commission of the offense and the initiation of prosecution.

🏛 RULE OF LAW
To prosecute a criminal defendant following investigative delay does not deprive him of due process, even if his defense might have been somewhat prejudiced by the lapse of time.

FACTS: Although the offenses of possessing firearms stolen from the U.S. mail and dealing in firearms without a license allegedly occurred between July 25 and August 31, 1973, Lovasco (D) was not indicted for those crimes until March 6, 1975. The initial report noted that he told government (P) agents just one month after the alleged commission of the crimes that he had possessed and sold five of the stolen guns. By that time, there was also strong evidence linking him to the remaining three weapons. However, the agents were unable to confirm or refute his claim that he had found the guns in his car when he returned to it after visiting his son, a mail handler, at work. Little additional information was uncovered in the 17 months that followed before the initiation of prosecution. Thus, the district court granted Lovasco's (D) motion to dismiss the indictment on the ground that the unreasonable and unnecessary delay in initiating prosecution had prejudiced his defense and thus violated his due process rights. Evidence showed that the two witnesses whom Lovasco (D) claimed would have helped his defense had died, one within nine months and the other more than a year after the initial investigative report on the crimes was completed.

ISSUE: Does it violate the Due Process Clause to prosecute a criminal defendant following investigative delay, even if his defense is somewhat prejudiced by the lapse of time?

HOLDING AND DECISION: (Marshall, J.) No. Even if his defense is somewhat prejudiced by the lapse of time between commission of the crimes and initiation of prosecution, prosecuting a defendant following investigative delay does not deprive him of due process. Proof of actual prejudice is a necessary prerequisite to, and makes, a due process claim concrete and ripe for adjudication, but it does not make the claim automatically valid. The determining question is whether compelling a particular defendant to stand trial after delay in a particular case violates those "fundamental conceptions of justice which lie at the base of our civil and political institutions." It does not in cases like this. Reversed.

▶ ANALYSIS

The Court is careful not to say that prejudicial pre-accusation delay could never be a due process violation. This may prove most important in the future, since the Sixth Amendment right to a speedy trial has been found inapplicable to pre-indictment delays.

Quicknotes

PROCEDURAL DUE PROCESS The constitutional mandate that if the state or federal government acts so as to deny a citizen of a life, liberty or property interest the individual is first entitled to notice and the right to be heard.

RIPENESS A doctrine precluding a federal court from hearing or determining a matter, unless it constitutes an actual and present controversy warranting a determination by the court.

CHAPTER 21

Discovery and Related Rights

Quick Reference Rules of Law

1. **Pretrial Discovery by the Prosecution.** The constitutional privilege against self-incrimination is not violated by a requirement that the defendant give notice of an alibi defense and disclose his alibi witnesses. (Williams v. Florida)

126

2. **Remedies and Sanctions.** A court may forbid a defense witness from testifying as a sanction for the defendant's failure to conduct pretrial discovery in good faith. (Taylor v. Illinois)

128

3. **The Defendant's "Constitutionally Guaranteed Access to Evidence."** Evidence is material and must be disclosed to the defense if there is a reasonable probability that, had the evidence been disclosed to the defense, the result of the proceeding would have been different. (United States v. Bagley)

129

Williams v. Florida

Robbery convict (D) v. State (P)

399 U.S. 78 (1970).

NATURE OF CASE: Appeal from conviction of robbery.

FACT SUMMARY: Florida (P) law requires that a defendant submit to a limited form of pretrial discovery by the State whenever he intends to rely at trial on the defense of alibi.

🏛 RULE OF LAW
The constitutional privilege against self-incrimination is not violated by a requirement that the defendant give notice of an alibi defense and disclose his alibi witnesses.

FACTS: Williams (D) was charged with robbery. Prior to his trial, Williams (D) sought a protective order to be excused from complying with a Florida (P) law which requires a defendant, on written demand of the prosecution, to give notice in advance of trial if the defendant intends to claim an alibi, and to furnish the prosecution with information as to the place he claims to have been and with the names and addresses of the alibi witnesses he intends to use. Williams (D) wanted to declare his intent to use an alibi, but objected to further disclosure on the ground that the rule would compel him to be a witness against himself in violation of the Fifth and Fourteenth Amendments. The rule also obligated the State (P) to notice a defendant of any rebuttal witnesses to the alibi defense the State (P) will call. Failure to comply, by either side, results in the exclusion of the defendant's alibi evidence or the State's (P) rebuttal evidence. When Williams's (D) motion for the protective order was denied, he complied with the rule. On the morning of his trial, the State (P) interviewed a Mrs. Scotty, Williams's (D) chief alibi witness. At trial, Mrs. Scotty gave testimony which contradicted her pretrial statements. The State (P) also furnished a rebuttal witness. Williams (D) was convicted.

ISSUE: Is a notice-of-alibi rule violative of the Fifth and Fourteenth Amendments by compelling a defendant to be a witness against himself?

HOLDING AND DECISION: (White, J.) No. The rule is fair to both the defendant and the State (P) in permitting liberal discovery. The State (P) has a legitimate interest in protecting itself against eleventh hour defenses: although based on an adversary system, a trial is not yet a poker game in which players may conceal their cards at will. No pretrial statements of Mrs. Scotty were introduced at trial; her pre-

trial testimony was only urged to find rebuttal witnesses. A defendant is always in a dilemma whether to remain silent or present a defense which may prove disastrous. Nothing in the rule obligates the defendant to rely on an alibi or prevents him from abandoning it as a defense. The rule only requires that a defendant accelerate the timing of his disclosure of information that he would have revealed at trial anyway. A defendant is not entitled to await the end of the prosecution's case against him before announcing the nature of his defense any more than he can await the jury's verdict on the State's (P) case before deciding to take the stand himself. Absent the rule, the prosecution would be entitled to a continuance at trial on the grounds of surprise; the rule thus serves to prevent a disrupted trial.

CONCURRENCE: (Burger, C.J.) The rule serves an added function of disposing of many cases before trial. If the prosecution interviews the defendant's alibi witnesses, and finds them to be reliable and unimpeachable, he might be strongly inclined to dismiss charges against the defendant. On the other hand, a defendant who knows that his alibi defense will be thoroughly investigated by the prosecution before trial, may well be induced to change his plea.

DISSENT: (Black, J.) Before trial, defense counsel can only guess at what the State's (P) case might be. The rule thus compels defendants with any thoughts at all of pleading alibi to be forced to disclose their intentions so as to preserve the possibility of later raising the defense—the decision goes to more than just "timing." Pretrial disclosure will adversely affect the defendant who then decides to forego raising an alibi defense. His alibi witnesses will still help the prosecution to new leads or evidence. The rule is a clear violation of the Fifth Amendment because it requires a defendant to give information to the State which may destroy him. The entire burden of proving criminal activity rests on the State: no constitutional provision is designed to make conviction easier. The defendant need not do anything to defend or convict himself. While a criminal trial is in part a search for truth, it also is designed to protect "freedom" by insuring that the State carries its burden. Efficiency is not a consideration. The majority's decision opens the way to compel complete pretrial discovery of a defendant's case, and any defenses he might raise.

Continued on next page.

▶ *ANALYSIS*

At the time *Williams* was decided, fifteen states other than Florida had notice-of-alibi requirements of varying kinds. One such rule, in *Wardins v. Oregon*, 412 U.S. 470 (1973), was struck down because it failed to provide reciprocal discovery rights to the defendant. The Court found this omission violative of the Due Process Clause of the Fourteenth Amendment. Because exclusion of the testimony of alibi witnesses is a drastic sanction for failure on the defendant's part to comply with the rule's disclosure requirements, other sanctions have been suggested. These include: (1) granting a continuance to the prosecution; (2) allowing the prosecution or court to comment on the defendant's failure to the jury; (3) placing the defense counsel in contempt when the failure was not in "good faith."

■══■

Quicknotes

DISCOVERY Pretrial procedure during which one party makes certain information available to the other.

PRIVILEGE AGAINST SELF-INCRIMINATION A privilege guaranteed by the Fifth Amendment to the federal Constitution in a criminal proceeding for communications made by an accused and protecting an accused or witness from having to give testimony that may incriminate himself.

■══■

Taylor v. Illinois

Attempted murder convict (D) v. State (P)

484 U.S. 400 (1988).

NATURE OF CASE: Appeal from conviction for attempted murder.

FACT SUMMARY: Taylor (D) contended he was deprived of his right to obtain favorable testimony by the trial court's refusal to allow a witness to testify whose identity had been withheld during pretrial discovery.

🏛 RULE OF LAW
A court may forbid a defense witness from testifying as a sanction for the defendant's failure to conduct pretrial discovery in good faith.

FACTS: Taylor (D) was charged with attempted murder. Well in advance of trial, the prosecution moved to compel a list of defense witnesses. Although Taylor's (D) attorney met with and spoke to Wormsley, he did not include this witness on the list. On the second day of trial, he sought to amend the list and add Wormsley, representing to the court that he had just been informed of his existence. The court refused to allow Wormsley to testify and Taylor (D) was convicted. He appealed, contending he had been deprived of his right to present favorable evidence. The appellate court affirmed, and the Supreme Court granted a hearing.

ISSUE: May a court preclude defense witness testimony as a discovery sanction?

HOLDING AND DECISION: (Stevens, J.) Yes. A court may forbid a defense witness from testifying as a sanction for a lack of compliance with discovery. The Sixth Amendment grants defendants a right to subpoena witnesses. It does not otherwise grant a right to testimony. The Sixth Amendment cannot be used to circumvent the adversary system. The court in this case did not abuse its discretion in precluding the testimony. Judgment of the appellate court is affirmed.

DISSENT: (Brennan, J.) Precluding a criminal defense witness from testifying bears an arbitrary and disproportionate relation to the purposes of discovery, at least absent any evidence that the defendant was personally responsible for the discovery violations. Direct punitive measures, such as contempt, can be used to graduate the punishment to correspond to the severity of a discovery violation.

DISSENT: (Blackmun, J.) Specific remedies for suppression should be fashioned on a case-by-case basis.

▶ ANALYSIS

Criminal discovery is much different from civil discovery. Criminal discovery is greatly restricted and runs heavily in favor of the defense. In civil actions, discovery is very wide and arguably favors neither party. It is generally believed that the apparent willfulness of the behavior in this case was the deciding factor in the use of the rather harsh sanction.

Quicknotes

ATTEMPT An intent combined with an act falling short of the thing intended.

DISCOVERY Pretrial procedure during which one party makes certain information available to the other.

United States v. Bagley

Federal government (P) v. Criminal suspect (D)

473 U.S. 667 (1985).

NATURE OF CASE: Appeal from narcotics conviction.

FACT SUMMARY: Bagley (D) contended it was reversible error for the prosecution to fail to disclose a financial arrangement between the state and prosecution witnesses.

> ## 🏛 RULE OF LAW
> Evidence is material and must be disclosed to the defense if there is a reasonable probability that, had the evidence been disclosed to the defense, the result of the proceeding would have been different.

FACTS: Bagley (D) was arrested for narcotics and firearm violations. His attorney filed a discovery motion seeking evidence of any deals made between the prosecution and witnesses for testimony. The prosecution failed to reveal a financial arrangement with two witnesses, and Bagley (D) appealed his conviction on the ground that he was denied the right to effectively cross-examine the witnesses due to this nondisclosure. The court of appeals reversed, and the Supreme Court granted certiorari.

ISSUE: Must evidence be disclosed if there is a reasonable likelihood that had it been disclosed, a different result would have resulted?

HOLDING AND DECISION: (Blackmun, J.) Yes. Evidence is material and must be disclosed to the defense if there is a reasonable probability that, had the evidence been disclosed to the defense, the result of the proceeding would have been different. The court of appeals held that the nondisclosure required automatic reversal. However, it made no determination regarding the materiality of the evidence so that application of the present rule could be performed. Reversed and remanded.

CONCURRENCE: (White, J.) The test of material it does not depend upon the specificity of the defense request.

DISSENT: (Marshall, J.) A presumption of materiality should be adopted and a rule of automatic reversal applied.

DISSENT: (Stevens, J.) While the result here is correct, however, a new rule of materiality should not be fashioned.

▌ANALYSIS

The Court in this case deemphasizes the manner in which the nondisclosure occurs in the analysis of reversible error. Previously, there were three situations analyzed separately which would provide difference levels of materiality. The first was where the prosecution knowingly introduced perjured testimony. The second was the failure to respond to a specific request, and the third was where no request was made.

Quicknotes

CROSS EXAMINATION The interrogation of a witness by an adverse party either to further inquire as to the subject matter of the direct examination or to call into question the witness's credibility.

PERJURY The making of false statements under oath.

Coerced, Induced, and Negotiated Guilty Pleas; Professional Responsibility

Quick Reference Rules of Law

Bordenkircher v. Hayes

Court (P) v. Forgery convict (D)

434 U.S. 357 (1978).

NATURE OF CASE: Appeal from a criminal conviction and penalty enhancement.

FACT SUMMARY: The prosecutor informed Hayes (D) that he would seek an indictment under the Kentucky Habitual Criminal Act if he did not plead guilty to the charge of uttering a forged instrument; Hayes (D) pled innocent, a jury convicted him, and his sentence was enhanced when the prosecutor initiated the Habitual Criminal indictment.

RULE OF LAW

A prosecutor can attempt to gain a defendant's assent to a plea bargain by informing the defendant that more severe charges will be brought if no bargain is struck.

FACTS: Hayes (D), who was charged with uttering a forged instrument (for $88.30), faced a sentence of two to ten years if convicted. The prosecutor offered a five-year sentence in return for a guilty plea and told Hayes (D) that refusal to take the "bargain" would result in his seeking an additional indictment under the Kentucky Habitual Criminal Act, which makes a life sentence mandatory if there are two prior felony convictions. When Hayes (D) declined the plea bargain, he was subjected to the additional indictment and sentenced to life imprisonment under the Habitual Criminal Act, after having been found guilty of the uttering charge. The two previous felonies in which Hayes (D) was involved had never resulted in his imprisonment, one was a rape charge reduced to a plea of detaining a female, and the other was a robbery conviction resulting in five years in a reformatory. Finding the prosecutor to have acted vindictively in securing the second indictment, the court of appeals reversed Hayes's (D) conviction for violation of due process of law.

ISSUE: Is it constitutionally permissible for a prosecutor to try to influence a defendant to accept a plea bargain by informing him that more severe charges will be brought if it is refused?

HOLDING AND DECISION: (Stewart, J.) Yes. As the constitutionality and utility of plea bargaining have been recognized, there is no bar to the prosecutor's use of the possibility of more severe charges being brought for purposes of persuading a defendant to accept a plea bargain. As long as the defendant is advised that the bringing of additional charges will accompany his refusal to bargain, the situation becomes similar to that where the prosecutor offers to drop a charge as part of the plea bargain. If plea bargaining is a recognized process, neither can be forbidden simply because the charging decision is influenced by what a prosecutor hopes to gain in plea bargaining negotiations. In accepting plea bargaining, it is implicit that there is acceptance of the notion that the prosecutor's interest is to persuade the defendant not to exercise his right to plead not guilty. As long as the prosecutor has probable cause to believe the accused committed the offense, and he properly exercises his discretion, decisions not being influenced by standards of race, religion, etc., there is no due process violation. Reversed.

DISSENT: (Blackmun, J.) Past cases indicate that prosecutorial vindictiveness resulting from a defendant's exercise of his rights is a constitutionally impermissible basis for discretionary actions. Here, it is admitted that such vindictiveness was the sole reason for the new indictment.

DISSENT: (Powell, J.) Discretion used to deter the exercise of constitutional rights is not constitutionally exercised. The prosecutor's initial failure to charge indicates his own appreciation of the unreasonableness of placing Hayes (D) in jeopardy of life imprisonment while many murderers and rapists face lighter sentences.

▶ ANALYSIS

The case in which the court first recognized plea bargaining as a legitimate practice was *Brady v. United States*, 397 U.S. 742 (1970). While the majority here suggests that such an acceptance implies sanctioning of prosecutorial use of charging powers to influence a defendant to plead guilty, the *Brady* decision specifically states that it makes no reference to such use by the prosecutor or a similar use by the judge of his sentencing power.

Quicknotes

PLEA BARGAIN An agreement between a criminal defendant and a prosecutor, which is submitted to the court for approval, generally involving the defendant's pleading guilty to a lesser charge or count in exchange for a more lenient sentence.

Santobello v. New York

Convicted felon (D) v. State (P)

404 U.S. 257 (1971).

NATURE OF CASE: Review of sentence following plea of guilty to a felony.

FACT SUMMARY: After a prosecutor promised no recommendation regarding sentencing, as an inducement to a guilty plea, a different prosecutor did recommend a sentence.

⚖ RULE OF LAW
When the prosecution makes a promise regarding sentencing recommendations as an inducement to a guilty plea, the prosecutor may not renege.

FACTS: Santobello (D) was charged with a felony. As an inducement to plead guilty, the prosecutor promised no recommendation regarding sentencing. Santobello (D) pled guilty. At the sentencing hearing, a different prosecutor recommended the maximum sentence, which the judge imposed. Santobello (D) moved to withdraw his plea. This was denied, and the court of appeals affirmed. The Supreme Court granted review.

ISSUE: When the prosecution makes a promise regarding sentencing recommendations as an inducement to a guilty plea, may the prosecution renege?

HOLDING AND DECISION: (Burger, C.J.) No. When the prosecution makes a promise regarding sentencing recommendations as an inducement to a guilty plea, the prosecution may not renege. To preserve the integrity of the plea bargaining process, due process requires the prosecution to live up to whatever promises it made to induce the guilty plea. Here, the prosecution reneged on a promise regarding sentencing. This was impermissible. (The Court then remanded to the trial court to determine whether Santobello (D) should be permitted to withdraw his guilty plea, or merely re-sentenced.)

CONCURRENCE: (Douglas, J.) The defendant's preference as to disposition in a case like this should be given considerable, if not controlling weight.

CONCURRENCE AND DISSENT: (Marshall, J.) Where a defendant wishes to withdraw his plea of guilty after the prosecution reneges on a sentencing promise, he should be allowed to withdraw his plea as a matter of right.

▶ ANALYSIS

A plea bargain is, in essence, a contract. This being so, it is logical to analogize the law of contracts to cases of broken plea bargain. This is to a large extent the rule. Differences do exist between plea bargains and typical contracts. The most important of these is that plea bargains have a constitutional dimension not usually found in contract law.

Quicknotes

FELONY A criminal offense of greater seriousness than a misdemeanor; felonies are generally defined pursuant to statute as any crime that is punishable by death or by a term of imprisonment exceeding one year.

PLEA BARGAIN An agreement between a criminal defendant and a prosecutor, which is submitted to the court for approval, generally involving the defendant's pleading guilty to a lesser charge or count in exchange for a more lenient sentence.

Newman v. United States

Convicted accomplice (D) v. Federal government (P)

127 U.S. App. D.C. 263, 382 F.2d 479 (D.C. Cir. 1967).

NATURE OF CASE: Appeal from conviction of housebreaking and petty larceny.

FACT SUMMARY: The United States Attorney refused to consent to plead on reduced charges for Newman (D), although Newman's (D) accomplice had been allowed to plead to less serious charges.

RULE OF LAW

The United States Attorney, as attorney for the Executive, is not constitutionally obligated to treat every offense and every offender alike in discharging his prosecutorial duties. The judiciary will not review his discretionary judgments.

FACTS: Newman (D) and Anderson (D) were indicted for housebreaking and petty larceny. After negotiations with an assistant U.S. Attorney, Anderson was allowed to plead guilty to a less serious charge of attempted housebreaking in return for having the housebreaking charge dropped. The U.S. Attorney, however, refused to consent to the same deal for Newman (D) who was then tried and convicted of housebreaking and petty larceny. Newman (D) claimed that because of the different treatment accorded him by the U.S. Attorney, he was denied "due process" and "equal protection" as guaranteed him by the Fourteenth Amendment, and "equal standing."

ISSUE: Is the decision of a U.S. Attorney to prosecute a defendant for a different offense than that charged against his accomplice reviewable by a federal court as an abuse of discretion?

HOLDING AND DECISION: (Burger, J.) No. When federal offenses are involved, the Executive branch (the President and, through him, the Justice Department) is charged with instituting criminal proceedings, formulating criminal charges and dismissing charges once brought. In carrying out these duties, the President is given broad discretion. As attorney for the Executive, a U.S. Attorney is imbued with the same broad discretion. Although a U.S. Attorney is, in one sense, an officer of the court and responsible for the manner of his conduct of a case (i.e., his demeanor, deportment, and ethical conduct), he is also an agent of the President, and accountable only to him for the execution of his duty within the framework of his professional employment. When two persons have committed the same legal offense, the prosecutor is free to exercise his own discretion and common sense. He might be influenced by their ages, criminal records, roles in perpe-

tration of the crime, relationship to one another, and other factors in deciding to prosecute each defendant differently. If a United States Attorney abuses his discretion, it is up to the President to deal with him. The conviction is affirmed.

ANALYSIS

It has been suggested that the Newman court would have had to reach a more difficult decision if Newman (D) could have shown that he and Anderson (D) came from almost identical backgrounds and played the same role in the commission of the alleged crime. A claim would thus arise under the Equal Protection Clause of the Fourteenth Amendment. Plea bargaining, in general gives rise to a host of problems: (1) widely disparate sentences which engender bitterness, and not remorse, by those convicted; (2) serious offenders are "let off the hook" because their cases superficially resemble those who are not as disposed to criminality; (3) the opportunity for a prosecutor to overinflate his case in pretrial negotiations (the same may equally be said for defense attorneys).

Quicknotes

EQUAL PROTECTION A constitutional guarantee that no person shall be denied the same protection of the laws enjoyed by other persons in life circumstances.

PROCEDURAL DUE PROCESS The constitutional mandate that if the state or federal government acts so as to deny a citizen of a life, liberty or property interest the individual is first entitled to notice and the right to be heard.

United States v. Ruiz

Government (P) v. Drug possessor (D)

536 U.S. 622 (2002).

NATURE OF CASE: Appeal by government from the vacating of a sentencing determination.

FACT SUMMARY: Angela Ruiz (D) argued that the Constitution prohibits a defendant from waiving the right to impeachment information before the defendant can enter into a plea agreement.

🏛 RULE OF LAW
The Fifth and Sixth Amendments do not require prosecutors, before entering into a plea bargain, to disclose impeachment information relating to any informants or other witnesses.

FACTS: After immigration agents found 30 kilograms of marijuana in Angela Ruiz's (D) luggage, federal prosecutors offered her a so-called "fast track" plea bargain in return for which the Government (P) agreed to recommend a more lenient sentence than otherwise would have been mandated. Such plea bargain agreement contained detailed terms, including that the defendant waive the right to receive impeachment information relating to any informants or other witnesses. Because Ruiz (D) would not agree to this waiver, the prosecutors withdrew their bargaining offer. Despite the absence of a plea agreement, Ruiz (D) pled guilty and requested that the sentencing judge grant her the same reduced sentence she would have received if she had accepted the "fast track" plea. The judge refused; however, the federal circuit court vacated the district judge's sentencing determination, taking the position that the Constitution prohibits defendants from waiving their right to impeachment information before they enter into a plea agreement. The Government (P) appealed.

ISSUE: Do the Fifth and Sixth Amendments require prosecutors, before entering into a plea bargain, to disclose impeachment information relating to any informants or other witnesses?

HOLDING AND DECISION: (Breyer, J.) No. The Fifth and Sixth Amendments do not require prosecutors, before entering into a plea bargain, to disclose impeachment information relating to any informants or other witnesses. Impeachment information is special in relation to the fairness of a trial, not in respect to whether a plea is voluntary ("knowing," "intelligent," and "sufficiently aware"). Of course, the more information the defendant has, the more aware he or she is of the likely consequences of a plea, waiver, or decision, and the wiser that decision will likely be. However, the Constitution does not require the prosecutor to share all useful information with the defendant. The law ordinarily considers a waiver knowing, intelligent, and sufficiently aware if the defendant fully understands the nature of the right and how it would likely apply in general in the circumstances—even though the defendant may not know the specific detailed consequences of invoking it. It is particularly difficult to characterize impeachment information as critical information of which the defendant must always be aware prior to pleading guilty given the random way in which such information may, or may not, help a particular defendant. The degree of help that impeachment information can provide will depend upon the defendant's own independent knowledge of the prosecution's potential case—a matter that the Constitution does not require prosecutors to disclose. Furthermore, since the proposed plea agreement provides that the government will provide any information establishing the factual innocence of the defendant, that fact along with other guilty-plea safeguards, diminishes the force of Ruiz's (D) concern that, in the absence of impeachment information, innocent individuals, accused of crimes, will plead guilty. Reversed.

CONCURRENCE: (Thomas, J.) The Court suggests that the constitutional analysis turns in some part on the degree of help such information would provide to the defendant at the plea stage, a distinction that is neither necessary nor accurate. The proper principle is avoidance of an unfair trial to the accused. That concern is not implicated at the plea stage regardless.

▶ ANALYSIS

In *Ruiz*, the Supreme Court found no decisional authority to support the Ninth Circuit position of required disclosure of impeachment witnesses. To the contrary, noted the Supreme Court, it would be difficult to distinguish, in terms of importance, (1) a defendant's ignorance of grounds for impeachment of potential witnesses at a possible future trial from (2) the varying forms of ignorance that could be at issue in any particular case.

In re United States

Federal Department of Justice (P) v. Federal judge (D)

345 F.3d 450 (7th Cir. 2003).

NATURE OF CASE: Writ of mandamus.

FACT SUMMARY: The federal government sought to compel a federal district judge to grant the government's motion to dismiss a criminal count against a defendant.

🏛 RULE OF LAW
A federal judge may not refuse to dismiss a count of an indictment when an agreement to do so was reached by a proper plea bargain agreement between the government and the defendant.

FACTS: Kenneth Bitsky, a police officer, was indicted on one count of depriving a citizen of civil rights under color of law and two counts of obstruction of justice. The government and Bitsky entered into a plea agreement by which the government agreed to dismiss the civil rights count. The federal district judge, however, refused to dismiss the civil rights count on the grounds that the government was trying to circumvent his sentencing authority because it considered the sentence that he would have imposed had Bitsky been convicted of the civil rights violation excessive, even though it would have been consistent with the sentencing guidelines. The government brought a writ of mandamus to compel the judge to dismiss the count.

ISSUE: May a federal judge refuse to dismiss a count of an indictment when an agreement to do so was reached by a proper plea bargain agreement between the government and the defendant?

HOLDING AND DECISION: (Posner, J.) No. A federal judge may not refuse to dismiss a count of an indictment when an agreement to do so was reached by a proper plea bargain agreement between the government and the defendant. While it is true that Rule 48(a) of the Federal Rules of Criminal Procedure requires leave of court for the government to dismiss an indictment, the principal purpose of the rule is to protect the defendant from harassment by the government repeatedly filing charges and then dismissing them before they are adjudicated. In such a case the judge might rightly condition dismissal on its being with prejudice. Here, there is no issue of that sort since it is the government who wants to dismiss the instant count with prejudice, and that is what the defendant wants as well. The district judge simply disagrees with the Justice Department's exercise of prosecutorial discretion. Those judicial decisions which state that a district judge may deny a motion to dismiss criminal charges even though the defendant has agreed to such dismissal, note that such a dismissal motion should be denied only if it is in bad faith or contrary to the public interest. This is not, however, the case here. Petition for mandamus granted.

▶ ANALYSIS

As *In re United States* observes, custom and limited prosecutorial resources, plea bargaining, federal statutes, and the federal sentencing guidelines themselves combine to lodge enormous charging discretion in the Justice Department, to the occasional frustration of judges.

■■■

Quicknotes

WRIT OF MANDAMUS A court order issued commanding a public or private entity, or an official thereof, to perform a duty required by law.

■■■

Quick Reference Rules of Law

Taylor v. Louisiana

Kidnapping convict (P) v. State (D)

419 U.S. 522 (1975).

NATURE OF CASE: Appeal from criminal conviction on the basis that the jury was unconstitutionally constituted.

FACT SUMMARY: Louisiana (D) had a statute which provided that women would be exempt from jury duty unless they specifically requested to serve.

RULE OF LAW

The exclusion of a segment of society from jury duty is sufficient to establish a per se violation of a defendant's constitutional right to a trial by jury of his peers guaranteed under the Sixth Amendment.

FACTS: Louisiana (D) enacted a statute which provided that women should not be selected for jury duty unless they filed a specific request to serve. The practical effect of this provision was that women (constituting 53 percent of potential jurors) were virtually unrepresented on juries within Louisiana (D). Taylor (P) was convicted of aggravated kidnaping. He moved to quash the conviction on the basis that no women were available to sit on the jury which tried him. He (P) claimed that this violated his rights to a trial by jury of his peers (i.e., a fair cross segment of the community). This was violative of the Sixth Amendment which was made applicable to the states under the Fourteenth Amendment to the U.S. Constitution. The motion was denied by the trial court.

ISSUE: Where the exclusion of a class of potential jurors makes the jury pool unrepresentative of the community, does this violate a defendant's rights under the Sixth Amendment?

HOLDING AND DECISION: (White, J.) Yes. A defendant is entitled to be tried by a representative cross-section of his community. The failure to provide such a cross-section is violative of the Sixth Amendment's constitutional guarantee of a trial by jury. It does not matter that the defendant has not established discrimination, for it is immaterial. The fact that he is a man and only women are being excluded is also immaterial. A Caucasian may complain that blacks are being excluded. The blanket exemption for women has the effect of practically excluding them from jury panels. The role of women in society (i.e., mothers) is insufficient grounds for the issuance of a blanket exemption. Liberal, specific exemptions are allowed where individual facts warrant. Since the jury was unrepresentative, the conviction must be overturned. Reversed and remanded.

DISSENT: (Rehnquist, J.) The conviction should not have been overturned without a showing of prejudice. There is no sound policy ground for arbitrarily overturning this conviction.

ANALYSIS

In *Hamling v. U.S.*, 418 US. 87 (1974), the Court held that exclusion of the young through a failure to update the master jury wheel for four years was not a per se violation of the defendant's Sixth Amendment guarantees. It would require a showing of prejudice to require a reversal of the conviction. The mere fact that persons who have become eligible for jury duty have been excluded is insufficient to establish purposeful discrimination. This last fact is what differentiates *Hamling* from *Taylor*.

Quicknotes

MOTION TO QUASH To vacate, annul, void.

RIGHT TO JURY TRIAL The right guaranteed by the Sixth Amendment to the federal Constitution that in all criminal prosecutions the accused has a right to a trial by an impartial jury of the state and district in which the crime was allegedly committed.

Hamer v. United States

Defendant at trial (D) v. Federal government (P)

259 F.2d 274 (9th Cir. 1958).

NATURE OF CASE: Appeal of conviction for fraudulently importing narcotic drugs and facilitating their sale.

FACT SUMMARY: During voir dire at Hamer's (D) trial, the prosecution used a jury book setting out how prospective jurors acted or voted while on previous juries.

🏛 RULE OF LAW
(1) Absent congressional authorization in non-capital offense cases, a defendant is not deprived of a right to a jury trial because he was denied a list of the names and addresses of prospective jurors prior to trial; (2) when coupled with a denial of personal voir dire, there is no constitutional violation so long as the defense counsel is able to submit voir dire questions to the court to ask; (3) prosecution use of "jury books," which show how members of a jury panel voted on previous juries, do not, as a rule, deprive a defendant of a fair jury trial.

FACTS: At Hamer's (D) trial, the judge himself conducted the voir dire (questioning of prospective jurors). The judge was willing to let Hamer's (D) counsel submit additional questions, but not to ask any questions. A pretrial request for a list of the names and addresses of prospective jurors was also denied. During voir dire, Hamer (D) discovered that the prosecutor had in his possession a "jury book" which indicated how various prospective jurors had voted on previous juries. The book, compiled by the prosecutor's office, characterized individual jurors as "pro-defense," listed instances in which a juror had "held up deliberations on 'easy cases'" and gave information—residence, age, number of children, etc.—on each.

ISSUE: Does prosecutorial use of "jury books," court-conducted voir dire, or denial of the defendant's request to be given a list of prospective jurors' names and addresses, prior to trial, taken singly or in conjunction with one another, violate the defendant's constitutional right to a jury trial?

HOLDING AND DECISION: (Barnes, J.) No. Although a congressional act requires that jury lists be supplied a defendant in capital offense cases, Congress has not so provided in less serious cases. Hammer's (D) remedy lies thus with Congress and not the courts. There is no constitutional right of a defendant to conduct his own voir dire. When both these requests are denied, so long as the selection of the jury, viewed as a whole, is fair and impartial, as here, there is neither a violation of a defendant's right to jury trial or of his due process rights. As for "jury books," many attorneys question their usefulness. However, nothing can prevent prosecutors from naturally discussing whether jurors are "good" or "bad" and sharing their experiences with one another. While most of the information in these books deals with concrete facts or impressions gathered in the courtroom, some of it deals with what actually transpires in the jury room itself. However, a juror cannot be prevented from discussing his opinion of his fellow jurors in public once the trial is over. Carrying Hamer's (D) claim to its ultimate limits, no defendant could be prosecuted by a government attorney who had more information about how jurors on a particular panel had voted in other cases than the defendant's own counsel possessed. Such a rule would break down law enforcement. Perfect equality in counsel can never be obtained.

▶ ANALYSIS

Some states have statutes which specifically entitle defendants to jury lists in all criminal cases, while others follow the federal practice and limit the right to only serious offense cases. Even where authorized, however, the lists only give names and addresses, but not other relevant data. In ten states, the court is given discretion to conduct the voir dire itself; in ten other states, the judge only can conduct voir dire; in 22 states, voir dire is the responsibility of both the court and counsel; in the remaining eight states, only counsel can do voir dire. Courts have not yet placed an affirmative obligation on prosecutors to divulge jury information to defense counsel.

■≡■

Quicknotes

PROCEDURAL DUE PROCESS The constitutional mandate that if the state or federal government acts so as to deny a citizen of a life, liberty or property interest the individual is first entitled to notice and the right to be heard.

RIGHT TO JURY TRIAL The right guaranteed by the Sixth Amendment to the federal Constitution that in all criminal prosecutions the accused has a right to a trial by an impartial jury of the state and district in which the crime was allegedly committed.

VOIR DIRE Examination of potential jurors on a case.

■≡■

Batson v. Kentucky

Black defendant (D) v. State (P)

476 U.S. 79 (1986).

NATURE OF CASE: Appeal of rejection of challenge to practice of exercising peremptory challenges to keep certain races off juries.

FACT SUMMARY: The prosecutor exercised his peremptory challenges to keep blacks off the jury in the trial of Batson (D), a black.

RULE OF LAW

A prosecutor cannot use peremptory challenges to keep members of the defendant's race off the jury on the assumption that they will not be impartial.

FACTS: During the jury selection process of the trial of Batson (D), the prosecutor used his peremptory challenges to disqualify all blacks from the jury. Batson (D), a black, argued that this constituted a violation of equal protection. The trial court rejected his contentions, and the state supreme court agreed. Batson (D) appealed.

ISSUE: May a prosecutor use peremptory challenges to keep members of the defendant's race off the jury on the assumption that they will not be impartial?

HOLDING AND DECISION: (Powell, J.) No. A prosecutor may not use peremptory challenges to keep members of the defendant's race off the jury on the assumption that they will not be impartial. Such generalizations are precisely what the Equal Protection Clause was meant to remove and cannot be approved, even when a time-honored practice such as peremptory challenges is concerned. If a defendant can demonstrate a pattern of racially motivated peremptory challenges in the selection of his jury, the burden falls on the prosecutor to make a legitimate explanation. Here, the prosecutor made no explanation at all. Reversed.

CONCURRENCE: (Marshall, J.) Peremptory challenges offer such a great potential for abuse that they should be abolished in the criminal justice system entirely.

DISSENT: (Burger, C.J.) Peremptory challenges are inherently based on hunches and other intangibles and one exercising them should not have to explain his/her reasons. The rule announced here can interfere with the defendant's use of peremptories if it is ever applied to him, which is likely.

DISSENT: (Rehnquist, J.) Where a party of any race may exclude members of any other race through peremptories, equal protection is not violated.

▶ ANALYSIS

Justice Rehnquist makes an interesting argument. According to him, as long as no particular race is precluded from using peremptories to keep off the jury members of any other race, no discrimination exists. This argument obviously would be wrong in most contexts, but in as fluid an area as peremptory challenges, it makes some sense, although practically speaking, black defendants have suffered most from the practice.

Quicknotes

EQUAL PROTECTION A constitutional guarantee that no person shall be denied the same protection of the laws enjoyed by other persons in life circumstances.

PEREMPTORY CHALLENGE The exclusion by a party to a lawsuit of a prospective juror without the need to specify a particular reason.

Quick Reference Rules of Law

Illinois v. Allen

State (P) v. Armed robbery convict (D)

397 U.S. 337 (1970).

NATURE OF CASE: Certiorari from reversal of a robbery conviction.

FACT SUMMARY: Allen (D) was convicted of armed robbery, after he was removed from the courtroom due to his disruptive behavior.

RULE OF LAW

The Sixth Amendment right of an accused to be present at his own trial and confront the witnesses against him can be lost if, after a warning by the judge, he continues to conduct himself in a manner so "disorderly, disruptive, and disrespectful of the court that his trial cannot be carried on with him in the courtroom."

FACTS: During his trial for armed robbery, Allen (D) argued with the judge continuously and in such an abusive, disruptive manner that it was impossible to carry on the trial. After repeated warnings from the judge that he would be removed, Allen (D) continued such behavior and was removed for most of his trial. Upon conviction and affirmation of the conviction by the Supreme Court of Illinois, Allen (D) brought a federal habeas corpus petition in the district court. The district court, finding no constitutional violation of Allen's (D) rights, declined to issue the writ, whereupon Allen (D) appealed to the court of appeals. The court of appeals reversed the conviction on the basis that an accused's Sixth Amendment right to "be confronted with the witnesses against him" can never be lost.

ISSUE: Where an accused is removed from his trial because of extremely disruptive behavior, after warnings by the judge that he would be removed if such behavior continued, has his right to be present at his trial been lost?

HOLDING AND DECISION: (Black, J.) Yes. The Sixth Amendment right of an accused to be present at his trial and confront the witnesses against him can be lost if, after a warning by the judge, he continues to conduct himself in a manner so "disorderly, disruptive and disrespectful of the court that his trial cannot be carried on with him in the courtroom." Of course, once the right is lost, it can be reclaimed when the accused is willing to conduct himself "consistently with the decorum and respect inherent in the concept of courts and judicial proceedings." It is essential to the proper administration of justice, that trial judges be given sufficient discretion to deal with disruptive behavior to preserve our system of justice, and there are at least three constitutionally permissible ways for a judge to handle such behavior: (1) bind and gag the accused in court, (2) cite him for contempt, or (3) take him out of the courtroom until he agrees to conduct himself properly. Each of these possibilities has disadvantages and infringes to a different degree upon an accused's Sixth Amendment right to confront witnesses. Therefore, discretion must be allowed to the trial judge to determine the appropriate sanction under the circumstances. Here, the trial judge decided that it was best to remove the extremely disruptive Allen (D), and did so only after repeated warnings and after telling him that he could be present whenever he decided to act properly. This may not have been the only solution to the problem, but it was properly within the discretion of the trial judge. Under these circumstances, Allen (D) lost his right to be present throughout his trial. The judgment of the court of appeals is reversed.

CONCURRENCE: (Brennan, J.) When an accused is excluded from his trial because of disruptive behavior, the court should still make reasonable efforts to allow him to communicate with his attorney and keep informed about the progress of his trial.

▶ ANALYSIS

This case illustrates one situation in which an accused's absence from the courtroom does not violate his Sixth Amendment right to confront the witnesses against him. Generally, this right guarantees that an accused must be present in the courtroom during any time when "testimony" is offered against him (though not necessarily during arguments on questions of law), unless he "waives" that right. Waiver not only occurs when the accused is disruptive, but also, in most jurisdictions, when he voluntarily absents himself from the trial once it has started. Note, however, that if an accused is not present at the start of his trial, the court cannot proceed without him, even if his absence is deliberate. Note, finally, that the Court here does not ignore the risk of prejudice to an accused who is bound and gagged in front of a jury. Rather, the Court states that this prejudice is one factor to be considered by the trial court when deciding whether such restraints should be applied or whether the disruptive accused should be removed from the court.

Quicknotes

HABEAS CORPUS A proceeding in which a defendant brings a writ to compel a judicial determination of whether he is lawfully being held in custody.

Griffin v. California

First-degree murder convict (D) v. State (P)

380 U.S. 609 (1965).

NATURE OF CASE: Certiorari from a murder conviction.

FACT SUMMARY: Griffin (D), during his trial for first-degree murder, did not testify on the issue of his guilt, and both the prosecutor and judge subsequently commented on this failure to the jury, before it convicted him.

RULE OF LAW

The Fifth Amendment SelfIncrimination Clause implicitly forbids comment by the prosecution on an accused's failure to testify, or instructions by the court that such failure is evidence of guilt.

FACTS: Griffin (D) refused to testify at his trial for first-degree murder, invoking the Fifth Amendment privilege against self-incrimination. Before the jury deliberated on the issue of guilt, the prosecutor commented on this failure to testify and suggested that guilt should be inferred therefrom. During instructions to the jury, the court stated that if Griffin (D) failed to explain facts within his knowledge which tended to indicate his guilt, then the jury could take that failure as "tending to indicate the truth of such evidence," but that such failure alone does not by itself "warrant an inference of guilt." Upon conviction, and affirmance of that conviction by the California Supreme Court, Griffin (D) brought a petition for certiorari to this court.

ISSUE: Does comment by a judge or prosecutor on an accused's failure to testify violate his Fifth Amendment privilege against self-incrimination?

HOLDING AND DECISION: (Douglas, J.) Yes. The Fifth Amendment Self-Incrimination Clause forbids comment by the prosecution on an accused's failure to testify, or instructions by the court that such failure is evidence of guilt. Such comment by the prosecution or court is a "remnant of the inquisitorial system of criminal justice which the Fifth Amendment protects against." Such comment penalizes the exercise of a constitutional privilege to refrain from self-incrimination and, as such, cannot be allowed. It may be true that there is a natural inference of guilt from a failure to testify as to facts within the knowledge of an accused, but the jury must make this inference on its own without comment from the court. Here, therefore, Griffin's (D) conviction must be reversed.

DISSENT: (Stewart, J.) In examining whether an accused's privilege against self-incrimination has been violated, "compulsion" is the focus of inquiry (i.e., such privilege has only been violated if the accused was "compelled to be a witness against himself"). The court however fails to identify any such compulsion in the comments of the court and prosecutor. First, such comment does not compel an accused's testimony by creating awareness in the jury of his failure to testify, since that failure is obvious by itself. Second, no compulsion may be assumed on the ground that the inferences drawn by the jury which has heard such comments will be detrimental to an accused, especially where the court has carefully controlled its comments. The trial court here carefully instructed the jury that Griffin's (D) failure to testify "does not by itself warrant an inference of guilt." It is doubtful that a jury without such instructions would have observed such a limitation. The comment in this case was a means of articulating and rationally discussing a fact that is necessarily impressed on the jury's consciousness (i.e., the failure to testify). The State has an important interest in such discussion, which should not arbitrarily be cut off.

ANALYSIS

This case illustrates the rule applicable to "direct comment" on an accused's failure to "testify." Note, however, that it does not prevent a prosecutor from commenting on an accused's "failure to offer evidence" on critical aspects of the case. It has been held that a court's comment that an accused's "failure to explain" possession of recently stolen property should be considered in determining whether he knew the goods were stolen, does not violate *Griffin* (*Barnes v. U.S.*). Of course, what is considered permissible depends upon the wording of the prosecutor's comments. If he emphasizes an accused's failure to present other evidence instead of the fact that he "personally" offered no explanation, there is probably no violation of *Griffin*. Note, further, that *Griffin* does not prevent a prosecutor from commenting to a jury upon an accused's "refusal to submit to reasonable tests or examinations," the results of which would have been admissible on the issue of guilt or innocence. Note, finally, that *Griffin* does prevent counsel for one of several codefendants from commenting on the failure of other codefendants to testify.

Quicknotes

PRIVILEGE AGAINST SELF-INCRIMINATION A privilege guaranteed by the Fifth Amendment to the federal Constitution in a criminal proceeding for communications made by an accused and protecting an accused or witness from having to give testimony that may incriminate himself.

Darden v. Wainwright

Murder convict (D) v. Court (P)

477 U.S. 168 (1986).

NATURE OF CASE: Appeal of denial of habeas corpus.

FACT SUMMARY: At the guilt phase of a murder trial, the prosecution made improper closing statements concerning the crime.

RULE OF LAW
Improper closing statements by counsel will void a conviction only if they make the trial so unfair as to violate due process.

FACTS: Darden (D) was charged with a particularly vicious series of crimes, including murder. At his trial, counsel for the prosecution made various improper closing arguments, which appealed to passion rather than facts, although evidence was not misstated, and no comments were made about the exercise of rights. Darden (D) was sentenced to death. This was affirmed on appeal, and the court of appeals denied habeas corpus. Darden (D) appealed.

ISSUE: Will improper closing statements by counsel void a conviction only if they make the trial so unfair as to violate due process?

HOLDING AND DECISION: (Powell, J.) Yes. Improper closing statements by counsel will void a conviction only if they make the trial so unfair as to violate due process. It is not enough to void a conviction that remarks by counsel are improper or incorrect. The relevant question is whether the remarks made the trial so unfair as to violate due process. Here, the remarks, while appealing to the passion of the jurors, did not misstate the evidence, and did not comment on the exercise of constitutional rights. The trial still was fundamentally fair. Affirmed.

DISSENT: (Blackmun, J.) The prosecution in this case offered personal opinions as to guilt, injected broader issues into the trial, and used arguments designed to inflame the passions of the jury. The result of all this was an unfair trial.

▶ ANALYSIS

The dissent did not appear to question the standard of review used by the Court. Due process would appear to be the standard the dissent proposed. However, the dissent disagreed with the Court's conclusion that the trial was not fundamentally unfair.

Quicknotes

PROCEDURAL DUE PROCESS The constitutional mandate that if the state or federal government acts so as to deny a citizen of a life, liberty or property interest the individual is first entitled to notice and the right to be heard.

26

Reprosecution and the Ban Against Double Jeopardy

Quick Reference Rules of Law

Illinois v. Somerville

State (D) v. Re-trial defendant (P)

410 U.S. 458 (1973).

NATURE OF CASE: Appeal of a judgment granting a petition for habeas corpus.

FACT SUMMARY: The judge declared a mistrial of Somerville's (P) first trial and Somerville (P) claimed that the second trial amounted to double jeopardy.

🏛 RULE OF LAW
If a trial judge grants a mistrial, over the objections of the defendant, because there is a manifest necessity to grant a mistrial or in order to meet the ends of public justice, a second trial for the same offense does not amount to double jeopardy.

FACTS: Somerville (P) was indicted by an Illinois grand jury for the crime of theft. Before any evidence was presented at his trial, the prosecuting attorney asked the court to declare a mistrial because Somerville's (P) indictment was found to be fatally defective. The defect could not be cured by an amendment and Somerville (P) could not waive the error as it was considered jurisdictional. The court felt that further proceedings under this indictment would be useless, and therefore declared a mistrial. Two days later, the grand jury handed down a second indictment. Somerville (P) claimed that the second trial constituted double jeopardy. The court rejected this contention and convicted Somerville (P), and the state appellate court upheld the verdict. Somerville (P) then sought a writ of habeas corpus in the federal district court, but the writ was denied and the Seventh Circuit Court of Appeals affirmed that decision. Somerville's (P) petition for certiorari was granted and the case was remanded for reconsideration in light of two recent court decisions. On remand, the Seventh Circuit held that Somerville's (P) petition for habeas corpus should have been granted because jeopardy had attached when the jury was impaneled and sworn in. A declaration of a mistrial by the court over Somerville's (P) objections precluded a retrial. Somerville (P) claims that once a jury has been selected and sworn in that jeopardy attaches, and that he has a right to have his case completed by the first court.

ISSUE: If a trial judge grants a mistrial, over the objections of the defendant, is a second trial for the same offense prohibited under the doctrine of double jeopardy because the mistrial was granted in order to meet the ends of public justice?

HOLDING AND DECISION: (Rehnquist, J.) No. If the court finds that there is manifest necessity for calling a mistrial or the ends of public justice would otherwise be defeated if a mistrial were not declared, the court may declare a mistrial over the objections of the defendant. The Court must consider all the circumstances in making its decision. In this case, it would have been useless to complete the first trial under the defective indictment because, on appeal, the decision would have been reversed and the case would have had to be retried. By declaring a mistrial, all parties were saved considerable time and expense. The Court also appointed out that the public has an interest in seeing all trials end in either a conviction or an acquittal. The Court held that even though a defendant has a valued right to have his trial completed by a particular tribunal, that right must, in some instances, be subordinated to the public's interest in fair trials ending in just judgments. Since the declaration of a mistrial implemented a reasonable state policy, Somerville's (P) interest in proceeding to verdict was outweighed by the competing and equally legitimate demand for public justice. The decision of the court of appeals was therefore reversed.

DISSENT: (White, J.) The right of the defendant not to be put in double jeopardy outweighs the public's interest in fair trials and there was no manifest necessity to grant the mistrial. Somerville (P) had the right to be tried by the jury chosen in the first trial.

▶ ANALYSIS

This case illustrates one of the situations in which a second trial is permissible, even though jeopardy would normally have been held to have attached at the first trial. Jeopardy attaches when the jury has been sworn in a jury trial, or when the first witness has been sworn in a trial without a jury. Usually, once jeopardy has attached, a second trial would constitute double jeopardy. Note, however, that there are several other situations in which a second trial is permissible after jeopardy has attached: (1) after a successful appeal by the defendant, (2) where a jury is unable to reach a verdict due to some "evident necessity" (e.g., death of judge or juror), (3) where there is a "hung jury," or (4) where "misconduct of a witness or a defendant" personally causes a mistrial.

■■■

Quicknotes

DOUBLE JEOPARDY A prohibition against a second prosecution for the same offense after an acquittal or conviction for that offense in a prior proceeding or against multiple punishments for the same offense.

■■■

Oregon v. Kennedy

State (P) v. Re-tried theft convict (D)

456 U.S. 667 (1982).

NATURE OF CASE: Appeal from dismissal of prosecution for theft.

FACT SUMMARY: After being granted a mistrial, Kennedy (D) contended the Double Jeopardy Clause barred reprosecution.

🏛 RULE OF LAW
Following a defendant's successful motion for a mistrial, the Double Jeopardy Clause will bar retrial only when the prosecution's objectionable conduct was done with the intent to provoke a mistrial motion.

FACTS: Kennedy (D) was charged with theft. During redirect of a State's (P) witness, the prosecutor made certain improper comments that resulted in a mistrial. It did not appear that the prosecutor intentionally provoked the motion. Kennedy (D) was retried and convicted. Kennedy (D) appealed, contending the Double Jeopardy Clause barred retrial. The Oregon Supreme Court agreed, and reversed the conviction. Oregon (P) appealed.

ISSUE: Following a defendant's successful motion for a mistrial, will the Double Jeopardy Clause bar retrial only when the prosecution's objectionable conduct was done with the intent to provoke a mistrial motion?

HOLDING AND DECISION: (Rehnquist, J.) Yes. Following a defendant's successful motion for a mistrial the Double Jeopardy Clause will bar retrial only when the prosecution's objectionable conduct was done with the intent to provoke a mistrial motion. The protection against double jeopardy is largely waived when the defendant himself moves for a mistrial. However, prosecutorial conduct may compel a defendant to move for a mistrial. There will always be an element of prejudicial prosecutorial conduct towards a defendant, so this alone does not justify barring retrial. A standard of intent by the prosecutor to provoke a mistrial motion is one easily applied. Any other standard would be very difficult to quantify. Only when the prosecutor intentionally provokes a motion should the prosecutor's conduct be such that a retrial should be barred. Reversed.

CONCURRENCE: (Powell, J.) A court should rely on objective evidence of intent.

CONCURRENCE: (Stevens, J.) Prosecutorial harassment or overreaching should also bar retrial.

▶ ANALYSIS

It is basic constitutional law that the U.S. Supreme Court is the final word on federal law. Several states have adopted rules broader than that enunciated here, based on state law. Oregon (P) did so later in this action. Kennedy (D) lost the battle but won the war.

Quicknotes

DOUBLE JEOPARDY A prohibition against a second prosecution for the same offense after an acquittal or conviction for that offense in a prior proceeding or against multiple punishments for the same offense.

MISTRIAL An erroneous or invalid trial.

United States v. Scott

Federal government (P) v. Narcotics indictee (D)

437 U.S. 82 (1978).

NATURE OF CASE: Appeal from dismissals of two counts of a criminal indictment.

FACT SUMMARY: Two of the three counts in the indictment against Scott (D) were dismissed on the ground that his defense had been prejudiced by preindictment delay, and the Government (P) sought to appeal.

🏛 RULE OF LAW
There is no violation of the Double Jeopardy Clause if the government appeals when the defendant has successfully sought to have his trial terminated without any submission to either judge or jury as to his guilt or innocence, whether it be by dismissal of the count or otherwise.

FACTS: Scott (D) successfully moved to have two of the three counts in his indictment for distributing narcotics dismissed on the ground that his defense had been prejudiced by preindictment delay. The offense allegedly occurred in September 1974, and the indictment was issued on March 5, 1975. A guilty verdict as to the third count was returned, but the Government (P) sought to appeal the dismissal of the first two counts. Concluding that any further prosecution on those counts was barred by the Double Jeopardy Clause, the appeal was dismissed and the Government (P) then sought review of that decision only as to the first count.

ISSUE: Can the government appeal when a defendant is successful in having the trial terminated without submission to judge or jury for determination of guilt or innocence?

HOLDING AND DECISION: (Rehnquist, J.) Yes. If a defendant manages to have his trial terminated without his guilt or innocence being submitted to judge or jury, as when he successfully moved for dismissal of a charge, the government may appeal without violating the Double Jeopardy Clause. The Double Jeopardy Clause looks askance at the government repeatedly seeking to try a person, but it does not come into play when the government is quite willing to continue a trial to conclusion but the defendant elects to seek termination of the trial on grounds unrelated to guilt or innocence. Unlike an insanity or entrapment defense, dismissal of a charge for preindictment delay represents a legal judgment that a defendant, although criminally culpable, may not be punished because of a supposed constitutional violation. It is a termination of a trial on grounds unrelated to guilt or innocence, and the Double Jeopardy Clause is not offended when such a dismissal is ap-

pealed by the government. In such a case, it is the government which has lost its right to "one complete opportunity to convict those who have violated its laws"; the defendant has voluntarily given up, as opposed to being deprived of, his valued right to go to the first jury. Judgment reversed.

DISSENT: (Brennan, J.) The majority's attempt to draw a distinction between "true acquittals," supposedly subject to the Double Jeopardy bar of government appeals, and other final judgments, supposedly subject to the bar, favoring the accused, is unsupported in logic or policy. The definition adopted for "acquittal" is overly restrictive, as is evidenced by the attempted distinction between a dismissal based on preaccusation delay and one based on a defense of insanity or entrapment. The Double Jeopardy Clause mandates that the government have just one complete opportunity to convict an accused and that retrial be barred when the first proceeding terminates in a final judgment favorable to the defendant, which is what occurred in this case. The reasons underlying preclusion of retrial after an acquittal are equally applicable to a final judgment entered on a ground "unrelated to factual innocence," so their disparate treatment is untenable. Furthermore, in this case, one of the "factual elements of the offense charged" was preindictment delay. If, indeed, acquittal is resolution of some or all of these elements, there was an acquittal and retrial is barred. In fact, there are few instances where defenses can be deemed unrelated to factual innocence.

▶ ANALYSIS

Prior to this case, the Court had determined that an appeal by the government is barred by double jeopardy considerations when there is a pre-verdict judgment of acquittal based on the Court's determination of the sufficiency of the evidence. Since the same result could be obtained by dismissing the indictment for failure to charge an offense, which would be more like a mistrial and could make appeal possible in certain circumstances, the Court would be left with two options on how to treat a particular case. One option would bar government appeal and the other would not. Regarding this situation, Wright, Miller, and Cooper, 15 Federal Practice and Procedure § 3919 (1978) (pocket part) states: "If this conclusion is correct, it means that the trial court has discretion to control the double jeopardy consequences of its ruling. It also means that the government

Continued on next page.

must be astute to argue for a disposition that leaves it free to appeal or start over. Although it is troubling that trial judges should be left free of appellate review, procedural punctilio at least has the advantage of helping the defendant to know whether further proceedings may be possible. Even this virtue may be reduced, however, until the 'manifest necessity' standard that limits retrials after a mistrial or dismissal without the defendant's consent is elaborated in the context of defective indictments."

■━■

Quicknotes

ACQUITTAL The discharge of an accused individual from suspicion of guilt for a particular crime and from further prosecution for that offense.

MISTRIAL An erroneous or invalid trial.

■━■

Lockhart v. Nelson

Court (P) v. Burglary convict (D)

488 U.S. 33 (1988).

NATURE OF CASE: Review of habeas corpus invalidating a conviction under a recidivist statute.

FACT SUMMARY: Nelson (D) was convicted under a recidivist statute, and when the conviction was shown to have been invalid, the State (P) attempted to retry him.

🏛 RULE OF LAW
When a conviction is based on evidence erroneously admitted and is reversed on appeal, the Double Jeopardy Clause does not prohibit retrial.

FACTS: Nelson (D) was convicted of burglary. Under a state recidivist statute, which required four prior felony convictions to be applicable, an enhanced sentencing hearing was held. Evidence of four prior convictions was introduced, although Nelson (D) contended one had been pardoned. Nelson was convicted under the recidivist law. In a habeas proceeding, Nelson (D) introduced proof of the pardon. The district court granted habeas. The State (P) announced an intention to retry, substituting another felony for the pardoned one. The district court held this to be barred by the Double Jeopardy Clause. The Eighth Circuit affirmed, and the Supreme Court granted review.

ISSUE: When a conviction is based on evidence erroneously admitted and is reversed on appeal, does the Double Jeopardy Clause prohibit retrial?

HOLDING AND DECISION: (Rehnquist, C.J.) No. When a conviction is based on evidence erroneously admitted and is reversed on appeal, the Double Jeopardy Clause does not prohibit retrial. It has long been settled that the clause does not bar retrial if a conviction is reversed on appeal. An exception to this rule has been created, that where a reversal is based on insufficiency of evidence, no retrial should occur, as such a reversal is tantamount to an acquittal. However, a reversal based on the erroneous admission of evidence is not the same situation. It may be that other evidence was not introduced for tactical reasons, because of the evidence which was erroneously admitted. The prosecution is entitled to present its best case. This differs from the above exception, because there the prosecution presumably has introduced its best case and still failed to obtain a conviction. Here, the prosecution wishes to introduce evidence of another, valid conviction, and it should be permitted to do so. Reversed.

DISSENT: (Marshall, J.) The decision here seems to rest on the notion that prosecutors hold back evidence, which is a questionable supposition at best.

▶ ANALYSIS

The rule that a defendant may be retried following a reversal is relatively new. Up until the latter part of the nineteenth century, there could be one trial, one judgment, and one appeal. If exonerating evidence was later found, there was no judicial remedy. Appeals for executive clemency were much more important then than now. There have been calls among a minority of authorities for a return to such a system.

■=■

Quicknotes

RECIDIVIST A habitual criminal.

■=■

Heath v. Alabama

Murder convict (D) v. State (P)

474 U.S. 82 (1985).

NATURE OF CASE: Review of murder conviction.

FACT SUMMARY: After being convicted of murder in Georgia, Heath (D) was convicted of murder in Alabama (P) for the same homicide.

🏛 RULE OF LAW
Successive prosecutions by two states for the same conduct are not barred by the Double Jeopardy Clause.

FACTS: Heath (D) was charged in Georgia with murder, arising out of his allegedly hiring certain individuals to kill his wife, who was in fact killed. Part of the crime occurred in Alabama. Heath (D) was convicted by a Georgia jury and sentenced to life imprisonment. He was then charged with murder by Alabama (P). He was convicted and sentenced to death. His double jeopardy claims were rejected at the trial level and on appeal as well. The Supreme Court accepted review.

ISSUE: Are successive prosecutions by two states for the same conduct barred by the Double Jeopardy Clause?

HOLDING AND DECISION: (O'Connor, J.) No. Successive prosecutions by two states for the same conduct are not barred by the Double Jeopardy Clause. A crime is an offense against the sovereignty of a government. When an individual breaks the laws of two states, he has committed two distinct offenses. Each sovereign is entitled to have its law adjudicated in its own courts, so it is no answer to the above principle that the trial in Georgia regarded the same sort of offense involved in Alabama (P). Essentially, when two laws derive from two difference ultimate sources, two separate offenses occur when the laws of each ultimate source are broken. Here, two separate sovereigns, Alabama (P) and Georgia, are involved, and consequently two different offenses occurred. Affirmed.

DISSENT: (Marshall, J.) When two states are involved in a single transaction, the issues of sovereignty for each state are identical. Vindicating the laws of one state in a prosecution automatically vindicates the laws of the other.

▶ *ANALYSIS*

The analysis of the Court here does not apply in all cases where the laws of multiple jurisdictions are broken. For instance, if a single act violates similar laws in a county and a state, the violator may not be tried twice. Counties are not sovereigns, but rather subdivisions of a sovereign state.

■=■

Quicknotes

FULL FAITH AND CREDIT Doctrine that a judgment by a court of one state shall be given the same effect in another state.

■=■

Sentencing

Quick Reference Rules of Law

Williams v. New York

Defendant (D) v. State (P)

337 U.S. 241 (1949).

NATURE OF CASE: Appeal from a death sentence.

FACT SUMMARY: The judge imposed a death sentence for a murder conviction after a jury had recommended life imprisonment.

⚖ RULE OF LAW
A sentencing judge can exercise a wide discretion in the sources and types of evidence used to assist him in determining the kind and extent of punishment to be imposed within limits fixed by law.

FACTS: Williams (D) was found guilty of murder in the first degree. The jury recommended life imprisonment. The trial judge, after considering information from the presentence investigation, imposed the death sentence. Williams (D) appealed, alleging that the judge's consideration of information obtained outside the courtroom, from persons whom Williams (D) had not been permitted to confront or cross-examine, violated his due process rights under the Fourteenth Amendment.

ISSUE: May a sentencing judge exercise a wide discretion in the sources and types of evidence used to assist him in determining the kind and extent of punishment to be imposed within limits fixed by law?

HOLDING AND DECISION: (Black, J.) Yes. A sentencing judge can exercise a wide discretion in the sources and types of evidence used to assist him in determining the kind and extent of punishment to be imposed within limits fixed by law. In addition to the historical basis for different evidentiary rules governing trial and sentencing procedures, there are sound practical reasons for the distinction. Modern concepts individualizing punishment have made it necessary that a sentencing judge not be denied an opportunity to obtain pertinent information by a requirement of rigid adherence to restrictive rules of evidence properly applicable to the trial. Affirmed.

DISSENT: (Murphy, J.) In our criminal courts the jury sits as the representative of the community; its voice is that of the society against which the crime was committed. A judge, even though vested with the statutory authority to do so, should hesitate indeed to increase the severity of such a community expression.

▶ ANALYSIS

The Court relied on information that Williams (D) had committed thirty other burglaries in the same areas, some of which he had confessed to. His probation report revealed certain sexual activities which the judge considered to be morbid. The judge found Williams (D) to be a menace to society, based on this information. Rule 32 of the Federal Rules of Criminal Procedure permits federal judges to consider reports made by probation officers in imposing sentences, reflecting the historical position.

■═■

Quicknotes

DISCRETION The authority conferred upon a public official to act reasonably in accordance with his own judgment under certain circumstances.

FIRST DEGREE MURDER The willful killing of another person with deliberation and premeditation; first-degree murder also encompasses those situations in which a person is killed within the perpetration of, or attempt to perpetrate, specified felonies.

FOURTEENTH AMENDMENT DUE PROCESS CLAUSE Provides that protections mandated by the Constitution and observed by the federal government are equally applicable, and therefore must be observed by the States.

■═■

United States v. Booker

Federal government (P) v. Convicted drug dealer (D)

___ U.S. ___, 125 S. Ct. 738 (2005).

NATURE OF CASE: Appeal from the reversal of a judge's sentencing enhancement.

FACT SUMMARY: When the sentencing judge found additional facts (not found by the jury) which resulted in an enhancement of Booker's (D) sentence under the Federal Sentencing Guidelines, the federal court of appeals reversed the enhancement on the grounds that a sentencing procedure which deprives the defendant of the right to a jury determination of all facts essential to the sentence, violates the Sixth Amendment under *Blakely v. Washington*.

> 🏛 **RULE OF LAW**
> Binding rules set forth in the Federal Sentencing Guidelines limit the severity of the sentence that a judge can lawfully impose on a defendant based on the facts found at trial by the jury.

FACTS: A jury found that Booker (D) possessed with intent to distribute 92.5 grams of crack cocaine, which authorized, under the Federal Sentencing Guidelines, 210 to 262 months in prison. At time of sentencing, the judge found by a preponderance of the evidence that Booker (D) actually possessed an additional 566 grams of crack, raising the Guidelines sentence to 360 months to life in prison. Booker (D) received 360 months. The federal court of appeals reversed on the basis of *Blakely v. Washington*, 124 S.Ct. 2531 (2004), which held a sentencing procedure that deprives the defendant of the right to a jury determination of all facts essential to the sentence, violates the Sixth Amendment. The Government (P) appealed. In a case decided together with Booker's (D) case, Fanfan (D) was convicted by a jury of conspiracy to distribute more than 500 grams of cocaine, which authorized a maximum Guidelines sentence of 78 months. At sentencing, the judge found by a preponderance of the evidence that Fanfan (D) actually controlled a much larger quantity of illegal drugs and that he was a leader of the operation, raising the Guideline maximum to 16 years. The judge, however, relying on *Blakely*, imposed the lower Guideline sentence authorized by the jury's verdict. The Government (P) appealed.

ISSUE: Do the binding rules set forth in the Federal Sentencing Guidelines limit the severity of the sentence that a judge can lawfully impose on a defendant based on the facts found at trial by the jury?

HOLDING AND DECISION: (Stevens, J.) Yes. Binding rules set forth in the Federal Sentencing Guidelines limit the severity of the sentence that a judge can lawfully impose on a defendant based on the facts found at trial by the jury. There is no distinction of constitutional significance between the Federal Sentencing Guidelines and the Washington procedures at issue in *Blakely*. This conclusion rests on the premise, common to both systems, that the relevant sentencing rules are mandatory and impose binding requirements on all sentencing judges. If the Guidelines as currently written could be read as merely advisory provisions that recommended, rather than required, the selection of particular sentences in response to differing sets of facts, their use would not implicate the Sixth Amendment. This Court has never doubted the authority of a judge to exercise broad discretion in imposing a sentence within a statutory range. The Guidelines as written, however, are not advisory; they are mandatory and binding on all judges. The statute specifically directs that the court "*shall* impose a sentence of the kind, and within the range" established by the Guidelines, subject to departures in specific, limited cases. The availability of a departure in specified circumstances does not avoid the constitutional issue. This Court rejects the Government's (P) arguments that *Blakely* should not apply to the Federal Guidelines because they were drafted by a commission, rather than the legislature itself; prior Court decisions had upheld the constitutionality of the Guidelines; and doing so would violate the principle of separation of powers because it would effectively convert the Guidelines into new criminal statutes. Newly developing enhanced sentencing practices have required this Court to address the question how the right of jury trial could be preserved, in a meaningful way guaranteeing that the jury would still stand between the individual and the power of the government under the new sentencing regimes. Affirmed. [Justice Breyer separately delivered part of the Court's opinion, concluding that in view of the Court's holding, the provisions of the Guidelines having the effect of making the Guidelines mandatory, must be invalidated.]

DISSENTING IN PART: (Stevens, J.) [Responding to Justice Breyer's portion of the opinion.] There is no need to invalidate provisions of the Sentencing Guidelines to avoid

Continued on next page.

violations of the Sixth Amendment. The Court's decision to do so constitutes an unnecessary "extraordinary exercise of authority."

DISSENTING IN PART: (Scalia, J.) Appellate review for unreasonableness may simply add another layer of unfettered judicial discretion to the sentencing process. It may become a mere formality, used by appellate judges only to ensure that district judges say all the right things when they explain how they have exercised their newly restored discretion.

DISSENTING IN PART: (Breyer, J.) [Responding to Justice Stevens's portion of the opinion.] Nothing in the Sixth Amendment forbids a sentencing judge to determine the *manner* or way in which the offender carried out the crime of which he or she was convicted.

▶ *ANALYSIS*

In *Booker*, the Supreme Court, while recognizing that in some cases jury factfinding may impair the most expedient and efficient sentencing of defendants, nevertheless emphasized that the interest in fairness and reliability protected by the right to a jury trial—a common law right that defendants enjoyed for centuries and that is now enshrined in the Sixth Amendment—has always outweighed the interest in concluding trials swiftly.

Quicknotes

SIXTH AMENDMENT Provides the right to a speedy and public trial by impartial jury, the right to be informed of the accusation, the right to confront witnesses, and the right to have the assistance of counsel in all criminal prosecutions.

CHAPTER **28**

Appeals

Quick Reference Rules of Law

North Carolina v. Pearce

State (P) v. Assault convict (D)

395 U.S. 711 (1969).

NATURE OF CASE: Petitions for writs of habeas corpus.

FACT SUMMARY: Pearce (D) obtained a reversal of his conviction. Upon retrial, he was sentenced to eight years in prison which, when added to the time he had already served, amounted to a longer total sentence than that originally imposed. Rice (D) also obtained a reversal of his conviction. Upon retrial, he was sentenced to a harsher sentence than his original sentence, and no credit was given for the time he had already served.

🏛 RULE OF LAW

(1) The Double Jeopardy Clause does not prohibit, upon a defendant's reconviction, the imposition of a harsher sentence than that imposed after the first conviction, but whenever a judge does impose a more severe sentence upon a defendant's reconviction, his reasons for doing so must be shown.

(2) The Double Jeopardy Clause requires that in computing a new sentence on retrial, credit be given for that part of the original sentence already served.

FACTS: Pearce (D) was sentenced to 12 to 15 years in prison for assault with intent to rape. He obtained a reversal of his conviction. Upon retrial, he was convicted and sentenced to eight years, which, when added to the time he had already served, amounted to a longer sentence than that originally imposed. Rice (D) was sentenced to ten years in prison after pleading guilty to burglary. He obtained a reversal of his conviction. Upon his retrial, he was convicted upon three of the original four counts and sentenced to a term totaling 25 years. No credit was given for the time he had already served. Pearce (D) was granted habeas corpus on the ground that the longer sentence was unconstitutional. Rice (D) was also granted habeas corpus as it was found that the state was punishing him for his having exercised his post-conviction right of review.

ISSUE:

(1) Does the Fifth Amendment prohibit the imposition of a more severe punishment after conviction for the same offense upon retrial?

(2) Does the Fifth Amendment require that, in computing a new sentence on retrial, credit must be given for that part of the original sentence already served?

HOLDING AND DECISION: (Stewart, J.)

(1) No. The guarantee against double jeopardy does not include restrictions upon the length of a sentence imposed upon reconviction. This rule rests upon the premise that the original conviction has, at the defendant's behest, been wholly nullified. However, it would be a flagrant violation of the Fourteenth Amendment for a state court to impose a heavier sentence upon every reconvicted defendant to the explicit purpose of punishing the defendant for his having gotten his original conviction set aside. The very threat inherent in the existence of such a policy would "chill the exercise of basic rights" by those still in prison. A court cannot put a price on an appeal, and a defendant's exercise of a right of appeal must be free and unfettered. In order to insure the absence of a motivation to punish, whenever a judge imposes a more severe sentence upon a defendant after a new trial, he must affirmatively show his reasons for doing so. These reasons must be based upon objective information concerning identifiable conduct on the part of the defendant after the original proceeding.

(2) Yes. The Double Jeopardy Clause protects against multiple punishments as well as multiple prosecutions. This basic constitutional guarantee is violated when punishment already exacted is not fully credited in imposing sentence upon a new conviction for the same offense. In both of these cases before us, no reason was offered to justify the imposition of the harsher sentence. The judgment below must be affirmed.

CONCURRENCE: (White, J.) The Court should authorize an increased sentence on retrial based on any objective, identifiable factual data not known to the trial judge at the time of the original sentencing proceeding.

CONCURRENCE/DISSENT: (Black, J.) I disagree that the Due Process Clause grants the court the power to require judges to state their reasons for the imposition of harsher sentences.

▶ ANALYSIS

In *Green v. U.S.*, 355 U.S. 184 (1957), mentioned in one of the concurring opinions, the defendant had originally been charged with first-degree murder, but was convicted of second-degree murder. His appeal resulted in the reversal of his conviction, and he was retried on the original charge. The second jury convicted him of first-degree murder. The

Continued on next page.

Supreme Court held that double jeopardy barred conviction on that charge, since Green had already been in peril of being convicted and punished for first-degree murder at his first trial. In *Tucker v. Peyton*, 357 F.2d 115 (1966), it was held that where a prisoner serving consecutive sentences succeeded in having one of the sentences invalidated after it had been fully or partially served, the state must give credit on the sentence remaining for the time served. In Miller v. Cox, 443 F.2d 1019 (4th Cir. 1971), it was held that a defendant who had served 21 years on a void conviction was not entitled to credit against subsequently committed felonies.

■━━■

Quicknotes

FIRST DEGREE MURDER The willful killing of another person with deliberation and premeditation; first-degree murder also encompasses those situations in which a person is killed within the perpetration of, or attempt to perpetrate, specified felonies.

PROCEDURAL DUE PROCESS The constitutional mandate that if the state or federal government acts so as to deny a citizen of a life, liberty or property interest the individual is first entitled to notice and the right to be heard.

SECOND-DEGREE MURDER The unlawful killing of another person, without premeditation, and characterized by either an intent to kill or by a reckless disregard for human life.

■━━■

Texas v. McCullough

State (P) v. Re-tried defendant (D)

475 U.S. 134 (1986).

NATURE OF CASE: Appeal from sentencing for murder.

FACT SUMMARY: McCullough (D) was tried twice for murder, receiving a harsher sentence upon retrial.

> **RULE OF LAW**
> A sentence upon retrial harsher than the original is permissible where new facts justify it.

FACTS: McCullough (D) was convicted of felony murder and sentenced by the jury to 20 years. McCullough (D) successfully moved for a retrial. At the second trial, new evidence was presented, indicating that McCullough (D) had done the actual killing. McCullough (D) was again convicted and was sentenced by the judge to 50 years. McCullough (D) appealed, and the Texas court of appeals reversed, holding that federal law prohibited a harsher sentence upon retrial unless it be for acts committed subsequent to the prior sentence. The Supreme Court granted certiorari.

ISSUE: Is a sentence upon retrial harsher than the original permissible where new facts justify it?

HOLDING AND DECISION: (Burger, C.J.) Yes. A sentence upon retrial harsher than the original is permissible where new facts justify it. Federal law only prohibits a harsher sentence upon retrial when this is done through personal vindictiveness on the part of the judge. Here, there was nothing to indicate vindictiveness. The harsher sentence came following new evidence regarding the nature of the offense and, hence, was made for acceptable reasons. Reversed and remanded.

CONCURRENCE: (Brennan, J.) A presumption of vindictiveness exists in a situation such as this, but the fact that the retrial was granted for prosecutorial misconduct would tend to negate this.

DISSENT: (Marshall, J.) Vindictiveness must be presumed. Nothing said or done by the judge was sufficient to rebut this. The mere fact that different evidence was introduced does not rebut vindictiveness.

▶ ANALYSIS

The seminal case in this area was *North Carolina v. Pearce*, 395 U.S. 711 (1969). It was there that the Court established a presumption of vindictiveness. In the instant case, the Court appears to demonstrate that great deference will be given to the trial court in the area of sentencing where new facts are brought to light on retrial.

■■■

Quicknotes

FELONY MURDER The unlawful killing of another human being while in the commission of, or attempted commission of, specified felonies.

■■■

Chapman v. California

Defendant who fails to testify (D) v. State (P)

386 U.S. 18 (1967).

NATURE OF CASE: Appeal from conviction of robbery, kidnapping and murder.

FACT SUMMARY: Chapman (D) et al. contended that because the prosecutor committed a constitutional error by commenting on his failure to testify in his own behalf, as a matter of law such error was reversible.

> **RULE OF LAW**
> A federal constitutional error may be found to be harmless where such is shown beyond a reasonable doubt.

FACTS: Chapman (D) and others were arrested for kidnapping, robbery, and murder. None of the defendants testified at trial. The prosecution commented heavily on Chapman's (D) failure to testify, and they were convicted. While the case was on appeal, the U.S. Supreme Court held that it was a deprivation of a defendant's constitutional rights for the prosecution to comment on his failure to testify. Chapman (D) contended that because the error was constitutional, as a matter of law it was reversible error. The California Supreme Court held the error to be harmless. The U.S. Supreme Court granted review.

ISSUE: May constitutional error be held harmless where such is shown beyond a reasonable doubt?

HOLDING AND DECISION: (Black, J.) Yes. It must be shown beyond a reasonable doubt that constitutional error was harmless or such will be considered reversible. Not all federal constitutional errors are reversible. However, the highest level of proof must be presented to hold such an error harmless. It is not harmless error to effectively deprive a defendant of his right against self-incrimination. By commenting on his failure to testify, the prosecution suggests that such failure is an admission of guilt. Thus this is reversible error. Reversed and remanded.

▶ ANALYSIS

Some commentators suggest this opinion implies that constitutional errors are, by their nature, more important errors than others. The abuse of constitutional as opposed to statutory or state common law standards is considered fundamentally more erosive of the justice system.

■═■

Quicknotes

HARMLESS ERROR An error committed during trial which is not sufficient in nature or effect of warrant reversal, modification, or retrial.

■═■

Neder v. United States

Criminal (D) v. Federal government (P)

527 U.S. 1 (1999).

NATURE OF CASE: Appeal from a guilty verdict and appellate court's holding that district court committed harmless error.

FACT SUMMARY: A jury found Neder (D) guilty on various charges and a judge sentenced him (D) to 147 months in prison. The defendant appealed and the court of appeals held that the district court's failure to instruct the jury on materiality was harmless error.

RULE OF LAW
When a trial judge omits an element of an offense in a jury instruction, the proper review on appeal is the harmless error analysis.

FACTS: Neder (D) was tried and convicted of fraud and tax offenses, and sentenced to 147 months imprisonment, 5 years' supervised release, and $25 million in restitution. On appeal, the court of appeals affirmed the conviction and held that the district court erred when it failed to submit the materiality element of the tax offense to the jury. The error, however, was harmless because materiality was not in dispute, therefore, the error did not contribute to the jury's verdict. Neder (D) appealed.

ISSUE: Is the harmless error analysis appropriate in reviewing a trial court's failure to instruct a jury on each and every element of an offense?

HOLDING AND DECISION: (Rehnquist, C.J.) Yes. The Federal Rules of Criminal Procedure Rule 52(a) states that any error, defect, irregularity, or variance that does not affect substantial rights will be disregarded. Although this rule applies to all alleged errors, there is a class of fundamental constitutional errors that goes beyond the harmless error examination. The error at issue here is a jury instruction that fails to include an element of an offense and is not an error that necessarily renders a criminal trial fundamentally unfair. The harmless error analysis is properly applied to an error as is involved in this case. The harmless error inquiry is whether it is clear beyond a reasonable doubt that a rational jury would have found the defendant guilty without the error. When an element of the offense is omitted from a jury instruction but supported by overwhelming and uncontroverted evidence, the above analysis balances society's interest in punishing the guilty and the method by which such decisions of guilt are made. Affirmed.

CONCURRENCE IN PART AND DISSENT IN PART: (Scalia, J.) A failure to include each element of the crime charged in an instruction can never be harmless error. The right to be tried by a jury necessarily means the right to have a jury determine whether one has been proved guilty of a charged offense, and that means a jury must determine all elements that were proved or not. The Court does not specify exactly how many elements of an offense can be omitted before the error is not viewed as harmless. Failure to prove one element should be treated the same as a failure to prove all elements of an offense and prevent a conviction.

ANALYSIS

Justice Stevens's concurrence noted that the Court took a narrow perspective in identifying those errors that required automatic reversal. For example, racial discrimination in the selection of grand juries is not to be tolerated, even if the defendant's guilt is later established in a fair trial with overwhelming evidence. Our Constitution and criminal justice system respects other values besides the reliability of a determination of guilt.

Quicknotes

HARMLESS ERROR An error taking place during trial that does not require the reviewing court to overturn or modify the trial court's judgment in that it did not affect the appellant's substantial rights or the disposition of the action.

MATERIALITY Importance; the degree of relevance or necessity to the particular matter.

Post-Conviction Review: Federal Habeas Corpus

Quick Reference Rules of Law

Stone v. Powell

Accused (D) v. State (P)

428 U.S. 465 (1976).

NATURE OF CASE: Writ for federal habeas corpus.

FACT SUMMARY: A prisoner sought habeas corpus relief on the grounds that he was convicted based on evidence obtained in an illegal search or seizure.

🏛 RULE OF LAW
Where the state has provided an opportunity for full and fair litigation of a Fourth Amendment claim, the Constitution does not require that a state prisoner be granted federal habeas corpus relief on the ground that evidence obtained in an unconstitutional search or seizure was introduced at his trial.

FACTS: Stone (D) alleged that his conviction was based on evidence illegally obtained, and requested habeas corpus review. After state habeas corpus proceedings, Stone (D) filed a writ for federal habeas corpus, alleging violation of Fourth Amendment rights guaranteed through the Fourteenth Amendment.

ISSUE: Where the state has provided an opportunity for full and fair litigation of a Fourth Amendment claim, does the Constitution require that a state prisoner be granted federal habeas corpus relief on the ground that evidence obtained in an unconstitutional search or seizure was introduced at his trial?

HOLDING AND DECISION: (Powell, J.) No. Where the state has provided an opportunity for full and fair litigation of a Fourth Amendment claim, the Constitution does not require that a state prisoner be granted federal habeas corpus relief on the ground that evidence obtained in an unconstitutional search or seizure was introduced at his trial. The primary justification for the exclusionary rule is the deterrence of police conduct that violates Fourth Amendment rights; the Fourth Amendment itself is not a personal constitutional right. Fourth Amendment concerns support the implementation of the exclusionary rule at trial and its enforcement on direct appeal of state court convictions. The additional contribution, if any, of the consideration of search and seizure claims of state prisoners on collateral review is small in relation to the costs. Writ denied.

DISSENT: (Brennan, J.) The Court today is ignoring the settled principle that for purposes of adjudicating constitutional claims Congress, which has the power to do so under Art. III of the Constitution, has effectively cast the district courts sitting in habeas in the role of surrogate Supreme Courts. The procedural safeguards mandated by the Congress are not admonitions to be tolerated only to the extent they serve functional purposes. Every guarantee enshrined in our Constitution is endowed with an independent vitality and value, and the court is not free to curtail those Constitutional guarantees even to punish the most obviously guilty.

DISSENT: (White, J.) Applying today's holding, a prisoner alleging that he is being held prisoner in violation of the U.S. Constitution and asserting that he did not have a full and fair hearing in the state courts would be refused even though a co-defendant was proved innocent on the same facts. Congress cannot have intended this result.

▶ ANALYSIS

The court has not extended the holding from this case to bar habeas corpus review of other claims based on violations of the Constitution. The Antiterrorism and Effective Death Penalty Act enacted in 1996 limited successive habeas corpus petitions. This Act did not, however, repeal the authority of the court to entertain original habeas corpus petitions.

━■━

Quicknotes

FOURTH AMENDMENT Provides that persons be secure as to their person and private belongings against unreasonable searches and seizures.

HABEAS CORPUS A proceeding in which a defendant brings a writ to compel a judicial determination of whether he is lawfully being held in custody.

SEARCH An inspection conducted in order to obtain evidence to be utilized for the prosecution of a crime.

SEIZURE The removal of property from one's possession due to unlawful activity or in satisfaction of a judgment entered by the court.

━■━

Wainwright v. Sykes

Court (D) v. Murder convict (P)

433 U.S. 72 (1977).

NATURE OF CASE: Habeas corpus challenge to a murder conviction.

FACT SUMMARY: Sykes (P) sought a review of his murder conviction via a habeas corpus proceeding, but he had failed to comply with state procedural rules in not raising the underlying claim at trial.

> ### 🏛 RULE OF LAW
> One who did not comply with state procedural rules by not raising his federal claim at trial cannot obtain federal habeas corpus review of his state criminal conviction unless he shows "cause" for noncompliance and shows "prejudice" as a result of the claimed error in the original proceeding.

FACTS: Sykes (P) violated a state procedural rule by not raising, at trial, his claim that the incriminating statements admitted against him were involuntary because he did not understand the Miranda warnings that he had been given. When he was convicted in state court for murder, Sykes (P) then presented a federal habeas corpus challenge to that conviction based on the aforementioned contention. Opposing such action, Wainwright (D) argued that the rule in *Francis v. Henderson* should be extended to cover this case. That rule was that federal habeas corpus review was barred absent a showing of "cause" and "prejudice" where the challenge was to the makeup of a grand jury. Sykes (P) argued that *Fay v. Noia*, 372 U.S. 391 (1963), had laid down an all-inclusive rule rendering state timely-objection rules ineffective to bar review of underlying federal claims in federal habeas corpus proceedings absent a showing of "knowing waiver" or a "deliberate bypass" of the right to so object.

ISSUE: In order to obtain federal habeas corpus review of his state criminal conviction, must one who did not comply with state procedural rules in raising his federal claim at trial show "cause" for noncompliance and show "prejudice" resulting from the claimed error in the original proceeding?

HOLDING AND DECISION: (Rehnquist, J.) Yes. If one who suffered a state criminal conviction did not comply with state procedural law by bringing up his federal claim at trial, he cannot obtain federal habeas corpus review of the conviction unless he shows "cause" for noncompliance and shows "prejudice" as a result of the claimed error in the original proceeding. A state's contemporaneous objection rule is designed to insure that constitutional claims are heard when they are fresh, not years later in a federal habeas corpus proceeding. Furthermore, to apply the "knowing waiver" or "deliberate bypass" standard, the more lenient of those suggested, would encourage "sandbagging" by lawyers who would take their chances on a not guilty verdict at trial with the intent to raise their constitutional claims in a federal habeas corpus court if their initial gamble does not pay off. The "cause" and "prejudice" rule herein adopted attempts to make the state trial on the merits the "main event" rather than a "tryout on the road." In this case, the required showing of cause was not made. Remanded with instructions to dismiss the petition for a writ of habeas corpus.

CONCURRENCE: (Stevens, J.) In applying the "deliberate bypass" standard, courts have found the client impliedly consents where, as here, his attorney decides as a tactical ploy not to raise a constitutional objection at trial. Furthermore, there is no evidence that the trial lacked fundamental fairness. So, there is no reason to allow collateral attack in this case regardless of which rule is chosen.

DISSENT: (Brennan, J.) The Court is not justified in imposing a stricter standard than the deliberate bypass test. It is the harshest test possible which still distinguishes between intentional and inadvertent noncompliance by counsel with procedural rules. Most procedural defaults are born of the inadvertence, negligence, inexperience, or incompetence of trial counsel, and it is unfair to make the criminal defendant accountable for the naked errors of his attorney. The mistakes of a trial attorney should be visited on the head of a federal habeas corpus applicant only when this Court is convinced that the lawyer actually exercised his expertise and judgment in his client's service, and with his client's knowing and intelligent participation, where possible.

▎ *ANALYSIS*

One possible result of this case may be that defendants are pushed into making more claims based on ineffectiveness of counsel to fulfill the requirement that they show "cause." That is, a particular procedural default will simply be cited as an example of general incompetence of counsel. The effect would be merely to transform the old claims alleging deprivation of constitutional rights to new claims alleging ineffectiveness of counsel, with all the attendant problems which will engender.

■=■

Teague v. Lane

Black felony convict (D) v. Court (P)

489 U.S. 288 (1989).

NATURE OF CASE: Review of denial of habeas corpus.

FACT SUMMARY: Teague (D) argued in a habeas proceeding that a post-conviction judicial decision had rendered his conviction invalid.

🏛 RULE OF LAW
Except in special circumstances, case law will not be retroactively applied in collateral review.

FACTS: Teague (D) was charged with various felonies. An all-white jury convicted Teague (D), a black man, of attempted murder, robbery, and battery. The prosecution had used all its peremptory challenges to exclude blacks from the jury. Teague (D) appealed, contending that this denied him due process. On appeal the conviction was upheld. Teague (D) subsequently petitioned for habeas corpus, contending that he had been entitled to a jury consisting of a cross-section of the community. The district court denied his petition on the merits, as did the court of appeals. The Supreme Court granted review.

ISSUE: Will case law be retroactively applied in collateral review?

HOLDING AND DECISION: (O'Connor, J.) No. Case law will not be retroactively applied in collateral review. Habeas corpus provides an avenue for upsetting judgments that otherwise would be final. It is not intended to be a substitute for direct review. Both the state and criminal defendants have an interest in leaving concluded litigation in a state of repose. If new rules of constitutional law were to be applied retroactively, any litigation might be reopened if the new rule were to be applicable. Further, the purpose of habeas is that its presence creates an incentive for trial and appellate judges to conduct their proceedings in a manner consistent with established constitutional principles. To apply new principles retroactively would actually subvert this purpose. Therefore, the Court concludes that, unless the post-conviction rule announced is so fundamental to the concept of ordered liberty that it would be unconscionable not to retroactively apply it, retroactive application will not be given. A necessary corollary to this rule is that no new rule of constitutional criminal procedure should be announced in a habeas proceeding. Here, to rule as Teague (D) urges would amount to that. Therefore, without ruling on the merits of the claim, the denial of habeas must be affirmed.

CONCURRENCE: (White, J.) The proper test for retroactivity should be whether the matter is on direct or collateral review, weighing of the purpose of the new rule, the extent of reliance on the old rule, and retroactivity's effect on the administration of justice.

CONCURRENCE: (Stevens, J.) The test adopted by the Court is essentially proper. However, as to the Court's discussion of the "fundamental fairness" exception, the Court gives an excessively result-oriented analysis.

DISSENT: (Brennan, J.) The 1867 Habeas Corpus statute was, from its inception, given an extremely broad jurisdictional reach. Nothing done by Congress since has indicated a wish to narrow its reach. Further, the ruling by the Court will foreclose decision upon important constitutional issues.

▶ ANALYSIS

The opinion in fact announces two rules, the first being that stated above and the second being that new constitutional issues cannot be announced in a habeas proceeding. The latter rule is potentially much more significant than the first. It is important to note, however, that only four justices joined the section announcing that rule, which limits its precedential value.

Quicknotes

HABEAS CORPUS A proceeding in which a defendant brings a writ to compel a judicial determination of whether he is lawfully being held in custody.

(Terry) Williams v. Taylor

Convicted murderer (D) v. Government (P)

529 U.S. 362 (2000).

NATURE OF CASE: Habeas corpus petition challenged validity of a death sentence.

FACT SUMMARY: Williams (D) brought a habeas corpus petition challenging his capital punishment sentence on the basis that he was denied effective assistance of counsel.

🏛 RULE OF LAW
The Antiterrorism and Effective Death Penalty Act of 1996 (AEDPA) requires that for a defendant to be entitled to federal habeas corpus relief the state court determination must be based on "clearly established federal law" and must be "contrary to, or involve an unreasonable application of" that clearly established law.

FACTS: Williams (D) was convicted of robbery and murder. At his sentencing hearing, the prosecution proved that Williams (D) had been convicted of armed robbery and burglary and grand larceny in two prior occasions. The prosecution also described two auto thefts and two assaults on elderly victims. Williams' (D) counsel asked the jury to give weight to the fact that he had turned himself in on four crimes. The weight of the closing was devoted to explaining that it was difficult to find a reason to spare Williams' (D) life. The jury sentenced Williams (D) to death and the Virginia Supreme Court affirmed. Williams (D) filed for state collateral relief and an evidentiary hearing was held by the same judge who presided over the trial on the claim that trial counsel had been ineffective. The Virginia Supreme Court disagreed that Williams (D) suffered sufficient prejudice to warrant relief. Williams (D) then sought a federal writ of habeas corpus and federal judge found that the death sentence was constitutionally infirm. The federal court of appeals reversed and this Court granter certiorari.

ISSUE: Does the AEDPA require that in order for a defendant to be entitled to federal habeas corpus relief the state court determination must be based on "clearly established federal law" and must be "contrary to, or involve an unreasonable application of" that clearly established law?

HOLDING AND DECISION: (Stevens, J.) Yes. The AEDPA requires that in order for a defendant to be entitled to federal habeas corpus relief the state court determination must be based on "clearly established federal law" and must be "contrary to, or involve an unreasonable application of" that clearly established law. When federal judges exercise their federal question jurisdiction under the judicial power of Article III,

it is their duty to say what the law is. A reading of the AEDPA that would cede such authority to the state courts would be inconsistent with Article III. In interpreting § 2254(d)(1) the requirement that the determinations of state courts be tested only against clearly established federal law and the prohibition on the issuance of the writ unless the state court's decision is contrary to or involved an unreasonable application of the clearly established law. In *Teague v. Lane*, 489 U.S. 288 (1989), this Court held that petitioner was not entitled to federal habeas corpus relief since he relied on a federal rule of law that had not been announced until after his conviction became final. The AEDPA codifies this holding to the extent that it requires courts to deny federal habeas corpus relief contingent upon a rule of law not clearly established at the time the state decision became final. *Teague* also provides that a federal habeas court may apply a rule dictated by precedent. A rule that breaks new ground or imposes a new obligation falls outside this scope. The AEDPA has further added to the clearly established law requirement a clause limiting the area of relevant law to that determined by the Supreme Court of the United States. A rule failing to satisfy these criteria is not available as a basis for relief in a habeas case to which the AEDPA applies. With respect to the "contrary to, or an unreasonable application of" requirement, it seems that Congress intended federal judges to invoke the utmost care to state-court decisions before concluding issuance of the writ was warranted, but does not require them to defer to the opinion of every reasonable state-court judge on the content of federal law. If after carefully weighing the reasons for accepting the state court's judgment a federal court is convinced that a prisoner's custody is unconstitutional, then that judgment should prevail. Here Williams (D) contended that he was denied his constitutionally guaranteed right to effective assistance of counsel when his lawyers failed to investigate and present substantial mitigating evidence to the sentencing jury. The initial inquiry under the AEDPA is whether Williams (D) seeks to apply a rule of law that was clearly established at the time his state-court conviction became final. Williams (D) is entitled to relief if the Virginia Supreme Court's decision was either "contrary to, or involved unreasonable application of" the clearly established law. It was both. Reversed.

CONCURRENCE: (O'Connor, J.) This case is not governed by the pre-1966 version of the habeas statute, but by the statute as amended by the AEDPA.

Continued on next page.

CONCURRENCE IN PART AND DISSENT IN PART: (Rehnquist, C.J.)

There is strong evidence petitioner would continue to be a danger to society, both in and out of prison. It is not unreasonable to assume that the jury would have viewed petitioner's mitigation as unconvincing upon hearing that he set fire to his cell while awaiting trial for the instant murder and has repeated visions of harming other inmates.

▶ ANALYSIS

The court concluded that Williams (D) had a fundamental right to provide the jury with mitigating evidence that his trial counsel either failed to discover or failed to offer. The Virginia court erred in requiring a separate inquiry into fundamental fairness even when Williams (D) was able to show that his counsel was ineffective and such ineffectiveness adversely affected the result of the proceeding. The court's decision also fulfilled the contrary to or unreasonable application of requirement with respect to the prejudice determination insofar as it failed to evaluate the totality of the mitigation evidence available and its decision turned on the erroneous view that a difference in outcome is not sufficient in itself to establish ineffective assistance of counsel.

Glossary

Common Latin Words and Phrases Encountered in the Law

A FORTIORI: Because one fact exists or has been proven, therefore a second fact that is related to the first fact must also exist.

A PRIORI: From the cause to the effect. A term of logic used to denote that when one generally accepted truth is shown to be a cause, another particular effect must necessarily follow.

AB INITIO: From the beginning; a condition which has existed throughout, as in a marriage which was void ab initio.

ACTUS REUS: The wrongful act; in criminal law, such action sufficient to trigger criminal liability.

AD VALOREM: According to value; an ad valorem tax is imposed upon an item located within the taxing jurisdiction calculated by the value of such item.

AMICUS CURIAE: Friend of the court. Its most common usage takes the form of an amicus curiae brief, filed by a person who is not a party to an action but is nonetheless allowed to offer an argument supporting his legal interests.

ARGUENDO: In arguing. A statement, possibly hypothetical, made for the purpose of argument, is one made arguendo.

BILL QUIA TIMET: A bill to quiet title (establish ownership) to real property.

BONA FIDE: True, honest, or genuine. May refer to a person's legal position based on good faith or lacking notice of fraud (such as a bona fide purchaser for value) or to the authenticity of a particular document (such as a bona fide last will and testament).

CAUSA MORTIS: With approaching death in mind. A gift causa mortis is a gift given by a party who feels certain that death is imminent.

CAVEAT EMPTOR: Let the buyer beware. This maxim is reflected in the rule of law that a buyer purchases at his own risk because it is his responsibility to examine, judge, test, and otherwise inspect what he is buying.

CERTIORARI: A writ of review. Petitions for review of a case by the United States Supreme Court are most often done by means of a writ of certiorari.

CONTRA: On the other hand. Opposite. Contrary to.

CORAM NOBIS: Before us; writs of error directed to the court that originally rendered the judgment.

CORAM VOBIS: Before you; writs of error directed by an appellate court to a lower court to correct a factual error.

CORPUS DELICTI: The body of the crime; the requisite elements of a crime amounting to objective proof that a crime has been committed.

CUM TESTAMENTO ANNEXO, ADMINISTRATOR (ADMINISTRATOR C.T.A.): With will annexed; an administrator c.t.a. settles an estate pursuant to a will in which he is not appointed.

DE BONIS NON, ADMINISTRATOR (ADMINISTRATOR D.B.N.): Of goods not administered; an administrator d.b.n. settles a partially settled estate.

DE FACTO: In fact; in reality; actually. Existing in fact but not officially approved or engendered.

DE JURE: By right; lawful. Describes a condition that is legitimate "as a matter of law," in contrast to the term "de facto," which connotes something existing in fact but not legally sanctioned or authorized. For example, de facto segregation refers to segregation brought about by housing patterns, etc., whereas de jure segregation refers to segregation created by law.

DE MINIMUS: Of minimal importance; insignificant; a trifle; not worth bothering about.

DE NOVO: Anew; a second time; afresh. A trial de novo is a new trial held at the appellate level as if the case originated there and the trial at a lower level had not taken place.

DICTA: Generally used as an abbreviated form of obiter dicta, a term describing those portions of a judicial opinion incidental or not necessary to resolution of the specific question before the court. Such nonessential statements and remarks are not considered to be binding precedent.

DUCES TECUM: Refers to a particular type of writ or subpoena requesting a party or organization to produce certain documents in their possession.

EN BANC: Full bench. Where a court sits with all justices present rather than the usual quorum.

EX PARTE: For one side or one party only. An ex parte proceeding is one undertaken for the benefit of only one party, without notice to, or an appearance by, an adverse party.

EX POST FACTO: After the fact. An ex post facto law is a law that retroactively changes the consequences of a prior act.

EX REL.: Abbreviated form of the term ex relatione, meaning, upon relation or information. When the state brings an action in which it has no interest against an individual at the instigation of one who has a private interest in the matter.

FORUM NON CONVENIENS: Inconvenient forum. Although a court may have jurisdiction over the case, the action should be tried in a more conveniently located court, one to which parties and witnesses may more easily travel, for example.

GUARDIAN AD LITEM: A guardian of an infant as to litigation, appointed to represent the infant and pursue his/her rights.

HABEAS CORPUS: You have the body. The modern writ of habeas corpus is a writ directing that a person (body) being detained (such as a prisoner) be brought before the court so that the legality of his detention can be judicially ascertained.

IN CAMERA: In private, in chambers. When a hearing is held before a judge in his chambers or when all spectators are excluded from the courtroom.

IN FORMA PAUPERIS: In the manner of a pauper. A party who proceeds in forma pauperis because of his poverty is one who is allowed to bring suit without liability for costs.

INFRA: Below, under. A word referring the reader to a later part of a book. (The opposite of supra.)

IN LOCO PARENTIS: In the place of a parent.

IN PARI DELICTO: Equally wrong; a court of equity will not grant requested relief to an applicant who is in pari delicto, or as much at fault in the transactions giving rise to the controversy as is the opponent of the applicant.

IN PARI MATERIA: On like subject matter or upon the same matter. Statutes relating to the same person or things are said to be in pari materia. It is a general rule of statutory construction that such statutes should be construed together, i.e., looked at as if they together constituted one law.

IN PERSONAM: Against the person. Jurisdiction over the person of an individual.

IN RE: In the matter of. Used to designate a proceeding involving an estate or other property.

IN REM: A term that signifies an action against the res, or thing. An action in rem is basically one that is taken directly against property, as distinguished from an action in personam, i.e., against the person.

INTER ALIA: Among other things. Used to show that the whole of a statement, pleading, list, statute, etc., has not been set forth in its entirety.

INTER PARTES: Between the parties. May refer to contracts, conveyances or other transactions having legal significance.

INTER VIVOS: Between the living. An inter vivos gift is a gift made by a living grantor, as distinguished from bequests contained in a will, which pass upon the death of the testator.

IPSO FACTO: By the mere fact itself.

JUS: Law or the entire body of law.

LEX LOCI: The law of the place; the notion that the rights of parties to a legal proceeding are governed by the law of the place where those rights arose.

MALUM IN SE: Evil or wrong in and of itself; inherently wrong. This term describes an act that is wrong by its very nature, as opposed to one which would not be wrong but for the fact that there is a specific legal prohibition against it (malum prohibitum).

MALUM PROHIBITUM: Wrong because prohibited, but not inherently evil. Used to describe something that is wrong because it is expressly forbidden by law but that is not in and of itself evil, e.g., speeding.

MANDAMUS: We command. A writ directing an official to take a certain action.

MENS REA: A guilty mind; a criminal intent. A term used to signify the mental state that accompanies a crime or other prohibited act. Some crimes require only a general mens rea (general intent to do the prohibited act), but others, like assault with intent to murder, require the existence of a specific mens rea.

MODUS OPERANDI: Method of operating; generally refers to the manner or style of a criminal in committing crimes, admissible in appropriate cases as evidence of the identity of a defendant.

NEXUS: A connection to.

NISI PRIUS: A court of first impression. A nisi prius court is one where issues of fact are tried before a judge or jury.

N.O.V. (NON OBSTANTE VEREDICTO): Not withstanding the verdict. A judgment n.o.v. is a judgment given in favor of one party despite the fact that a verdict was returned in favor of the other party, the justification being that the verdict either had no reasonable support in fact or was contrary to law.

NUNC PRO TUNC: Now for then. This phrase refers to actions that may be taken and will then have full retroactive effect.

PENDENTE LITE: Pending the suit; pending litigation underway.

PER CAPITA: By head; beneficiaries of an estate, if they take in equal shares, take per capita.

PER CURIAM: By the court; signifies an opinion ostensibly written "by the whole court" and with no identified author.

PER SE: By itself, in itself; inherently.

PER STIRPES: By representation. Used primarily in the law of wills to describe the method of distribution where a person, generally because of death, is unable to take that which is left to him by the will of another, and therefore his heirs divide such property between them rather than take under the will individually.

PRIMA FACIE: On its face, at first sight. A prima facie case is one that is sufficient on its face, meaning that the evidence supporting it is adequate to establish the case until contradicted or overcome by other evidence.

PRO TANTO: For so much; as far as it goes. Often used in eminent domain cases when a property owner receives partial payment for his land without prejudice to his right to bring suit for the full amount he claims his land to be worth.

QUANTUM MERUIT: As much as he deserves. Refers to recovery based on the doctrine of unjust enrichment in those cases in which a party has rendered valuable services or furnished materials that were accepted and enjoyed by another under circumstances that would reasonably notify the recipient that the rendering party expected to be paid. In essence, the law implies a contract to pay the reasonable value of the services or materials furnished.

QUASI: Almost like; as if; nearly. This term is essentially used to signify that one subject or thing is almost analogous to another but that material differences between them do exist. For example, a quasi-criminal proceeding is one that is not strictly criminal but shares enough of the same characteristics to require some of the same safeguards (e.g., procedural due process must be followed in a parole hearing).

QUID PRO QUO: Something for something. In contract law, the consideration, something of value, passed between the parties to render the contract binding.

RES GESTAE: Things done. In evidence law, this principle justifies the admission of a statement that would otherwise be hearsay when it is made so closely to the event in question as to be said to be a part of it, or with such spontaneity as not to have the possibility of falsehood.

RES IPSA LOQUITUR: The thing speaks for itself. This doctrine gives rise to a rebuttable presumption of negligence when the instrumentality causing the injury was within the exclusive control of the defendant, and the injury was one that does not normally occur unless a person has been negligent.

RES JUDICATA: A matter adjudged. Doctrine which provides that once a court of competent jurisdiction has rendered a final judgment or decree on the merits, that judgment or decree is conclusive upon the parties to the case and prevents them from engaging in any other litigation on the points and issues determined therein.

RESPONDEAT SUPERIOR: Let the master reply. This doctrine holds the master liable for the wrongful acts of his servant (or the principal for his agent) in those cases in which the servant (or agent) was acting within the scope of his authority at the time of the injury.

STARE DECISIS: To stand by or adhere to that which has been decided. The common law doctrine of stare decisis attempts to give security and certainty to the law by following the policy that once a principle of law as applicable to a certain set of facts has been set forth in a decision, it forms a precedent that will subsequently be followed, even though a different decision might be made were it the first time the question had arisen. Of course, stare decisis is not an inviolable principle and is departed from in instances where there is good cause (e.g., considerations of public policy led the Supreme Court to disregard prior decisions sanctioning segregation).

SUPRA: Above. A word referring a reader to an earlier part of a book.

ULTRA VIRES: Beyond the power. This phrase is most commonly used to refer to actions taken by a corporation that are beyond the power or legal authority of the corporation.

Addendum of French Derivatives

IN PAIS: Not pursuant to legal proceedings.

CHATTEL: Tangible personal property.

CY PRES: Doctrine permitting courts to apply trust funds to purposes not expressed in the trust but necessary to carry out the settlor's intent.

PER AUTRE VIE: For another's life; during another's life. In property law, an estate may be granted that will terminate upon the death of someone other than the grantee.

PROFIT A PRENDRE: A license to remove minerals or other produce from land.

VOIR DIRE: Process of questioning jurors as to their predispositions about the case or parties to a proceeding in order to identify those jurors displaying bias or prejudice.

Casenote Legal Briefs